AF471027

TO CATCH A SUNBEAM

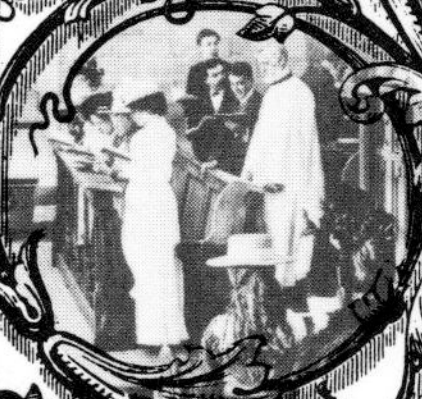

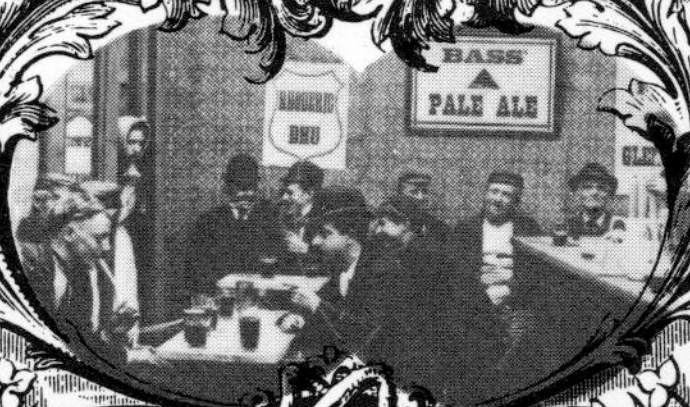

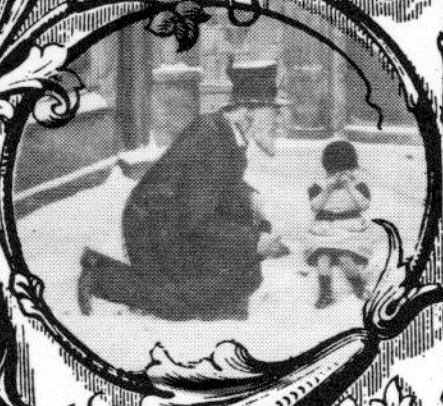

TO CATCH A SUNBEAM

Victorian reality
through the magic lantern

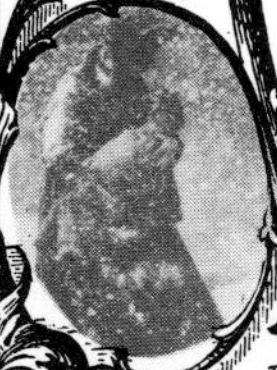

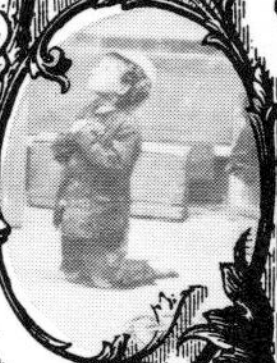

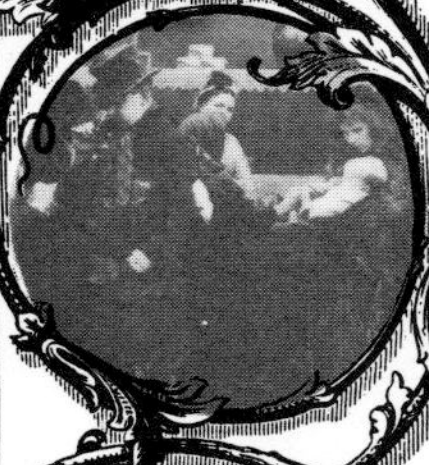

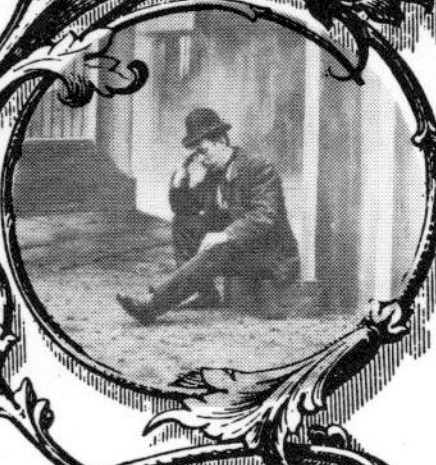

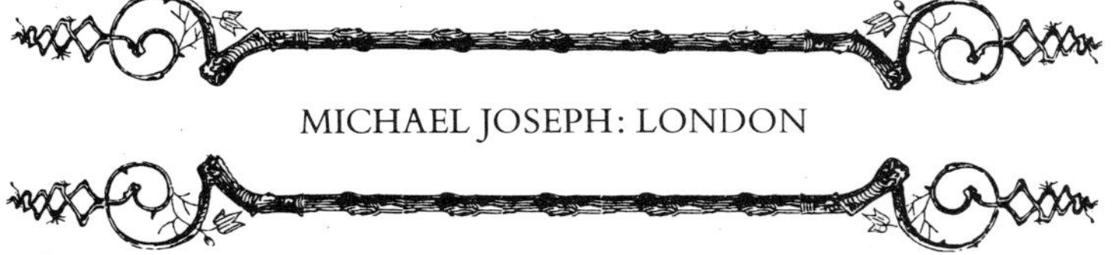

Designed and Edited
by
G. A. HOUSEHOLD
from the collection of
L. M. H. Smith

MICHAEL JOSEPH: LONDON

First published in Great Britain by
Michael Joseph Limited
44 Bedford Square, London WC1
1979

ISBN: 0 7181 1861 8

Printed in Great Britain by
Cripplegate Printing Company Limited
and bound by Dorstal Press Limited, Harlow

CONTENTS

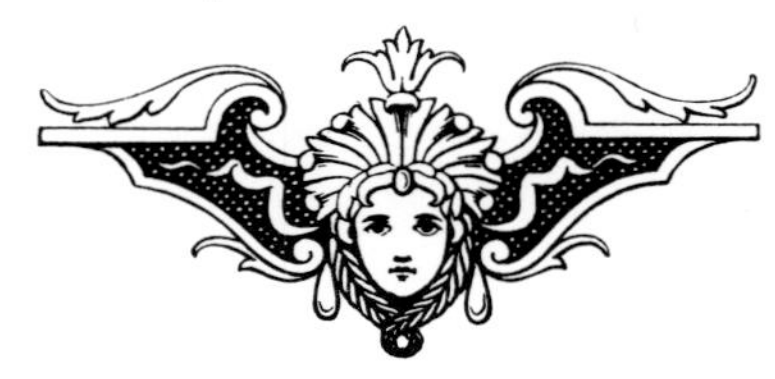

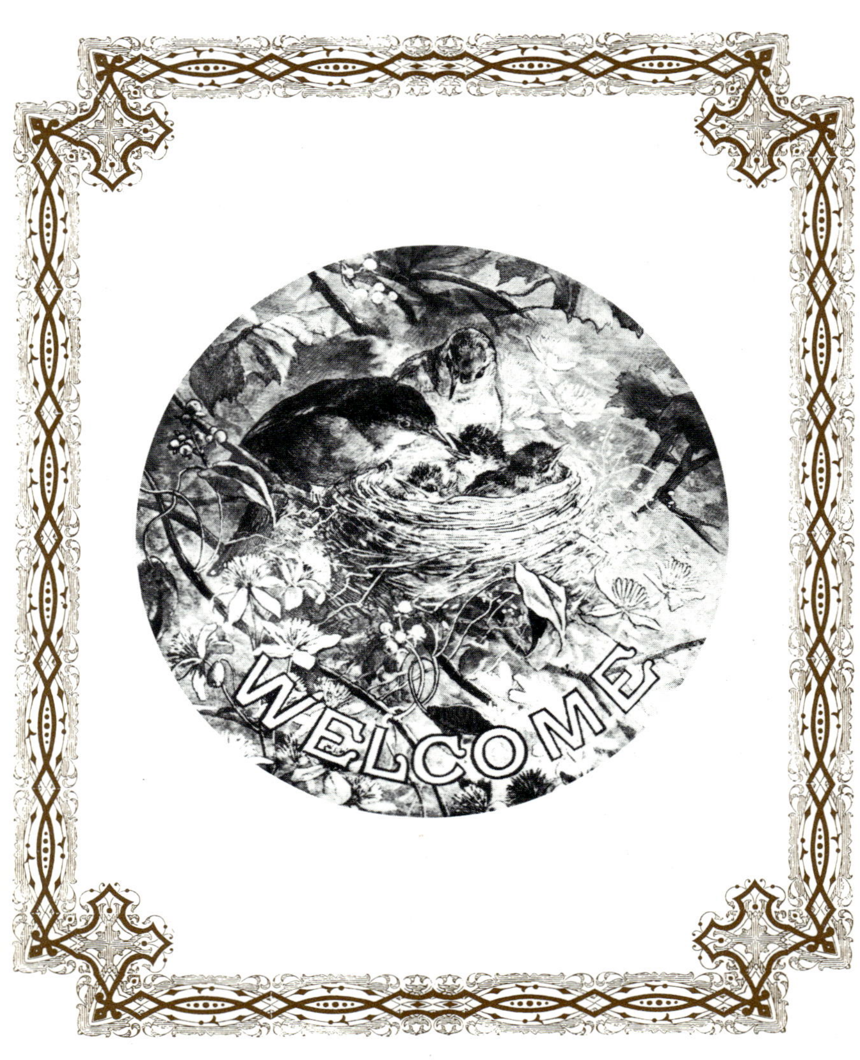
WELCOME

INTRODUCTION

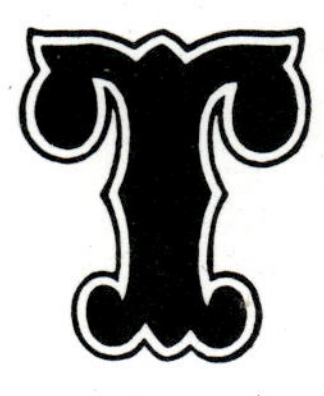owards the end of the last century the magic lantern was a very popular form of entertainment. This was the heyday of the magic lantern show and stories of the kind illustrated in this collection were shown in church halls and community centres up and down the country. The stories highlight the social problems of the day, drunkenness, poverty and unemployment.

While these shows were frequently organised by charitable organisations, the non-conformist churches and temperance societies, they were viewed as entertainment and not just as something socially instructive. The Victorians loved Sentiment; it was a necessary ingredient of any mass medium of the time. It was because a morally or socially relevant message could be put across so effectively with the use of Sentiment that both writers and manufacturers of lantern slides exploited it. They were selling a message but the public were reading and viewing what they wanted.

The magic lantern was probably invented in about 1650 but while the principles of optical projection had been known for 200 years before the Victorian era, no one had been able to develop a sufficiently powerful source of light to project an image far enough for an audience to be able to participate. The magic lantern had been a novelty or a toy. The breakthrough came with the invention of 'limelight' – oxygen and hydrogen jets were played on to lime and the mixture ignited – which produced a brilliant flame powerful enough to project the image depicted on the glass slide on to a screen seventy feet away.

The invention of photography was the second factor that revolutionalised the magic lantern. But it was not until about 1850 that the use of photographic glass slides for the magic lantern was really explored and it took a further twenty years for the slide manufacturers to develop the idea. By the early 1870s the mass production of magic lantern slides had begun.

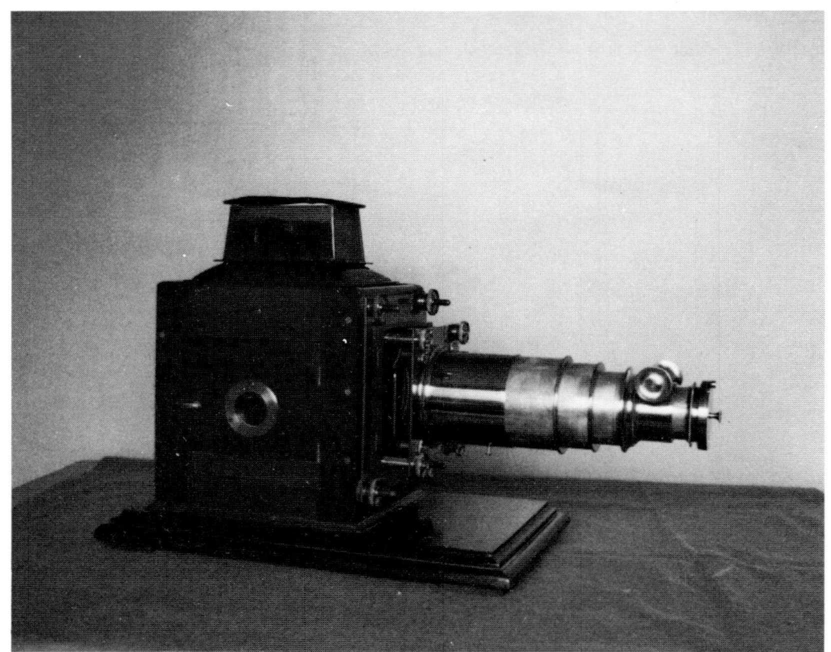

Slides were produced in sets on a wide variety of subjects: some were educational, some humorous and some illustrated the popular fiction and verses of the time.

The largest manufacturer of slides in Britain was James Bamforth of Holmfirth in Yorkshire. He set up what was virtually a film studio, using live models rather than actors, but building sets in which to pose his characters. He worked to a script.

The illustrations in this book come almost entirely from the Bamforth studios. (The firm of Bamforth still exists, making greeting cards and calendars, but between 1908 and 1914 they had a brief success in producing comedy films and were one of the earliest pioneers of motion pictures before the Hollywood era.)

James Bamforth was no doubt influenced in his work by the non-conformist area in which he lived. The chapel was the focal point of the community and religious and moral instruction was preached with the aid of magic lantern slides. Bamforth must have realised that this form of 'instruction' might reach a much wider audience if the slides could be manufactured in sufficient numbers. He set out to produce slides in volume and therefore undercut most of his competitors on price.

Bamforth himself designed and painted the backcloths and sets and arranged the models and props in readiness for the photographer. The sets were frequently re-used and there are several examples of the same scene being used to illustrate different stories in this collection.

For models Bamforth employed mostly local untrained people as well as members of his family and staff. They were poorly paid, if at all, but probably posed for fun, in which case a free set of photographs is all they would have wanted in recompense. These anonymous early stars of the screen wore no make-up and therefore their faces tend to contrast vividly with the coloured scenery.

The colours that could be used for painting lantern slides were restricted by their opacity. Some colours are naturally transparent whereas others are naturally opaque; the lantern slide artist could use only those colours which remained true when projected on to a screen. Vermilion, for example, is opaque and when viewed through glass appears black because light cannot filter through it.

The Victorian lantern slide artists skilfully mixed transparent colours, like Prussian Blue, Indigo and Raw Sienna, to produce a remarkably colourful image, though the lack of a strong red gives the slides their characteristic rich mellow effect.

The artists, probably all women trained and employed specially for the purpose, developed considerable skill in working in detail on glass plates only $3\frac{1}{4}$ in. square. Their paintings had to stand up to very large magnification and it was due to their skill that black and white lantern slides quickly became unacceptable to the public.

The production of the slides was carried out seasonally. The photography was done in summer, either in the studios or 'on location', the manufacturing of the slides in winter.

The number of slides in each set could vary from three to fifty or more. A text accompanied each set. The text would be read aloud and frequently the show would include a song or hymn which would be projected on to the screen so that the audience could participate in community singing.

The influence the magic lantern shows had on early motion pictures is immediately obvious in many of the illustrations and stories; particularly 'A Word for Sally' which at a glance might seem to be illustrated with stills from an early Chaplin movie, but, of course, it predates the first Chaplin film by fifteen years or more.

The magic lantern was capable of producing effects on the screen which are astonishing to anyone who has never seen them before. It was possible to dissolve one image into another, or superimpose one image on top of another. The 'thought' pictures in the story 'One Winter Night' are examples of this. Continuous movement for a short time was also possible by using banked projectors – in effect two or more lanterns placed on top of each other, or side by side. By this means a long background slide could be cranked slowly across, to give the effect, say, of a train pulling into a station. It took many years before motion pictures could provide such flowing and unflickering movement, but the magic lantern could, of course, only do it in short bursts. These effects cannot be reproduced in a book, but otherwise the stories, verses and illustrations give a good impression of a magic lantern show in about 1885.

The theme of many of the stories in this collection is Temperance, so, perhaps, we should conclude with a note about the temperance movement, before getting on with the show.

In the middle of the seventeenth century the introduction of a beer tax caused the working people of England to turn to gin – originally as a protest. This error was never properly rectified. Over the years law after law was passed in an attempt to regulate the sale of liquor. By the mid-nineteenth century a social disaster of quite horrible proportions had been allowed to get totally out of control.

There were 133,840 licenced breweries in England and Wales in 1870 and one pub for every 182 head of the population. Spirits were sold in the streets as well as in the pubs.

The temperance movement, which had begun in Maine, U.S.A., in 1851 gradually gained strength in Britain. By 1880 it was made illegal for an habitual drunkard to be sold liquor. By the end of the century legislation had lessened the worst excesses, but it was not until World War I that the problem was got under control. Even then Lloyd George said, 'Drink is causing more damage in the war than all the German submarines put together.'

The War also put paid to the era of Sentiment. It was replaced by the great era of silent comedy films in which Chaplin satirised social problems rather than sentimentalised them.

*   *   *

The church hall is packed, there is an air of expectancy as we wait for the gas lights to be turned down. The projectionist is busy preparing the magic lantern. We hope that he knows what he is doing. Everyone has heard stories of how the gases which ignite the lime can explode. There is a smell of hot mahogany and brass as the limelight flares into brilliance and a shaft of light is projected on to the screen.

The first slide is placed in the magic lantern.

The lights are dimmed. . .

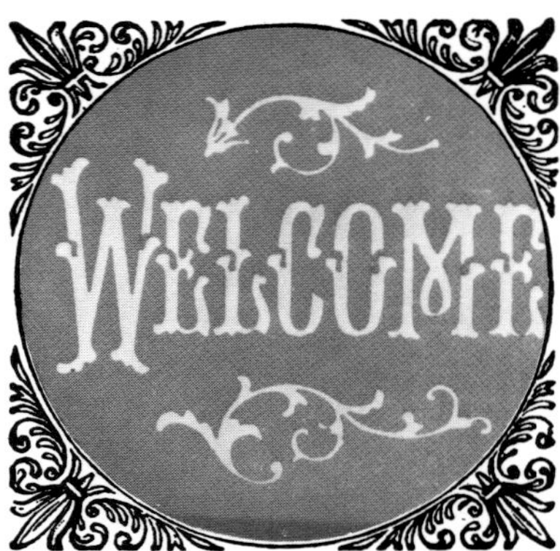

THE LITTLE HERO

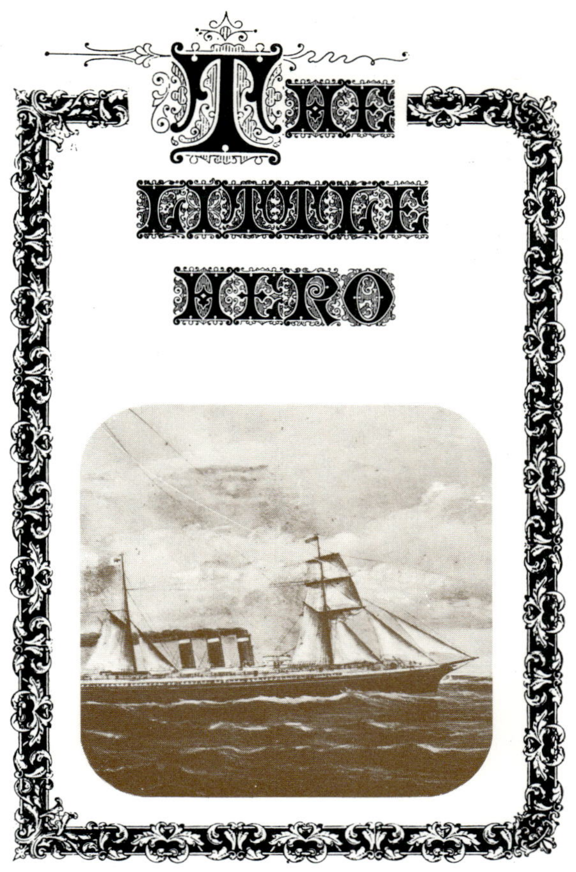

Triumph of engineering skill,
How beautiful to see!
Thy mighty powers, with wonder fill
Me as I gaze on thee.

Within thy borders broad and fair,
Some hundreds dwell secure;
All orders represented there—
A town in miniature.

Thus mused I, as at utmost speed,
And buoyant as a cork,
I saw, as you may see, proceed
The City of New York.

'Twas thus she sped upon her way,
As if possessed of soul,
Her throbbing ceasing night nor day,
Until she reached her goal.

And then it came into my mind,
A story I had heard
Of that same ship, which you will find,
Seems true in every word.

One day when lost to England's view,
And on the Atlantic wild,
Appeared among the sailor crew,
a fair-haired little child.

And there he stood—the sailor's pest—
Dragged to the light of day;
And standing there himself confessed
A useless *stowaway*.

For there was one more mouth to feed—
The mate felt very sore—
One more that anxious care would need,
Before they reached the shore.

Among the goods within the hold,
For two days and a night,
That little waif, hungry and cold,
Had kept himself from sight.

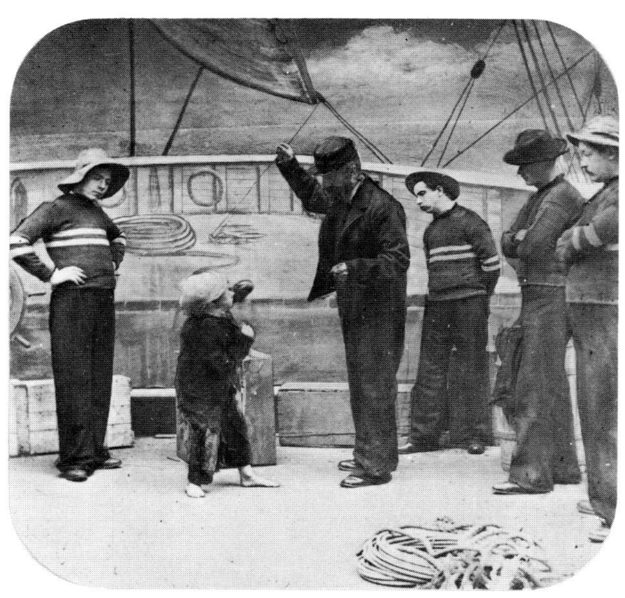

The mate in anger questioned him,
With voice that almost roared;
And sought to know *which* sailor's whim,
Had smuggled him aboard.

At first the little fellow's fears
Quite took his speech away;
But soon between his sobs and tears,
He managed thus to say:—

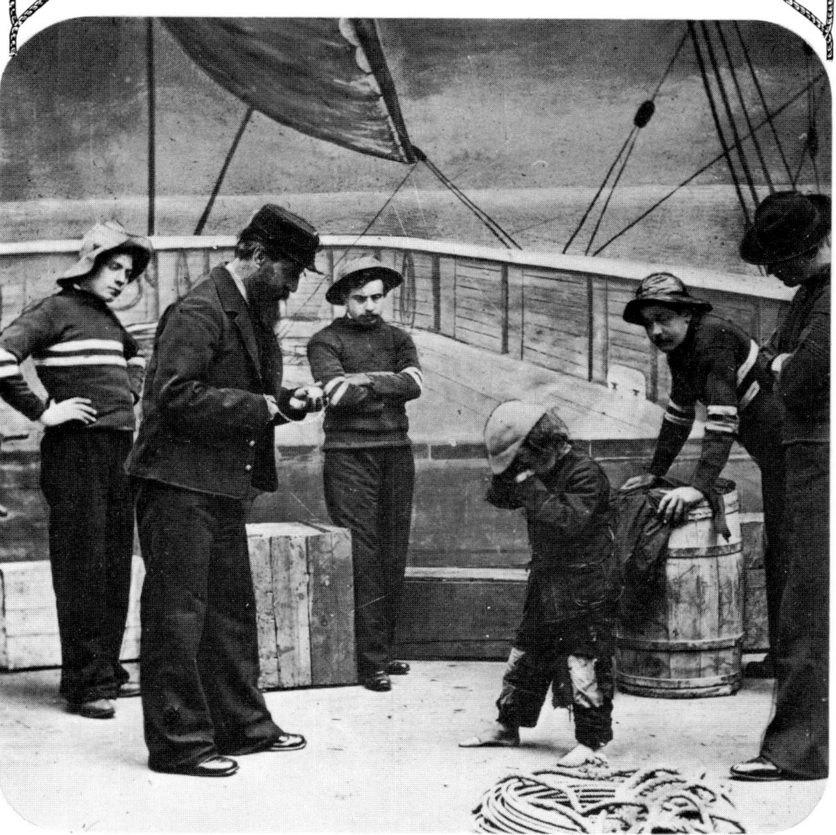

"Oh, sir, 'tis true as true can be—
It is not as you fear—
I don't know them, they don't know me,
Nor know how I came here."

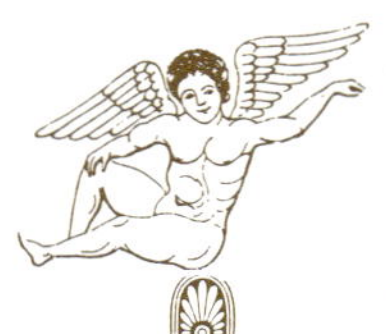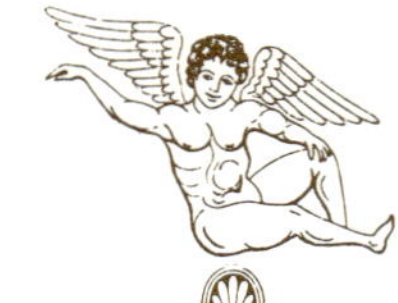

"Then tell me, boy," again he roared,
"And mind you tell me true,
What rascall *did* put you on board?
Or I will make you rue."

The little fellow dried his eyes,
And looked up in his face
Beseechingly, as if he tries
Some pity there to trace.

"Some time ago my father died,
And mother oft would brood
Upon her loss, and I oft cried
I know for want of food.

A man came to our house one day—
We were no longer poor—
And mother seemed as glad and gay
As she had been of yore.

He had not long been there when he,
Told me, in future I
Must call him 'father'; but you see,
I couldn't tell a lie.

For father, as I said before,
Was dead and gone to heaven;
I knew I ne'er should see him more,
Though I was only seven.

So though we then had many a feast,
I oft got many a cuff,
And oft he called me 'little beast,'
And wished me 'far enough.'

'Twas he who brought me here, and hid
Me in the hold below,
He said 'they'd never hurt a kid
So small as me,' you know.

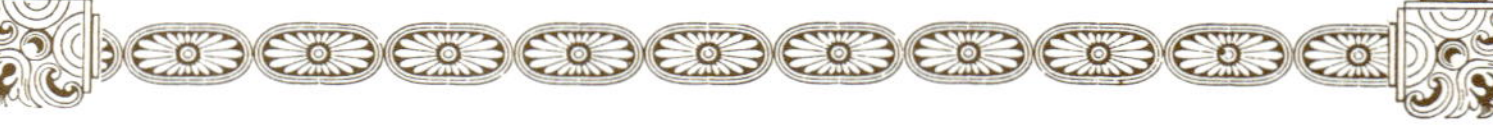

He told me that I had an aunt,
In Canada somewhere;
And she would see to every want
As soon as I got there.

Within that hold I've been, and would
Have been I guess there still,
If it had not been want of food
Has made me feel quite ill."

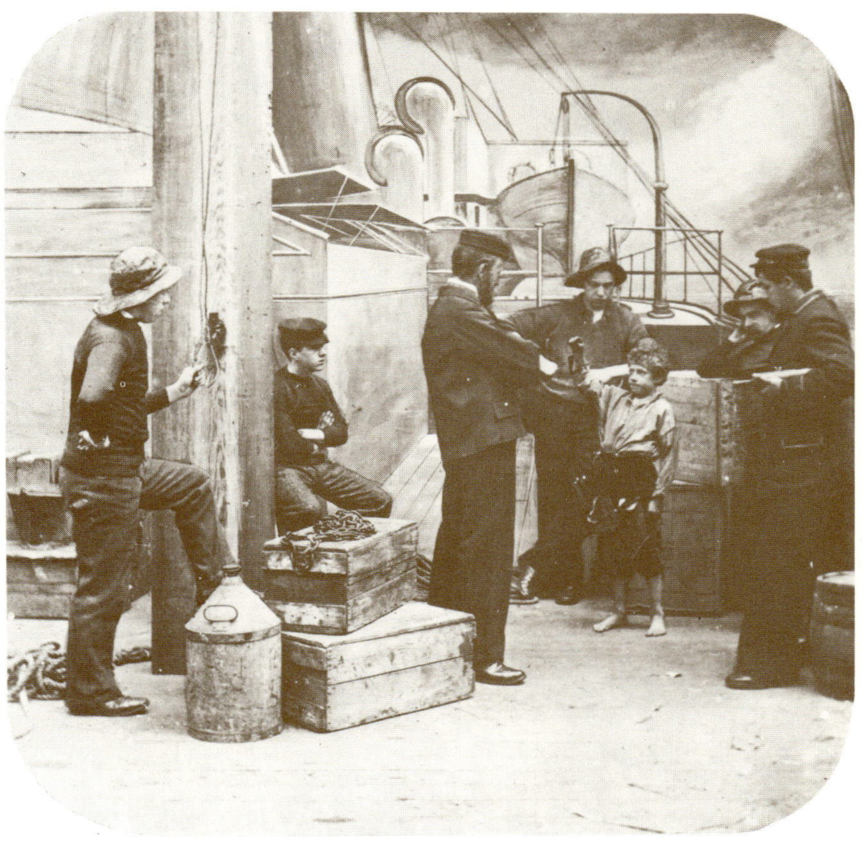

While listening to his simple tale,
The mate had often winced;
His cheek had more than once grown pale;
He was almost convinced.

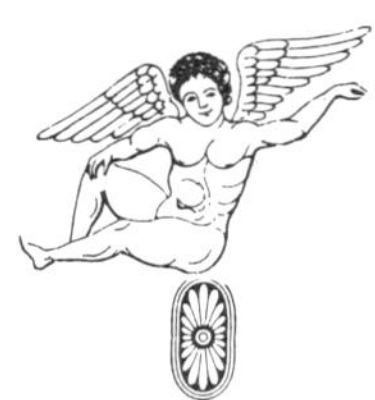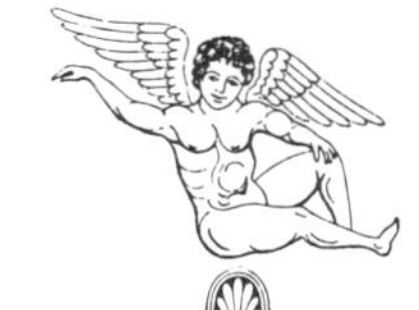

But stowaways must be suppressed,
He sternly said once more,
And so he thought another test,
Would make the matter sure.

"Look here, my lad," he said again,
"You've got your tale quite pat;
But you will find that it is vain
To spin a yarn like that.

You are a most precocious youth;
Ten minutes more I'll give,
And if you do not tell the truth,
Why then you'll cease to live.

For I will hang you like a dog,
With that rope at your feet,
And throw you o'erboard like a log,
To give the fish a treat."

The youngster now renewed his tears;
He'd not the slightest doubt,
The sentence that had reached his ears,
Would now be carried out.

But all at once he ceased his tears—
His eye the mate's did seek—
His face shows now no trace of fears—
He seems about to speak.

Eight minutes of the ten had flown;
The mate again now spoke,
And—painful had the silence grown—
That solemn silence broke.

"Two minutes more you've got to live,
So if you've ought to say,
The best advice that I can give
Is, say it, straight away."

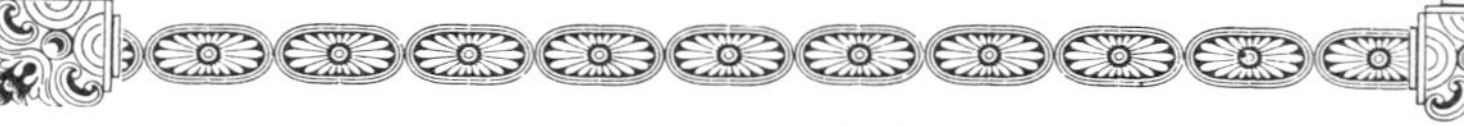

"What I have told you is no lie,"
The little boy did say,
"But if you'd let me, ere I die,
I'd like to kneel and pray."

The mate too much o'ercome to speak,
Now merely gave a nod,
While down the poor child knelt, to seek
An audience with God.

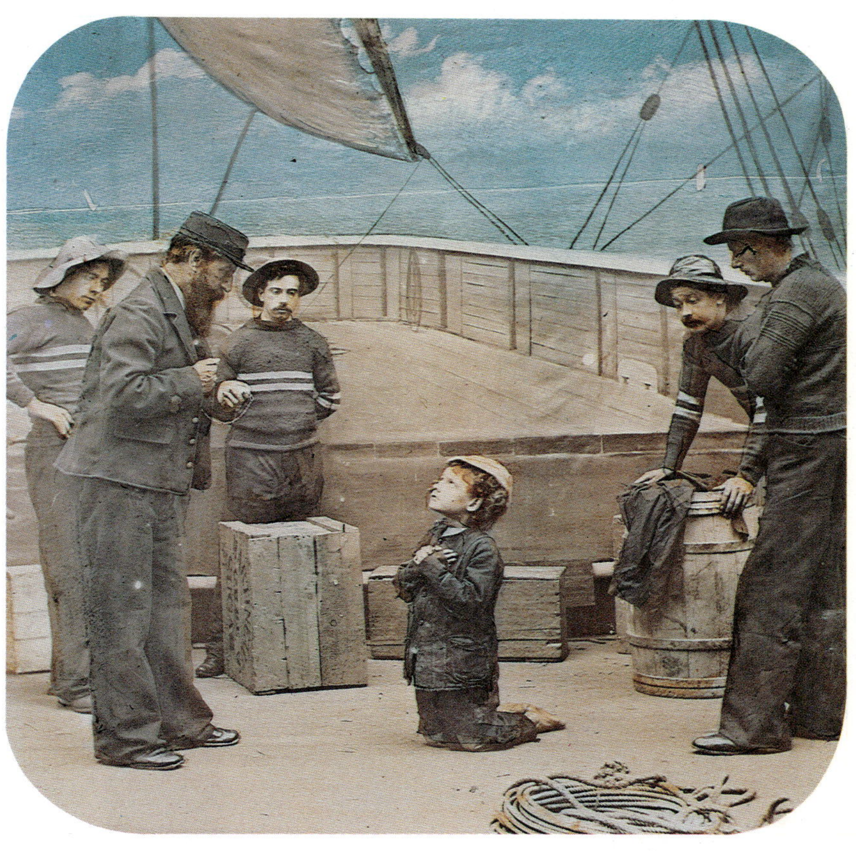

With hands across his little breast,
And eyes upturned to heaven,
He prayed that he might be at rest,
And all his sins forgiven.

And then 'Our Father' he began—
The mate ne'er heard the rest;
With streaming eyes he to him ran,
And snatched him to his breast.

"God bless you, boy, I have no doubt,
Your story is quite true;
And nobly you have carried out
What hundreds could not do.

There may be, but I've never seen
On board this ship, a youth
Or man, as ready as you've been
To suffer for the truth.

I'll see you safely to your friends,
To them your worth make known;
If they don't want you—there it ends—
I'll claim you as my own."

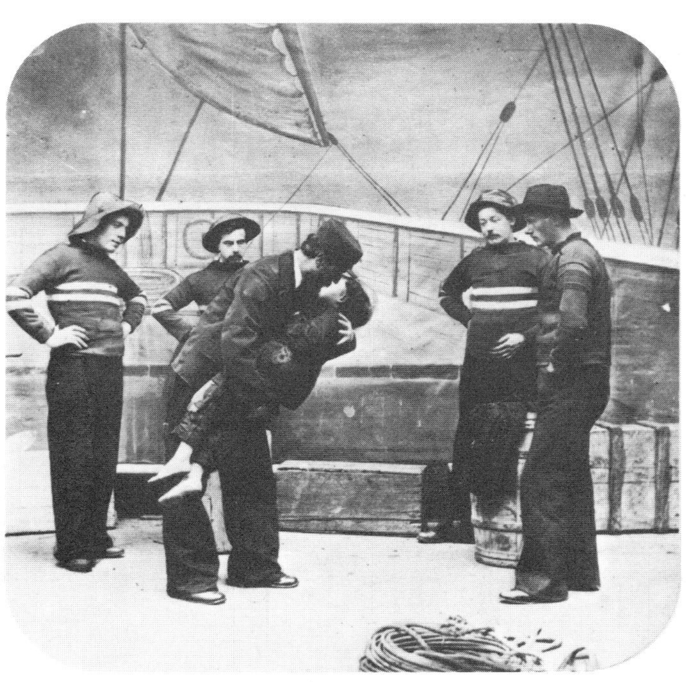

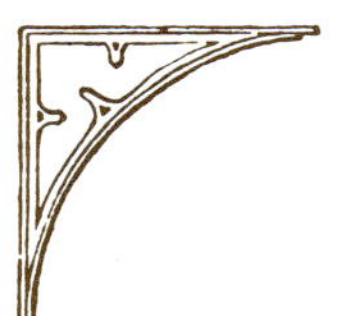

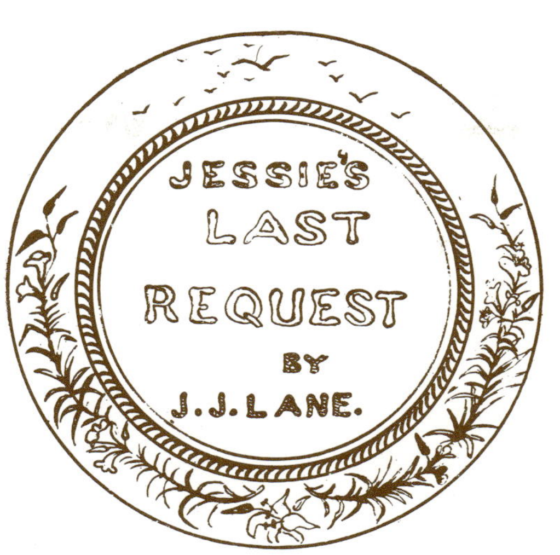

"Father," said a voice in a whisper,
    "I'm glad you've come again;
Bring a stool, and sit beside me,
    For I am so full of pain.
It was kind of you, dear father,
    Just to cheer me up a bit;
And I wanted so to see you
    Before the lamp is lit.

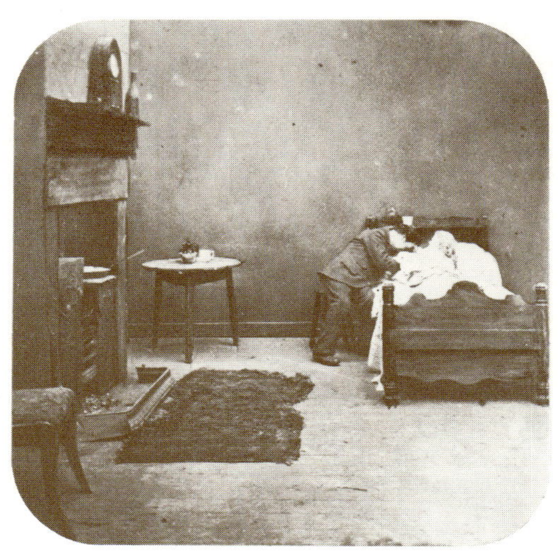

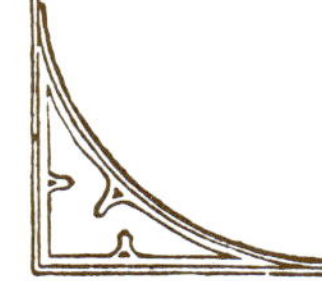

"Or poor mother comes from washing,
    Or Johnny from the loom, —
I shall not live till morning,
    They're waiting in the room,
So beautiful and white, father,
    With long and radiant wings;
They've beckoned twice, and pointed up
    To bright and lovely things.

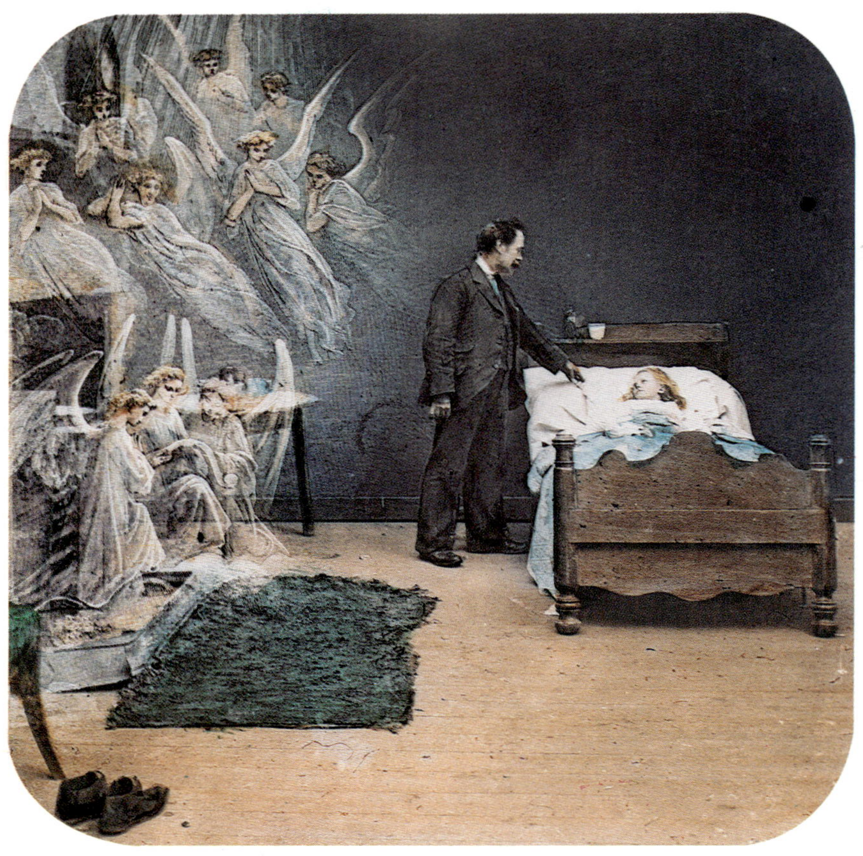

"Now put your hand in mine, father,
    It feels quite stiff and cold,
Though I see you have been drinking,
    I do not mean to scold.
Can you remember, father, just
    Three years last month ago,
When the trees were dark and naked,
    And earth was white with snow,

"A lady kind who came to see us,
    A pledge book in her hand?

She pressed us all to sign, father,
    And join a Temperance band;
She said that none were safe who took
    The drink in little drops,
It led to drinking more and more
    At home, and liquor shops;

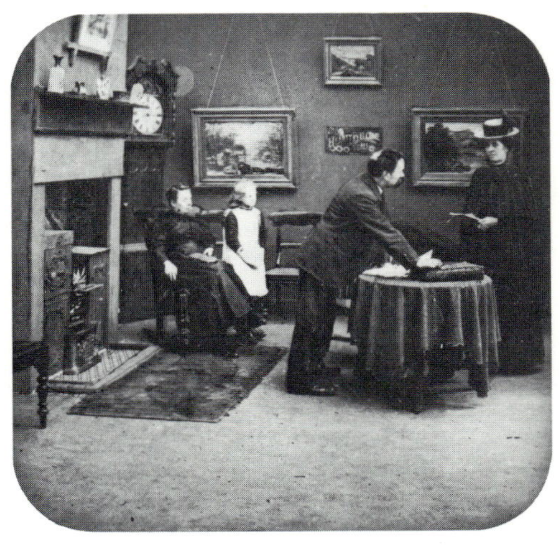

"She said that tens of thousands, through
    Drink, die every year,
Who proudly boasted once they drank
    Only a glass of beer.
You got angry with her, father,
    You said your moderate plan
Was sanctioned by the Holy Book,
    And drink was good for man;

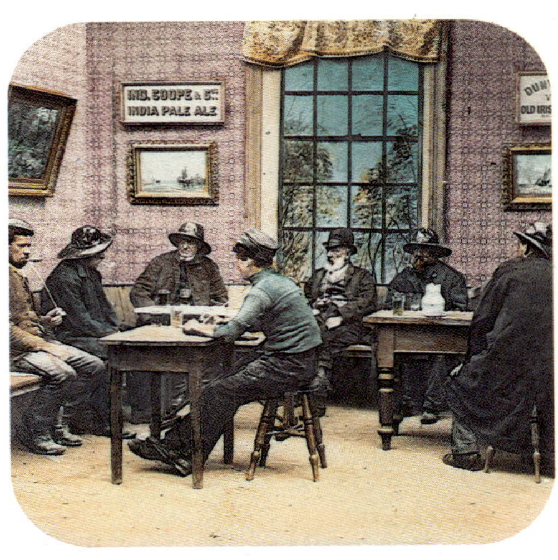

"That you could not help men drinking
     Until they got the *worse*;
What Heaven had made a blessing,
     They turned into a curse.
She went, but left a card behind, —
     It is lying in my box;
I've kept it nice, and clean, and new,
     Between my little frocks:

"You will find it wrapp'd in paper; —
     Things now are not the same,
Our mother never went to work
     Before that lady came;
When you came home from work, father,
     You romp't and talked, and read,
And heard us say our evening prayers,
     Then kissed us off to bed.

"Oh! they were happy, happy times;
     Now, mother cries to think
The home she made so neat and clean,
     Has gone to pay for drink.
I have prayed the gentle Saviour,
     In the shadow where I lie,
To look down in loving pity,
     And make you fit to die:

"Or you can never, never come
     Where I am going to-night,
Unless you give the drinking up,
     And strive to do the right.
The Bible says of drunkards, father,
     They cannot enter there,
I've prayed to Jesus o'er and o'er
     To answer Jessie's prayer.

"Father, promise ere I leave you
     For the mansions of the blest;
You will heed my solemn warning
     And follow my request.
Do not falter, — tell me, father, —
     God will help you, I know:"
"I will, I will, my Jessie, love,"
     And his tears began to flow.

Silent long he stood beside her,
    Looking on her darling face;
Thinking of her sinless nature,
    Thinking of his own disgrace.
While the deeds of shameless manhood,
    Crowded o'er his fevered brain;
Down he sank upon her pillow,
    Groaning with his load of pain; —

Then he started — gazed upon her,
    Pressed her little ice-cold brow,
Clasped her hand again, — and staggered, —
    It was all too lifeless now
She had heard his faithful promise,
    Heard her wayward father say
He would sign the pledge and keep it,
    Then her spirit passed away.

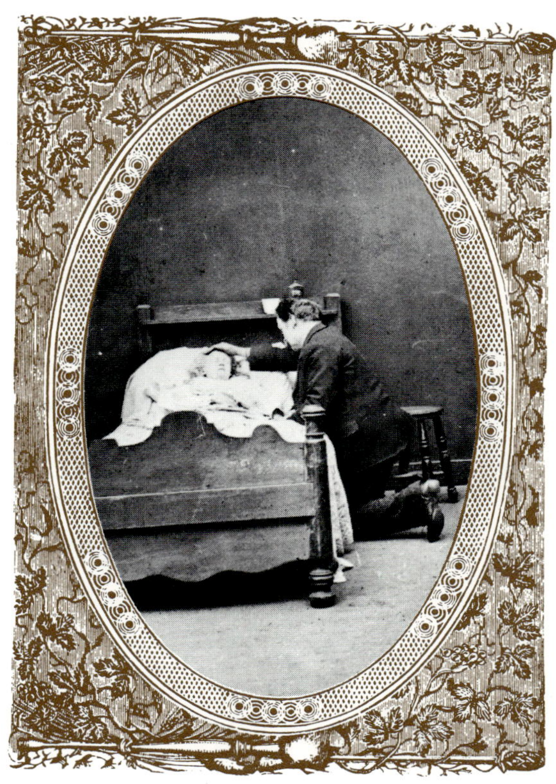

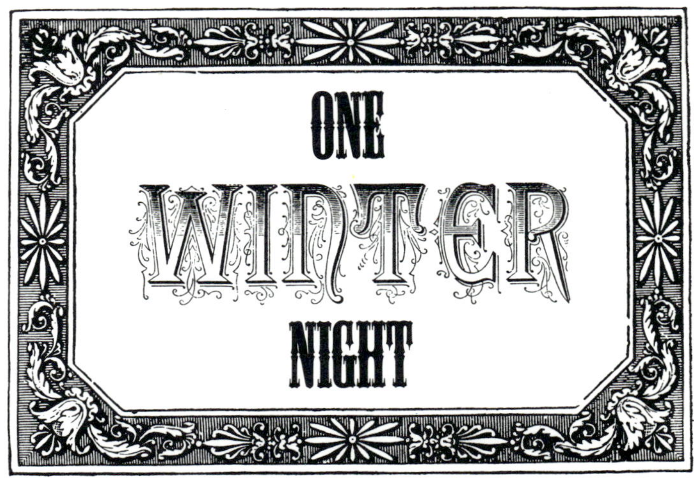

Ragged, wretched, worn and weary,
    Come the casuals, creeping in,
Where the Parish nightly shelters
    Shame and sorrow, sloth and sin;
Where the wounded in life's battle,
    Pushed aside and trodden down,
Share the Poor Law's tender mercy
    With the refuse of the town.

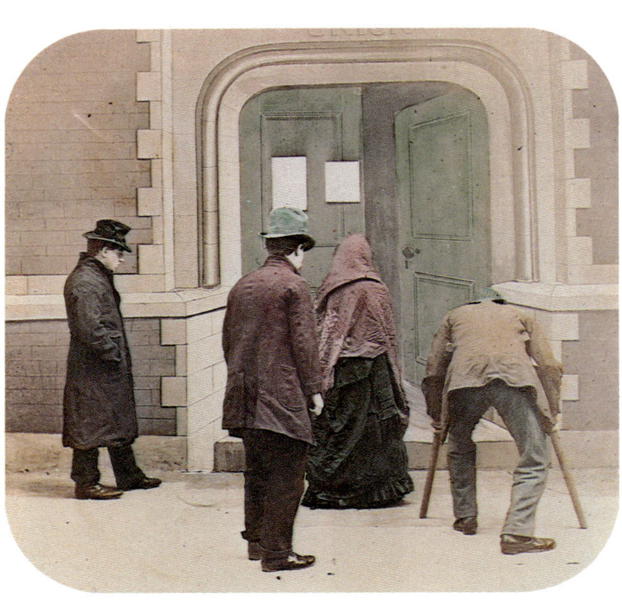

When the night has flung her mantle
    Rags and tatters kindly o'er,
Come the outcasts, meekly knocking
    At the black, forbidding door.
All the storm-tossed human wreckage,
    Sport for fortune's changing tide,
Hither drifts as to a harbour—
    Foul and fair float side by side.

Here, through all the long night watches,
    Want and woe can rest their heads:
Who shall say what bygone blisses
    Hover round these narrow beds?
Stained with travel, bent and broken,
    Here the starving outcast lies,
Yet he smiles—some happy vision
    Sleep has drawn across his eyes.

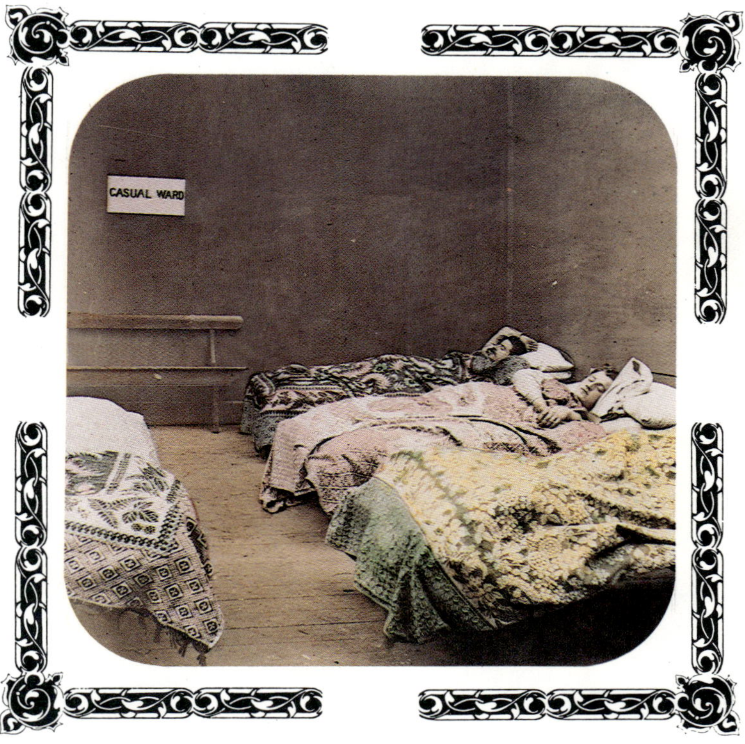

Sleep has come to weary eyelids,
    Dreams have come to tortured brains,
And in dreams perchance they wander
    Freely o'er life's pleasant plains.

Look where lies a woman sleeping,
　　Moaning even in her rest,
With a wee, wan baby pillowed
　　On her chill and shrivelled breast.

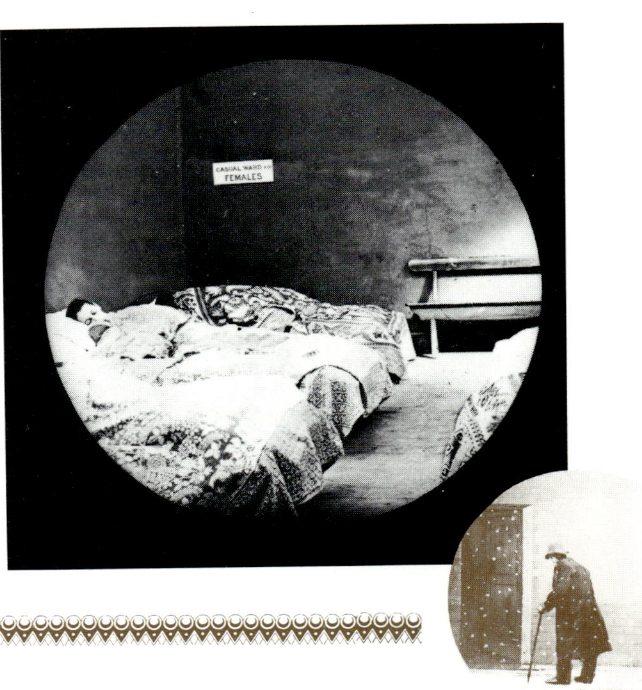

In her sleep she sees the husband
　　Whom the cruel fever slew,
While he sought the honest labour
　　He was all too weak to do.
Faint and footsore, broken-hearted,
　　Cold and hunger did their work:
Charity that might have saved him
　　Went abroad to help the Turk.

When the throes of death were on him,
　　With a groan he raised his head,
And he cried, "O God, have mercy
　　On my darlings when I'm dead!"
Then his dying kiss he gave them—
　　All that he had left to give—
Still the craved-for mercy tarries,
　　For his wife and baby *live*.

26

'Tis the Sabbath, and a woman,
    With a baby on her knee,
Sits among the poor who worship
    In the sittings labelled "Free"
From the cutting blast of winter
    She has sought a refuge there,
Though the peasants eye her fiercely,
    Wondering "how such creatures dare".

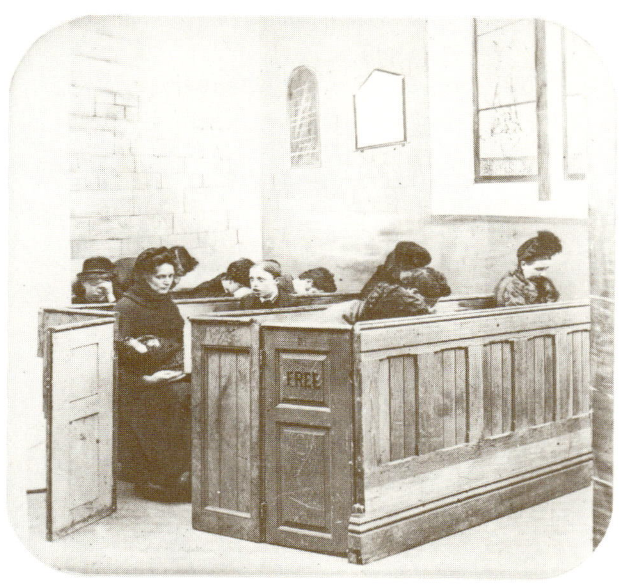

Rent and ragged are her garments,
    Pinched and pallid is her face;
She is tramping from the workhouse
    To her distant native place.
Here she rests awhile and listens
    In the warm and cosy church,
While the vicar reads a sermon
    From his velvet-cushioned perch.

For a special sermon chosen
    Is the Saviour's gentle speech,
When He blessed the little children,
    Laying loving hands on each;
And the parson tells his people
    How God loves the children well,
And will take them to his bosom
    In the golden land to dwell.

"Dry your eyes," he says, "O mourners,
    When your cherished darlings die;
Think how warm within God's bosom
    In that happy land they lie.
There no more can pain and anguish
    Wring the heart and cloud the brow—
They are past all sin and sorrow,
    They are happy angels now."

Peals the music of the organ
    As the people pass away;
O'er the fields they hurry homeward,
    For the skies are ashen grey;
And a homeless creature totters
    From God's temple with the rest;
In her heart her loving promise,
    And a baby at her breast.

*   *   *

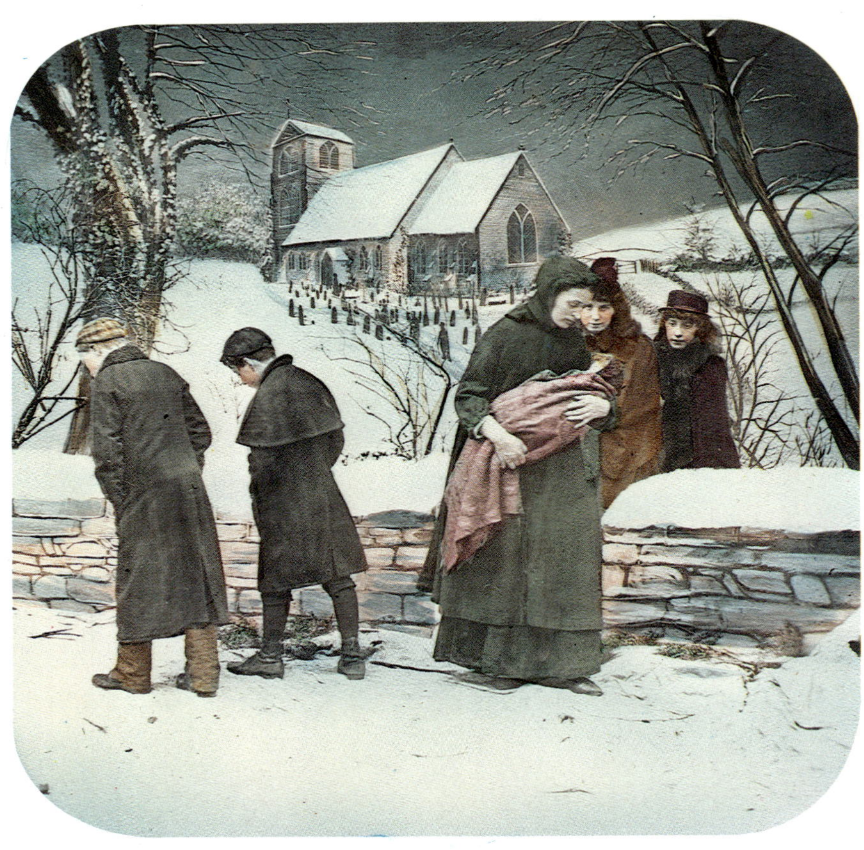

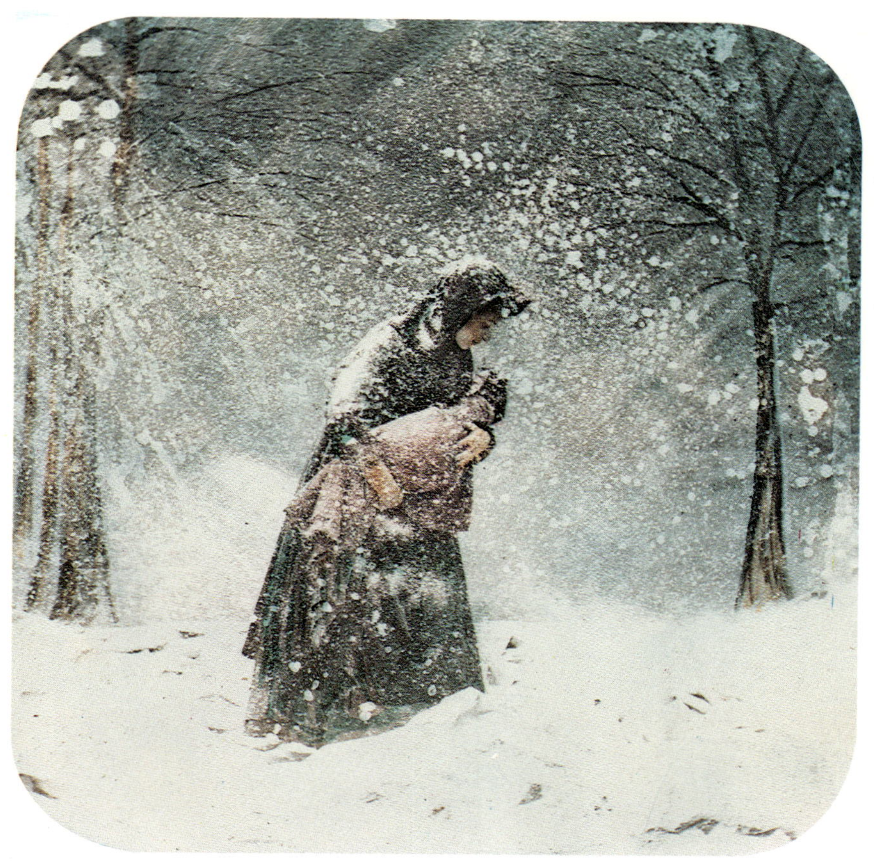

Hark, the tempest howls in fury,
   And the snow is falling fast,
As an outcast sinks exhausted,
   For her strength gives way at last.
She is lost upon the moorland,
   Daylight's last faint glimmer fled,
And the shelter that she seeks for
   Lieth weary miles ahead.

She is blinded by the snowstorm,
   And her limbs are numb with cold;
In her rags she wraps the baby
   That her weak arms scarce can hold.
She can feel its frozen body,
   She can hear its piteous cry,
And she thinks as on she staggers,
   What—O God—if she should die!

If her senses should desert her,
    And through all the cruel night
Here her babe should slowly perish—
    Ah, thank God!—she sees a light.
No, her eyes are dim with anguish,
    'Twas a star peeped through a cloud.
Hark, the blast grows fierce and fiercer,
    And the baby moans aloud.

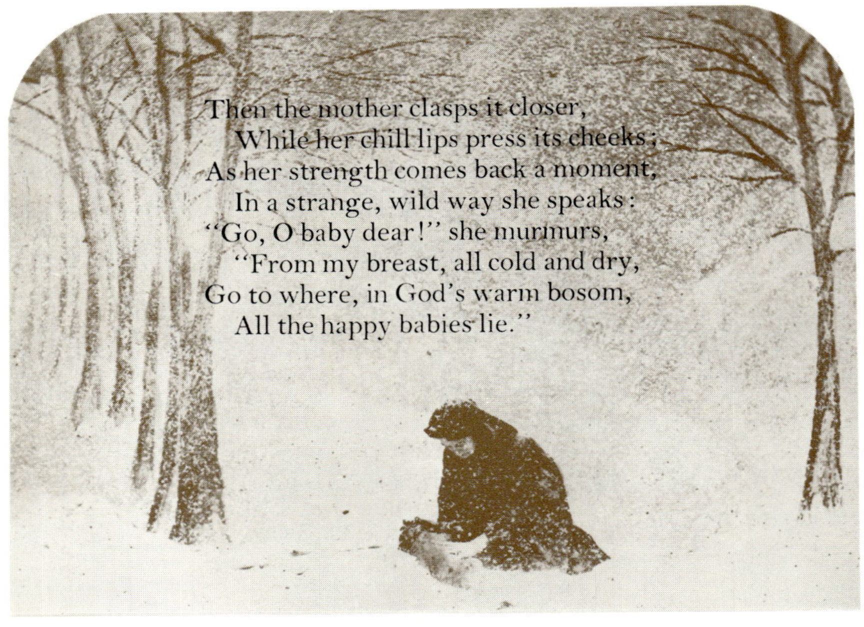

Then the mother clasps it closer,
    While her chill lips press its cheeks;
As her strength comes back a moment,
    In a strange, wild way she speaks:
"Go, O baby dear!" she murmurs,
    "From my breast, all cold and dry,
Go to where, in God's warm bosom,
    All the happy babies lie."

Pass the preacher's words of comfort
    Swiftly through her tortured brain;
High above her stretch the heavens
    Where they know not grief and pain.
What had earth to give her baby?
    What could be its life below?
Just one long, long spell of torture,
    Years of hunger, want, and woe.

*   *   *

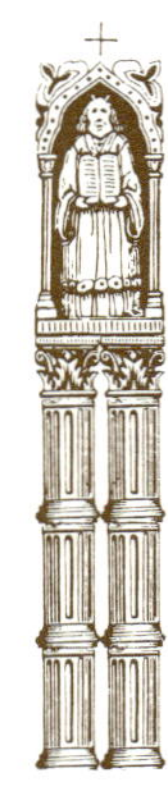

Late that night they found her, living,
    And the law condemned her crime.
"Death!" cried Justice, passing sentence.
    But before the fatal time,
He who took her burden from her
    Flung her prison gates ajar—
He perchance lets tortured mothers
    Pass to where their babies are.

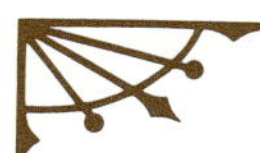

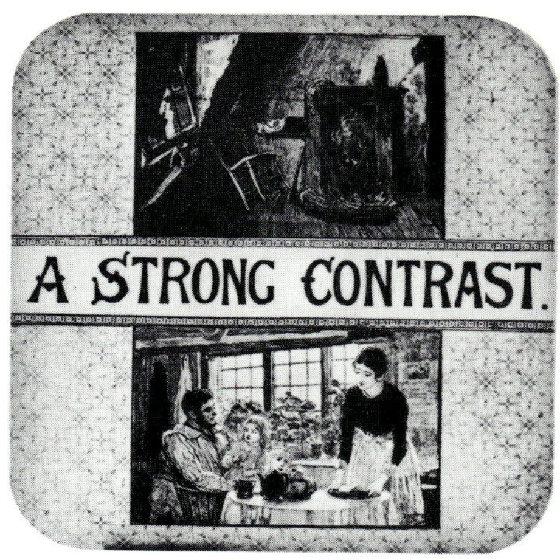

Each picture as shown tells its own story.
There is nothing like such contrasts
for enabling one to take in at a glance
the great width of the gulf
that lies between the abstainer and the drunkard.
And yet its width may be easily bridged
from either side.

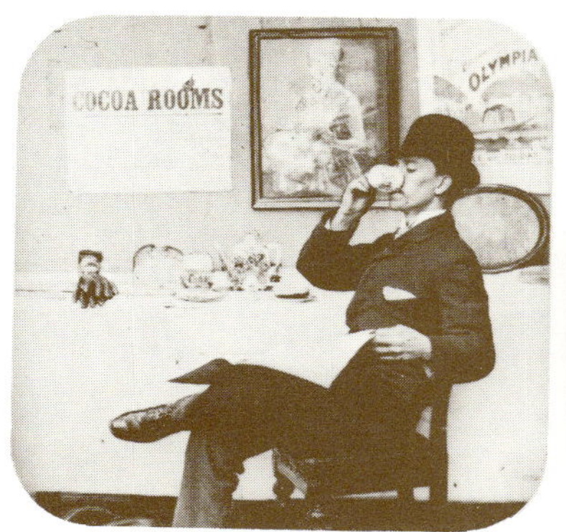

Temperance

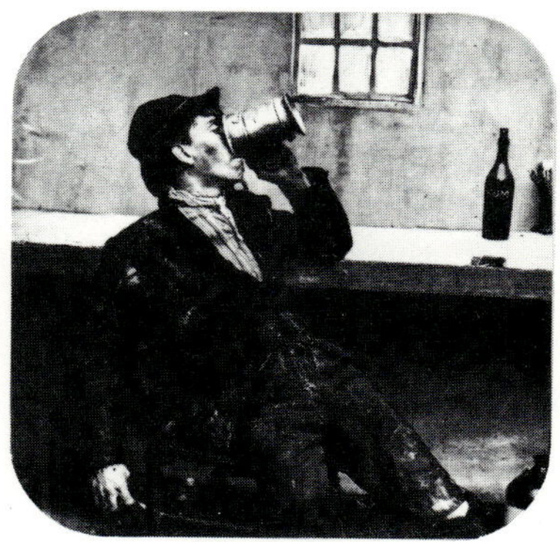

Intemperance

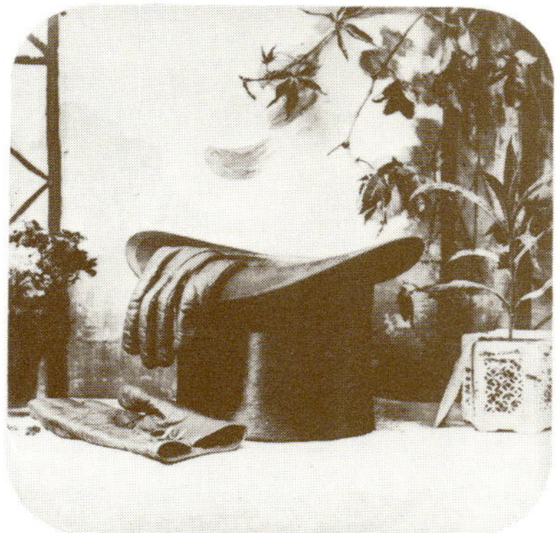

I am worn by a man who works and thinks

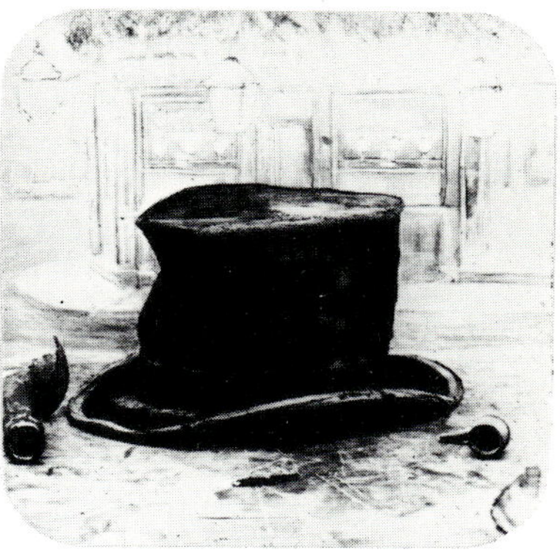

And I by one who don't and drinks

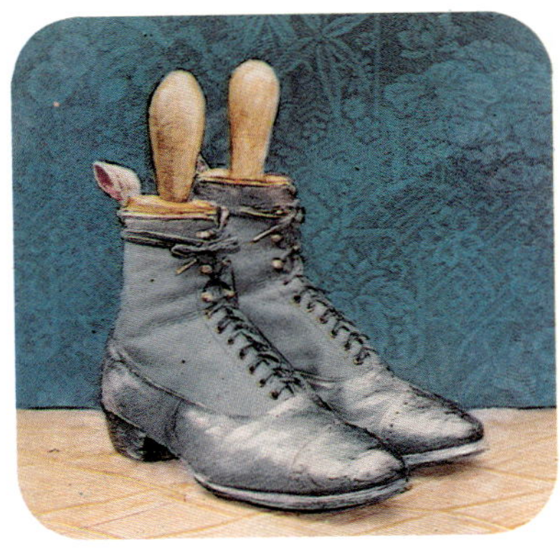

We guard his feet from damp and dust

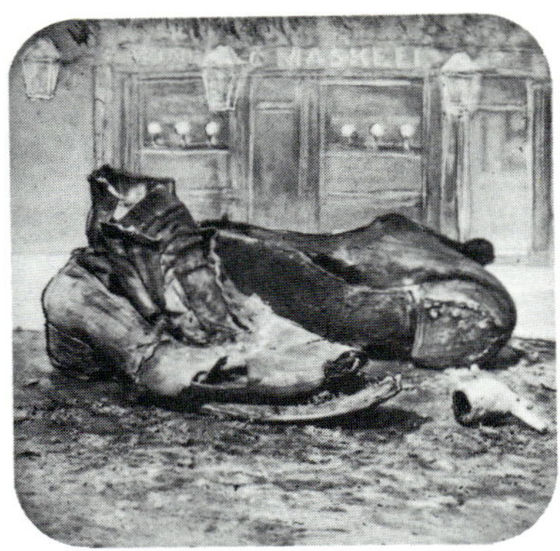

Like him we are always on the "bust"

Have you resolved that none of your money shall be spent for strong drink?
We hope so.
In that case your clothing will not resemble
the worthless sort pictured this evening.

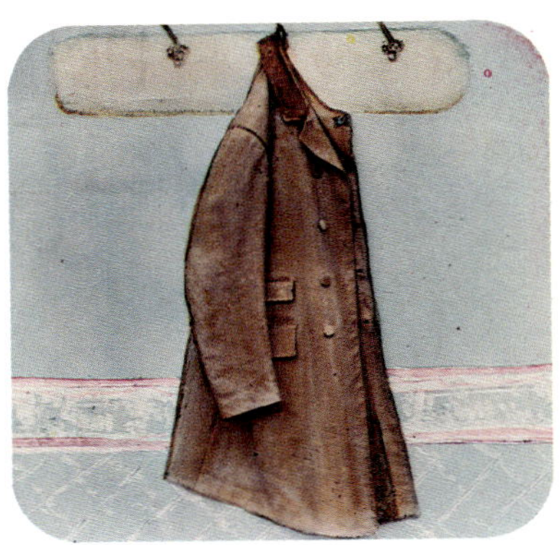

I am the coat my master wears

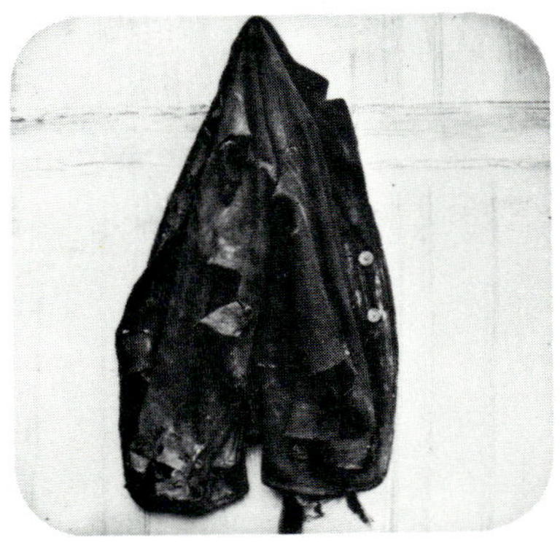

I resemble mine in terrible tears

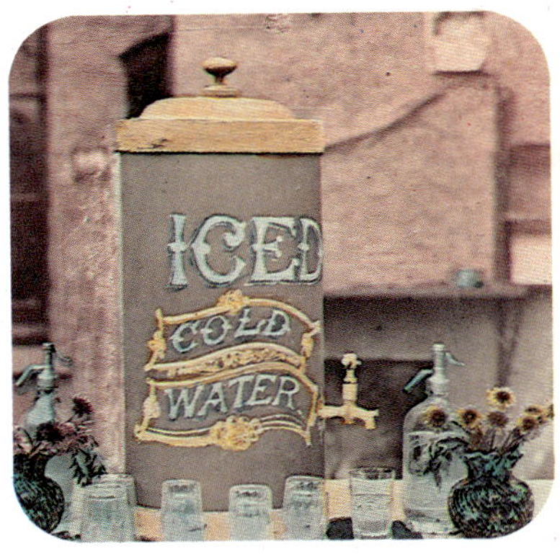

When master thirsts he comes to me,
I cost him nothing; to all I'm free

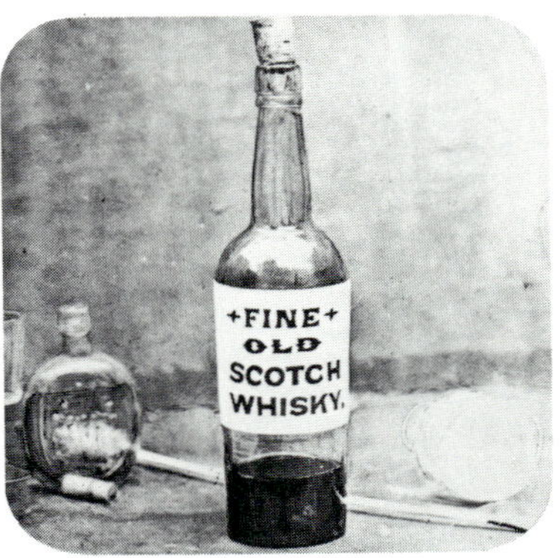

My master's throat I only burn,
And cost him all he can borrow or earn

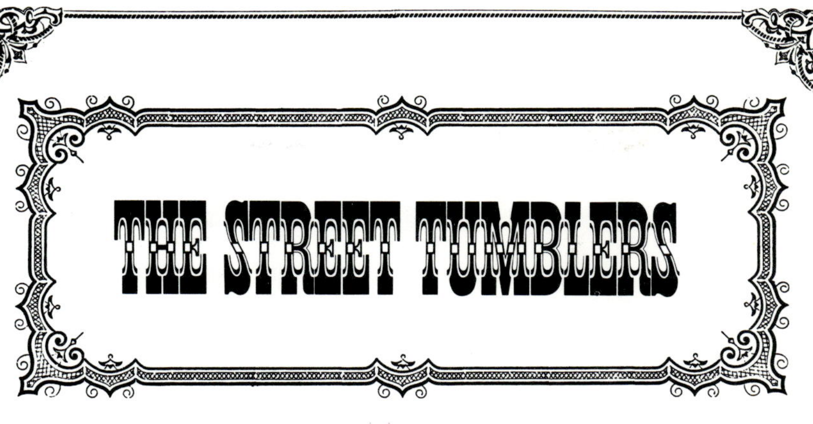

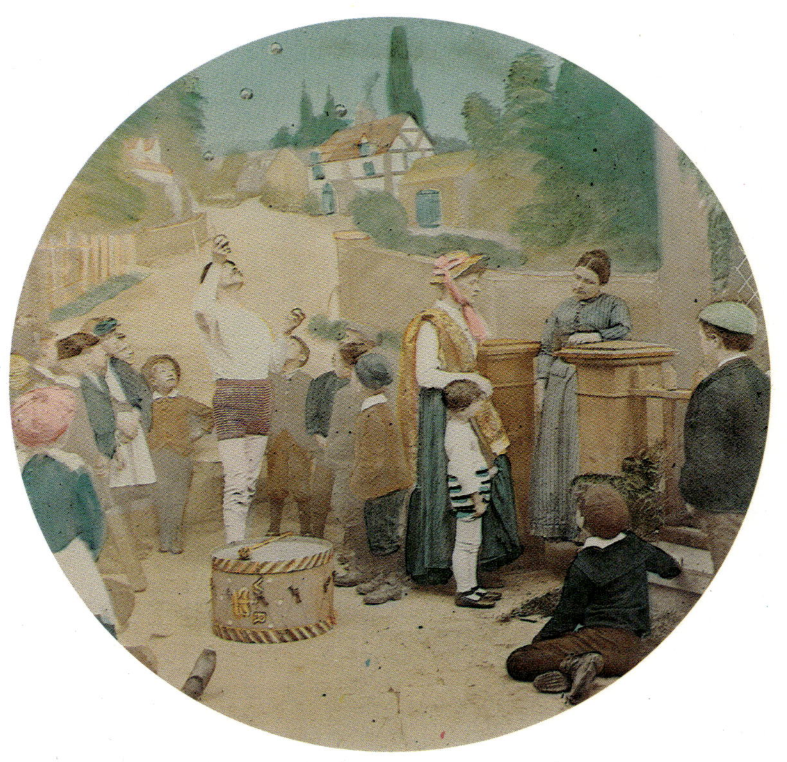

Thank the lady, Johnny, and give the money to dad;
Yes, I'm his mother, lady—don't say, "Poor little lad!"
For he likes the tumblin' rarely—took to it from the first.
Accidents?—nothing to speak of—a bruise or two at the worst.
It's him as draws the money; he's pretty and looks so smart,
He gets many a bit o' silver, with a "Bless your little heart!"
Danger—because his father flings him up like a ball?—
He's been at the game too long ,ma'am, to let our Johnny fall.

You'd sooner your child was dead, ma'am, than leading a life like this?
Come here a minute, Johnny, and give your mammy a kiss;
Look at his rosy cheeks, ma'am! look at his sturdy limbs!
Look how his dark eyes glisten! there's nothing their brightness dims.
We live in the air and the sunshine, we tramp thro' the long green lanes,
We know where to get good shelter, and we never have aches or pains.
We're happy we three together as we roam from place to place,
We should die pent up in cities, for we come of a gipsy race.

The rough and smooth together, it isn't so hard a life.
Yes, I've had my troubles—the biggest, the year I was mother and wife.
'Twas a hard black frosty winter the year that our baby came,
The master had sprained his ankle, and hobbled along dead lame.

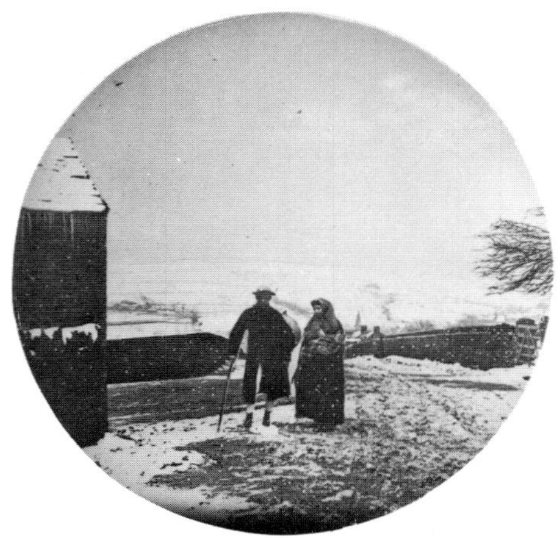

He'd had to give up performin', for the agony made him shriek,
And I had a month-old baby, and illness had left me weak.
We couldn't do much for a livin', and we weren't the folks to beg;
The master was fond o' baby, but, Lord, how he cursed his leg!

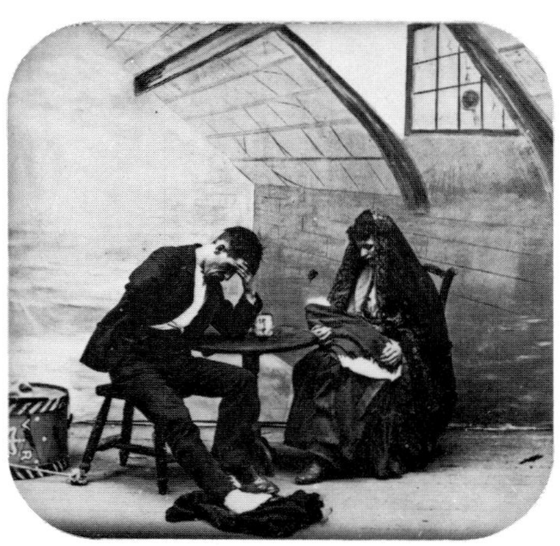

We wouldn't go in the workhouse, so we just kept tramping on,
Till the last of our little savin's hoarded for months had gone.
The master he got no better, and I got worse and worse,
And I watched the baby wastin' as I hadn't the strength to nurse.
I was cross and low, and I fretted, and I'd look at the child and think
As p'r'aps it 'ud be a mercy if the Lord 'ud let it sink—
Sink and die and be buried before it grew to know
What a road life is to travel when the luck's agin' your show.

At last, with the miles of trampin', Jo's leg grew quite inflamed,
And the doctor who saw it told him if he didn't rest he'd be lamed;
You can fancy what that meant, lady, to him as could lie in the street
And toss a weight up and catch it, and spin it round with his feet.

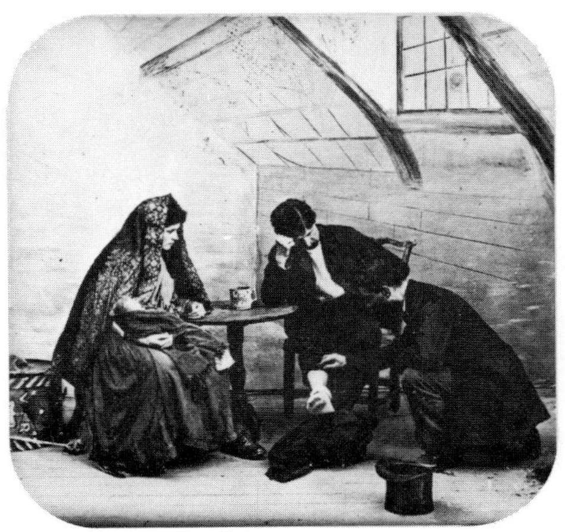

Now we couldn't earn a copper, and at last we wanted bread,
So we had to go to the workhouse for the sake of a meal and bed.
We had to go to the workhouse, where they parted man and wife,
And that was the wretchedest time, ma'am, of all my wand'rin' life.

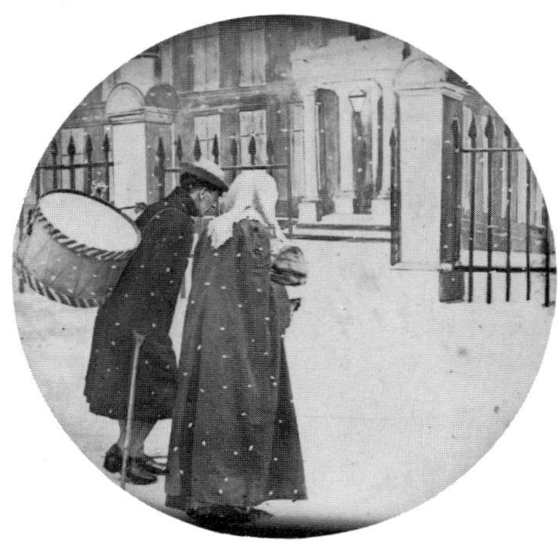

It's only folks like ourselves, ma'am, as can tell what artists feels,
When they're treated like common loafers that tramps and cadges and steals.
It seemed to us like a prison, with all them heartless rules,
So we started again, but often I'd stop by one o' them pools
That lie in a quiet corner, dark and slimy and still,
And wonder what drownin' felt like—you see I was weak and ill.
I know it was bad and sinful, but my thoughts were strange and wild;
You can pity a homeless mother, who loved her ailin' child.

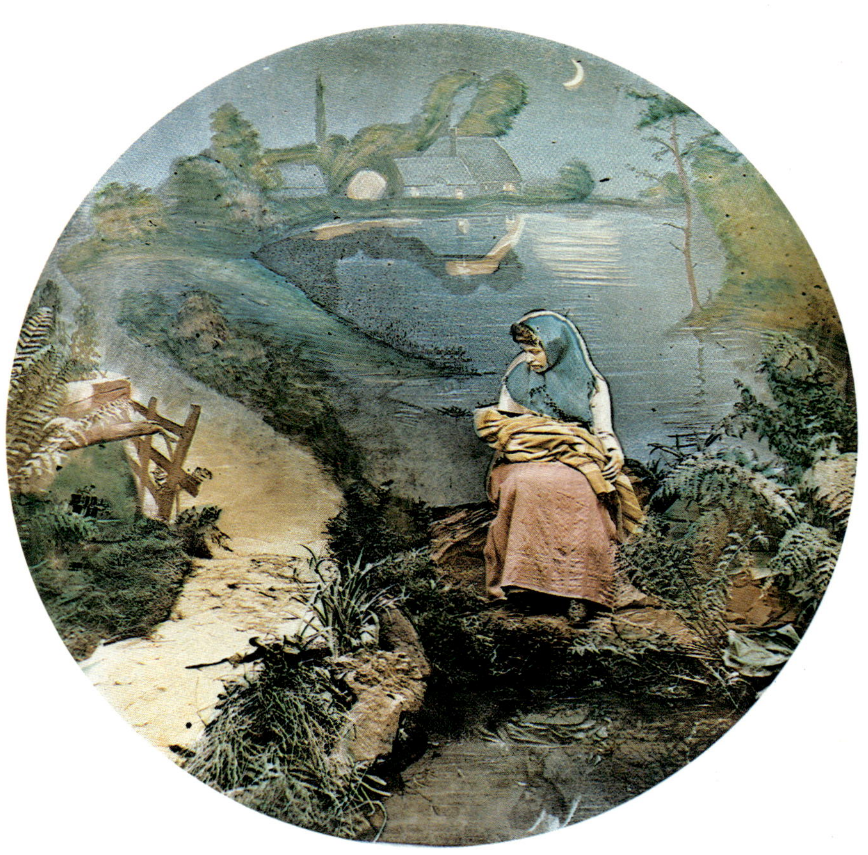

I hated the healthy babies I saw in their mothers' arms,
I'd look at my pale thin darlin' with a thousand wild alarms,
And think of what lay before us if the master didn't mend,
And our means of earnin' a livin' had come to a sudden end.
I envied the sturdy children when I looked at my poor wee mite.
I sometimes fancy now, ma'am, maybe as my head weren't right;
But I never envied another after a certain day,
As Providence gave me a lesson in a wonderful sort o' way.

It was through your a-sayin' you'd rather your child was stiff and dead
Than leadin' a life like Johnny, and as put it into my head
To tell you my bit o' story, and how as I came to see
It's better to be contented, no matter how bad things be.
Now look at him yonder, lady—handsome and firm o' limb;
There isn't a mother in England as mightn't be proud o' him.
Yet the day as I had my lesson I looked at his poor pinched face,
And I envied a little creature as came of a high-born race.

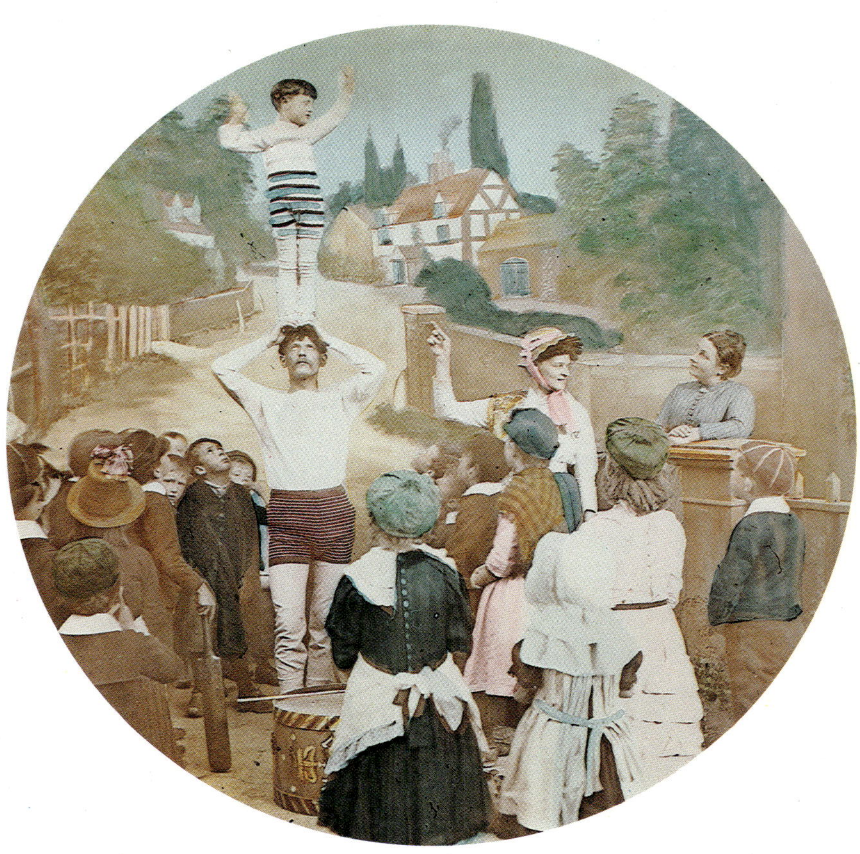

We'd tramped to a country village, and passin' the village church
Sat down in the porch a minute, for Joe had begun to lurch
And stagger a bit and murmur, for his ankle was awful bad;
But we hadn't sat down a second when a beadle came up like mad,
And ordered us off, and bellowed, and went nigh black in the face;
We saw what was up directly, when a big crowd filled the place,
And carriages full of ladies came drivin' up to the gate;
I never saw such a christenin'—'twas the heir to a grand estate.

We were pushed along by the people, and got mixed up in the crowd,
And I heard 'twas a countess's baby, for the women talked aloud.
The great folks filled the chancel—all friends of my lord the earl's,
For this was the first boy-baby—the others had all been girls.
I heard that one-half the county would come to that baby-boy;
I watched as his grand nurse held him, and I saw the mother's joy.
Then I thought of the life of pleasure, of the love and the tender care,
Of the fortune that God had given that white-robed baby-heir.

Then I looked at my half-starved Johnny, and thought of his hapless lot,
A lame street-tumbler's baby, by God and by man forgot.
And my heart was filled with passion as I looked at the tiny heir,
And thought, "Ah, if only Johnny had future half as fair!"
I envied my lady countess—no fear had she for her child;
My eyes were red with weepin'—her proud lips only smiled,
And I cried in my bitter anguish, "Oh God, if my little son
Could have such a fate as Heaven intends for that pampered one!"

So we stood in that church—two mothers—she blessed and me accursed,
And my heart was full of envy, when suddenly with a burst
Of a music loud and joyous the organ filled the place;
And stoopin', the lovely countess pressed her lips on her baby's face.
And then—it was all in a moment—I heard a sudden cry,
And a shriek from the lady-mother—then a murmur from low and high.
For the baby-heir to the title, guarded from every harm,
Lay dead in its christenin' garments—lay dead in its nurse's arm!

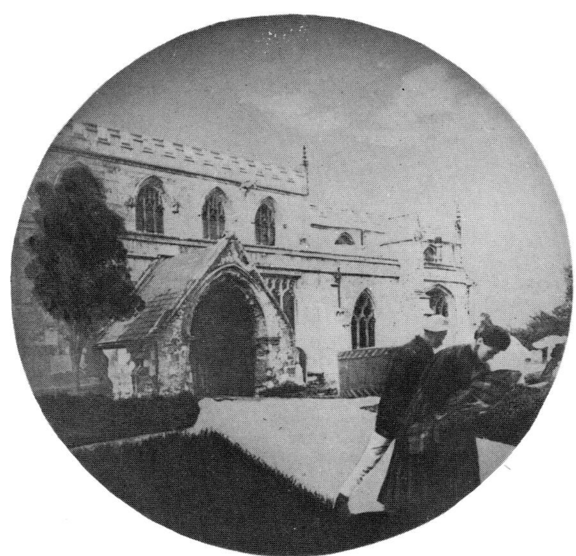

I rushed from the church that moment, my senses seemed to reel,
And I hugged my poor wee baby, with my hand on its heart to feel

The beatin' that seemed like music—then I clasped it to my breast
And smothered its face with kisses till I woke it from its rest.
Then its eyes looked up so sweetly, like an angel's, into mine,
And I thanked the God of Mercy for a blessing so divine.
For I had my babe—my darlin'—what matter the workhouse bed?
I could pity the noble lady, whose little child lay dead.

But our luck got round soon after, for I got better so quick
I was able to dance and juggle, and spin the hat with a stick;
And Johnny grew plump and pretty, and learnt to hold the shell,
To lisp out "Ta" for the pennies, and the master's leg got well;
And then when the boy grew bigger he took to the tumblin' so
That he learnt the tricks directly, and was quite a part of the show.

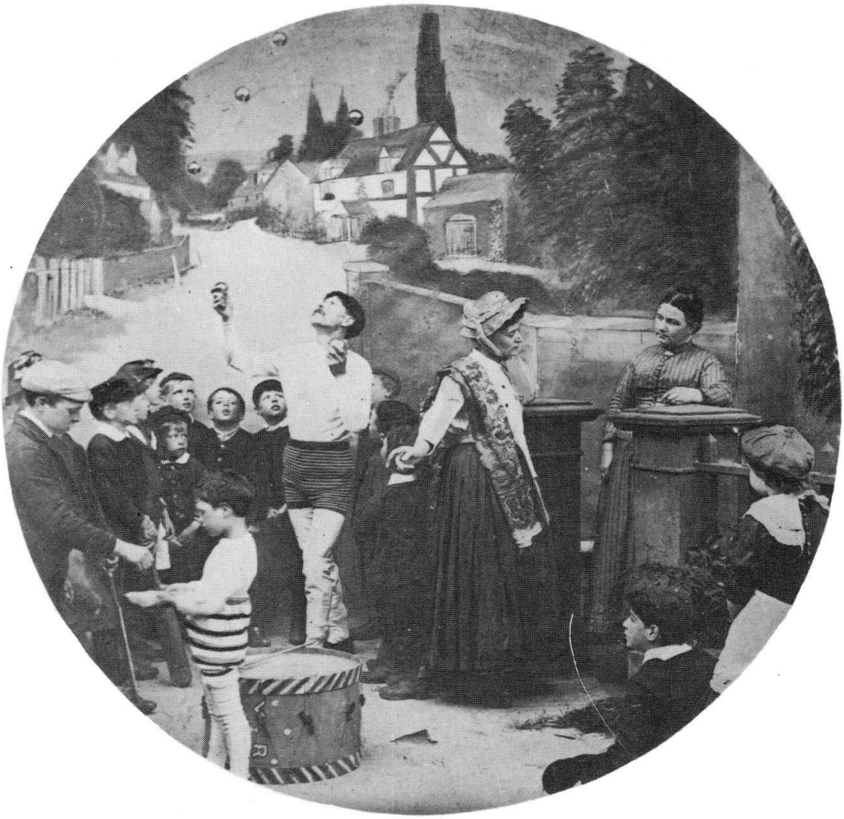

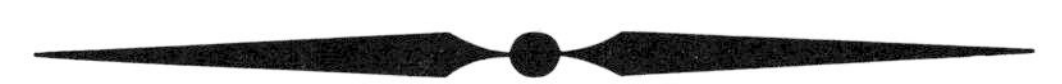

Street tumblin' ain't a fortune, but you know how I came to see
As it's better to rest contented, to be what you've got to be.

39

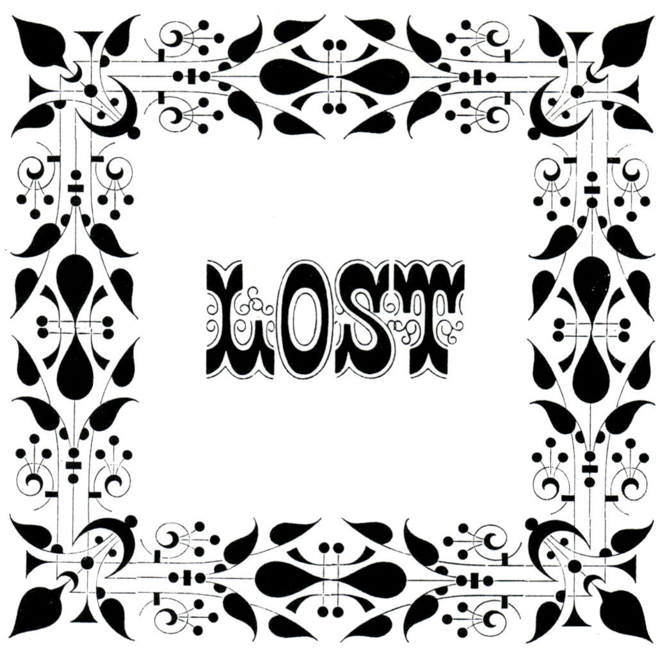

You have listened to many a story told of a shipwrecked man,
Cast on a desert Island where the painted savages ran,
And the monkeys climbed and chattered : cast there, and lost for years.
And you've listened, maybe, to ballads, that have filled your eyes with tears,

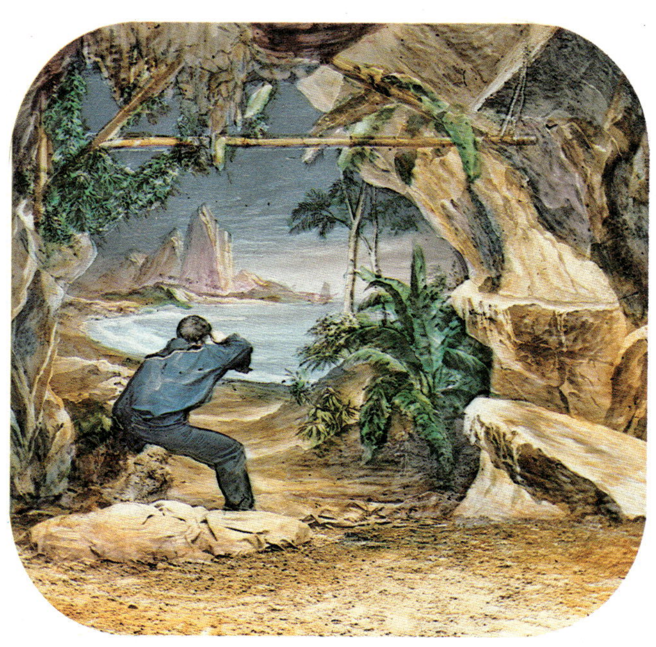

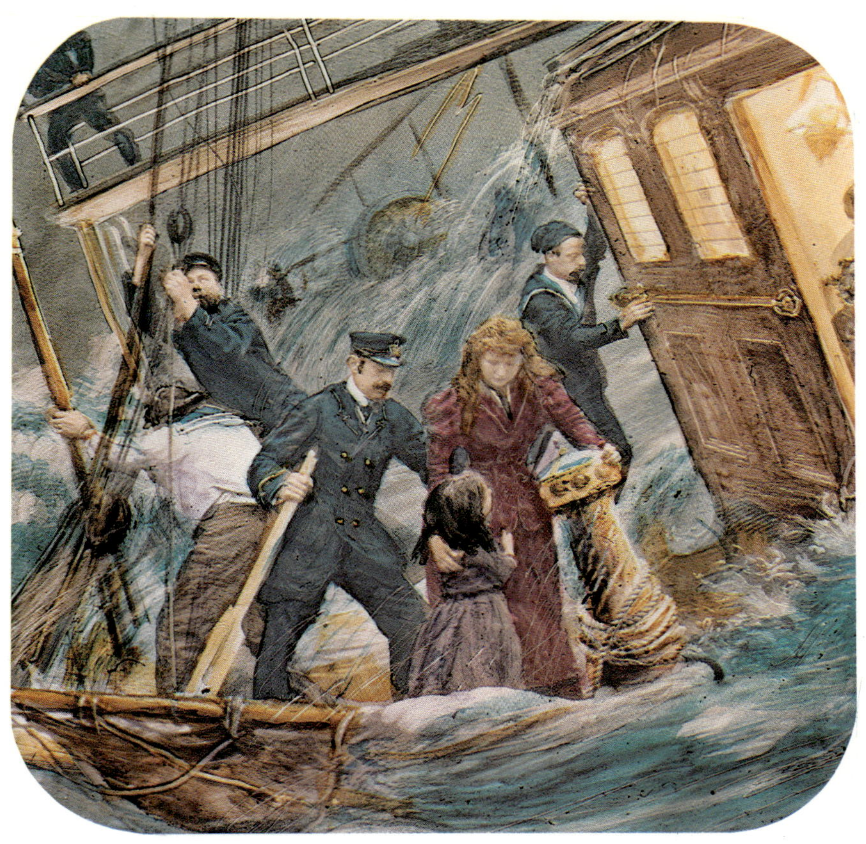

Of women and little children lost in the sand, or the snow:
Lost on the sea, when the vessel struck on the reefs below.
And the losing of our poor bodies is tragic enough, God knows!
But there are other stories, stranger, wilder, than those.
Tales of SOULS *that are lost. And I come to you this time*
With the truth of one such story. A tale of sin and crime,
But one of the most wonderful that ever was told in rhyme.

*   *   *

'T was after Jim had the fever. We were dreadful poor for a spell.
For there was a bill at the Baker's, and arrears of rent as well.
And me and Jim, we've a feeling that debt is a sort of sin!
So to help us through the trouble we took a lodger in.

Dave he was called, or Davey. I didn't like his eyes.
They used to make me fancy he'd be good at telling lies.
He never looked you straight in the face, and always shuffled his feet:
Though a bigger-made man than he was you couldn't pass in the street.

41

He told us he was an orphan: that he hadn't a human tie
In the world: and that, at starting, was a regular, downright lie!
For we found, a long time after, his parents were both alive!
And his wife! – whom he'd deserted – and a son! of four or five.

He never went to Chapel, nor to Church with Jim and me.
"Why don't you come? It's lovely!" I says to him pleasantly.
He turned and swore. *He* comin'! He'd as lief be hung or be shot
As sit in a place o' Worship and listen to Parson's rot.
Devil take this and the other! Did I take him for a saint?
"Well, no," I says, "I didn't! But," I says, "if you ain't,
Nor more am I: and maybe, you'll like it when you're there."
But he wasn't one for preaching: nor for Bible: nor for prayer.
And it made me think of demons to see him about the place,
With his hang-dog eyes, and his shuffles, and his evil-looking face.

Once he fell ill and I nursed him. Well, I take no praise for that.
It was nothing but my duty, and I'd nurse a dog or cat
That was under my roof, and ailing – but when he was up again,
He never so much as said "Thank you," though he knew I'd had a strain
To get him little comforts; for at that time we were bent
On saving every penny we could scrape towards the rent.

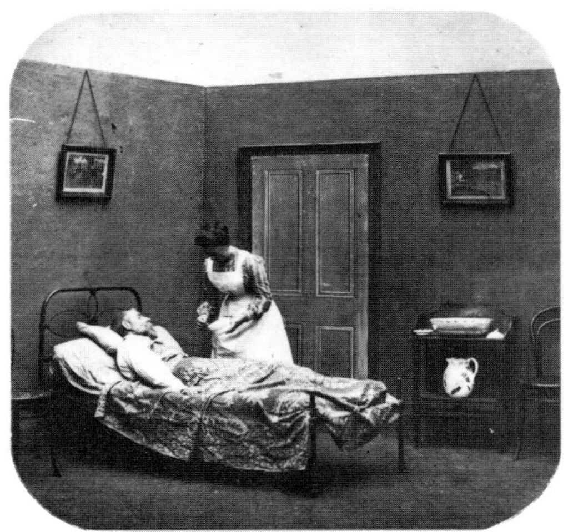

As long as there's back-rent owing you can't call your soul your own.
That's how I felt about it. And it wasn't my feel alone,
For we felt it all together. The children says to me –
"Mother, we don't mind having no sugar in our tea,
And that will save a little!" And Jim he says, says he –
"I'll stop my beer and baccy till this blessed debt is through."
And I says – "Well, I'm shabby! – But not a stitch that's new
Will I wear . . . till we've paid it." And so our savings grew
Till in my old cracked tea-pot I'd got the whole round sum,
And felt that happy-hearted I could have played the drum!

The Monday I meant to pay it – it was three o'clock about –
I reached me down the tea-pot to count the money out.
I'd a sovereign on the table, Jim gave me Saturday night –
And as I stood there, counting, to see that all was right,
I heard the door shut softly, and turned my head to see,
And there was Dave, our lodger, standing up close to me.

Friends! It's a fearful moment when a soul beneath this sun
Stands face to face, on a sudden, with the power of the Evil One.
The Devil was in that man. And looked at me out of his eyes.
I knew he had come to rob me. And quick as the lightning flies
I knew that I couldn't stop him! There was none in the house but me.
The children away at school, and Jim at the factory.

"Quick!" he says, "Give me the money! If you move, or lift your hand,
Or speak above a whisper, I'll brain you where you stand."
I didn't move, but I faced him – "Dave!" I says, "I've no fear,
I'm not a going to struggle or scream, for there's none to hear.
You can rob us of our savings. You! That have shared our bread.
But as sure as a God of Justice is watching overhead
You will take a *curse* with this money that will follow you into Hell . . ."
And I said no more, for he struck me: a murderous blow, and I fell
Straight down at his feet like a dead thing, and remembered nothing more
Till Jim came in at tea-time and lifted me from the floor.

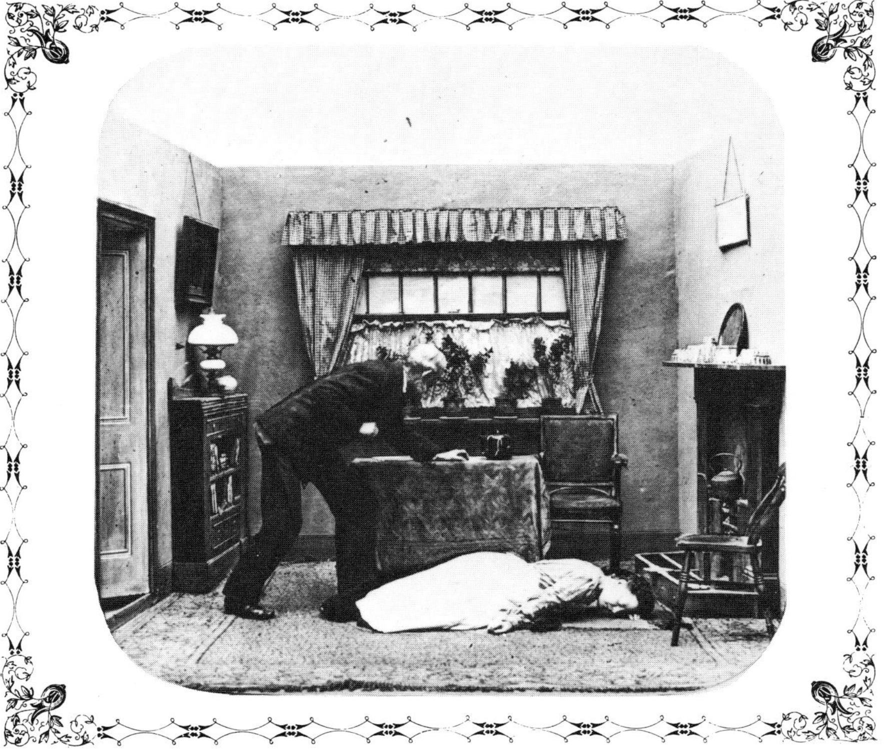

I was ill for a long time after, with the blow, and the shock, and the pain,
And the sickness of heart at thinking we must save all over again.
For he'd robbed us of every sixpence, and cleared right out of the place,
And though the Police were a searching they never set eyes on his face.

I've known bad men, and bad women, but never one worse than him,
For, mind you, he'd been our lodger, living friendly with me and Jim!
He'd known our shifts and our struggles. And yet he was bad, that *bad*,
He could rob poor folks as we were of the little that we had!

Well. The full years went over – nine of them, one by one,
Jimmy was Foreman, and working as hard as he's always done.
We were busy, and hearty, and happy. And I'd ceased to give a thought
To Davey and his doings, or to wonder if he'd been caught.
The summer was stifling sultry, and one night I pushed my chair
Beside the open window, to get a breath of air.
And as I sat there, dreamy, for a minute in the heat –
The face of the man who had robbed me rose out of the dark of the street.

Only a moment I saw it! – pale! – like a face from the grave.
A moment it stared in my eyes, and was gone! But I knew it was Dave.
And on the impulse I started, and screamed to the others, and ran . . .
And found him lying across our step like a drunken man.
Not drunk. He had fainted. And Jimmy, he lifted and carried him in.
Oh! It's the truth in the Bible that hard is the service of sin.

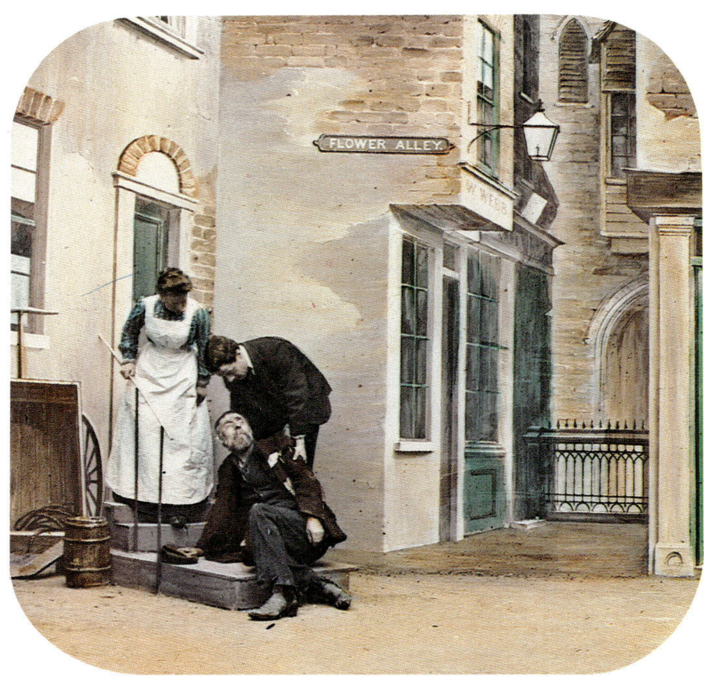

We didn't need words to tell us, as we stood by our enemy,
That he'd done more harm to himself by his crimes than he'd done to we.
The man was a ghost to look on! a wreck! a half-starved hound!
We had to fetch the doctor before we could bring him round.

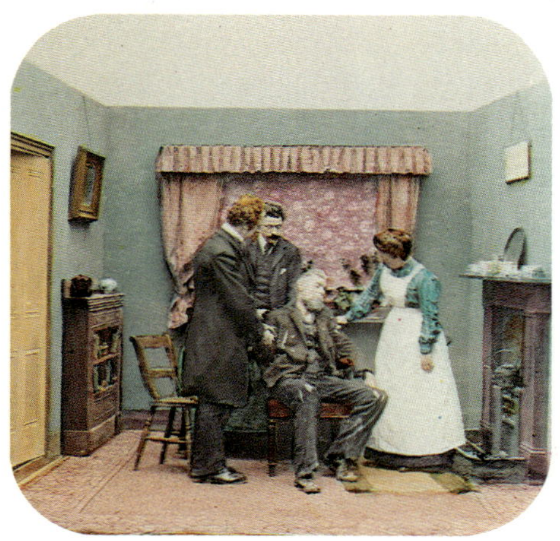

I sent the others to bed, and through the hush and the gloom
Of that live-long night I watched him, in our little sitting-room.
Just after midnight he spoke to me, raising a heavy lid –
"You here! . . . I meant to kill you that day . . ." "Yes, I know you did."
"Listen!" He says! "I *must* speak –." And oh! May there never be
In my ears again a voice of such desperate misery.
"I took a curse with that money . . . you said I should . . . you was right.
It's dragged, it's hunted me down, it's followed me, day an' night.
You wasn't the last I robbed. I'm dyin' . . . I knows it well . . .
And I'm lost . . . And that CURSE you spoke of, *will* follow me . . . into Hell!"

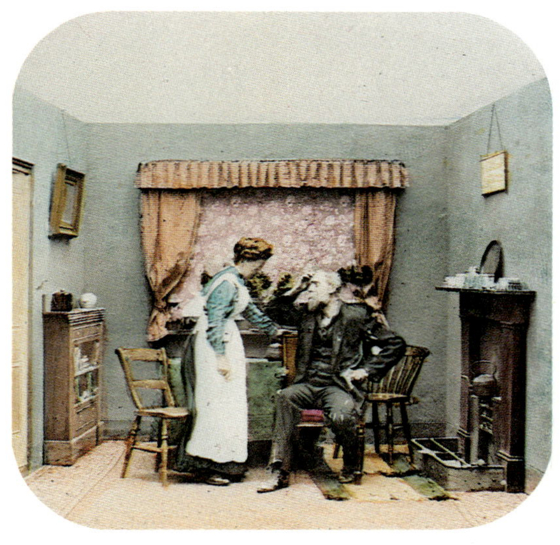

Friends! It's not given to many who draw our mortal breath,
To hear a lost soul wailing on the very edge of death.
Thank God, it was given to me! Thank God as I saw him there,
Bad as he'd been, thief – outcast – in the last gasp of despair –
There rushed on my soul the message Christ brought to wrecks like him.
And the glory of that message thrilled me through every limb!
It seemed as if an Angel lifted a golden rod
And showed me the Hope, and Pity, that rolls through the Word of God!

Lost! But the *lost* may be *found*: Christ's truth!
      I knelt down on the floor.
"Dave, you were lost, but you're found – found – rescued for evermore.
It's the truth of the blessed Gospel – I can show you chapter and verse
The Lord whom you have forgotten will take away the curse.
I know you are black: but never was a man, or a woman, so vile
That the blood of the Lord couldn't cleanse them. Oh Dave!" – and I couldn't but
      smile –
"You've nothing to say but – '*Forgive me! . . . I'm sorry! . . . I've sinned!*' and at last
The love of the Father can reach you, and blot out your wretched past.
When the wicked man turns to his God – it is writ in the Bible plain –
The sins which he hath committed shall not be mentioned again!"
"Nothing to say but . . . *forgive me*:"
      It seemed too much to be true.
He stared at me unbelieving.
      "And can you forgive me? You!
That I robbed . . . and struck?" "Forgive you! Poor soul," I says, "I do.
If forgiveness of mine will show you the forgiveness of God more clear,
I'll forgive you every day and every night in the year!"
      Oh friends! The wonder of it! I looked and I saw on his face
A look there must be on the faces of those in the Happy Place.
It came in a blaze to him! Pardon! Hope! Mercy! for him – the defiled!
He'd not shed a tear for thirty year, but he sobbed like a little child.

He didn't die. He recovered. He was granted another span
Of life in this world, was Davey. And he lived it – an altered man.

I could show you a little cottage, to-day, in a Surrey lane,
Where the clematis and roses climb round the window pane,
And the birds sing in summer. A man lives there, with his wife,
And his son – whom he'd deserted: – and he's living an honest life.
That's him! That's Dave! They're happy. He's working at a trade.
And he looks you full in the face now: eyes steady, and straight as a blade.
We were friends, all friends together, in London, before they went.
And he's paid us back that money. Every penny! every cent!

O Glory to God for the Hope that girdles the whole world round.
The sinner may be forgiven. And the lost, the LOST – can be Found!

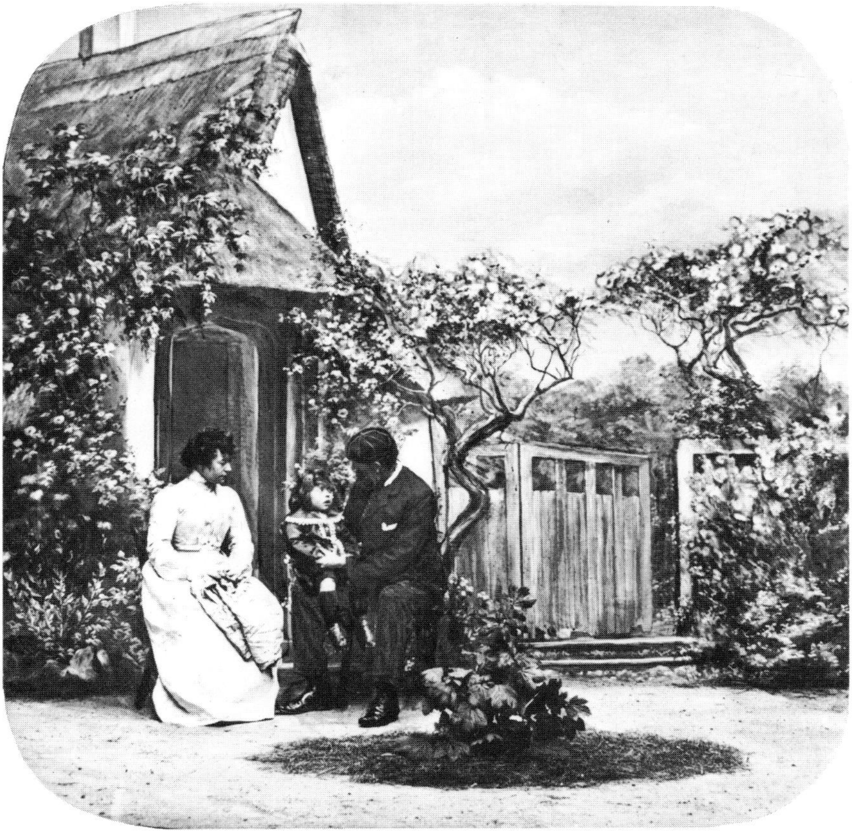

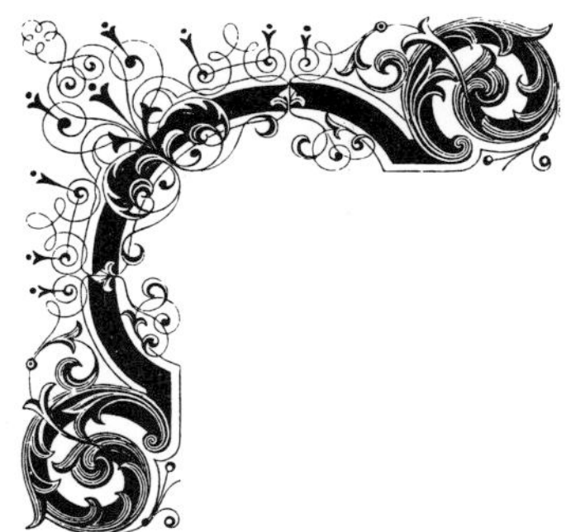
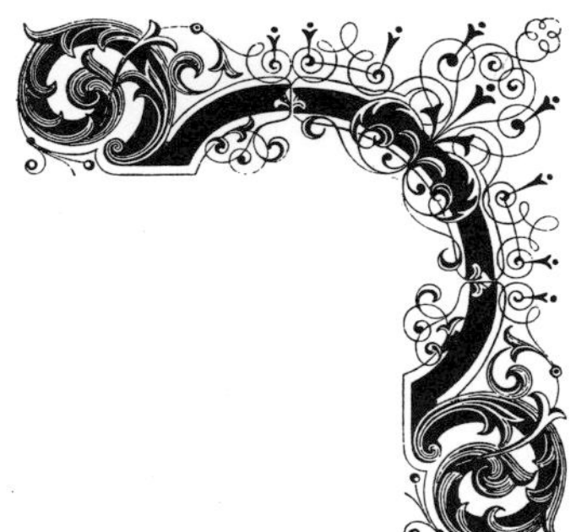
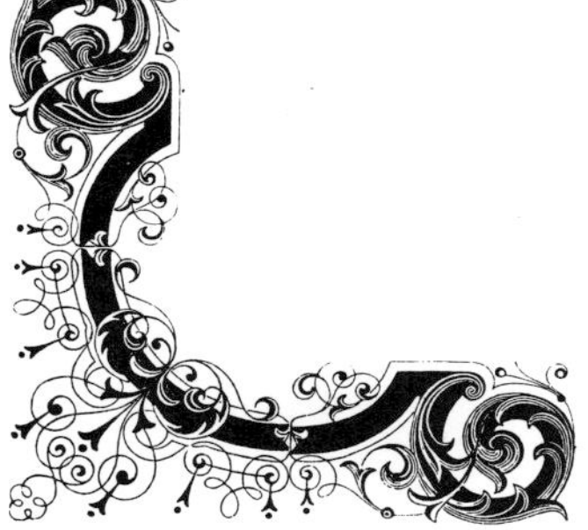
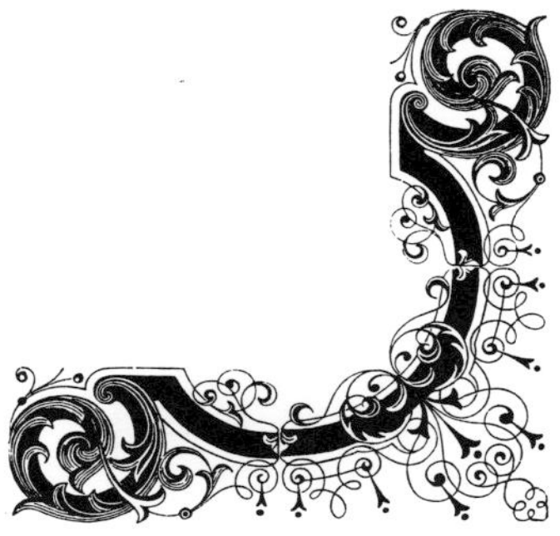

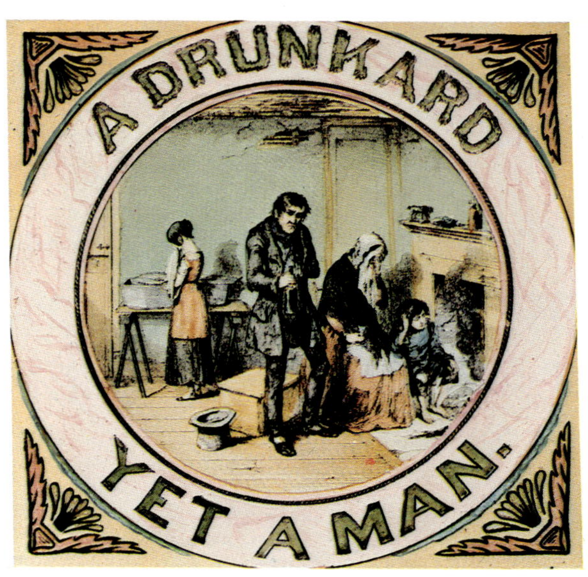

A drunkard stood in his cheerless home,
 In deep distress he seem'd,
For poverty and want had come
 Where hope and joy once beamed.
"Ah me!" he sigh'd, with tearful eye,
 And call'd on Him above:
"No bread for these my children dear,
 No food for her I love!"
At their hungry cry he turn'd around
 Their slender forms to scan,
Said he, "How fearful is my fate—
 A drunkard, not a man."

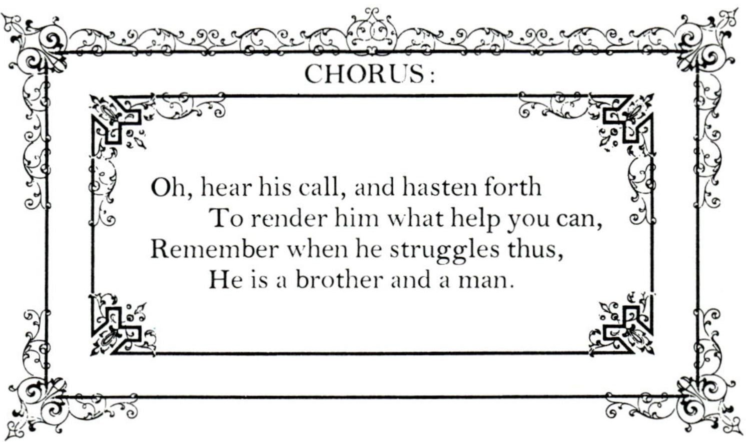

CHORUS:

Oh, hear his call, and hasten forth
 To render him what help you can,
Remember when he struggles thus,
 He is a brother and a man.

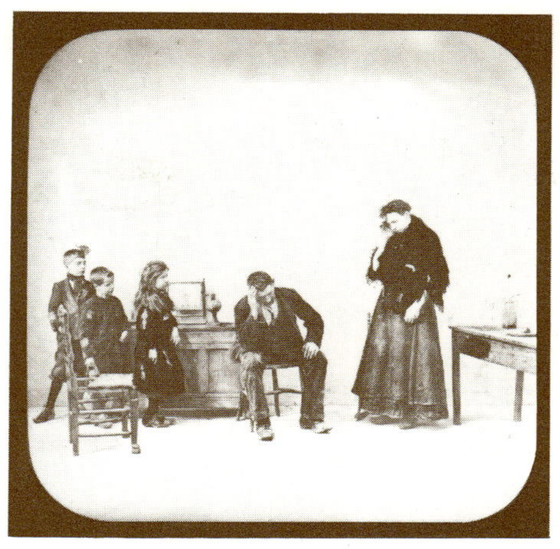

The mother wept as well she might,
    To see her husband's grief;
"I've done my best," she feebly cried,
    "Will God not send relief?"
She toil'd so hard from morn till night—
    She work'd with heart so brave,
Till fainting in his arms she fell;
    What could he do to save?
Oh, Father! who in heav'n above
    Hath all things in Thy span,
The drunkard's wife,—God spare her life
    To love him when a man.

[CHORUS]

Her drooping head he sadly rais'd,
    He call'd her by her name,

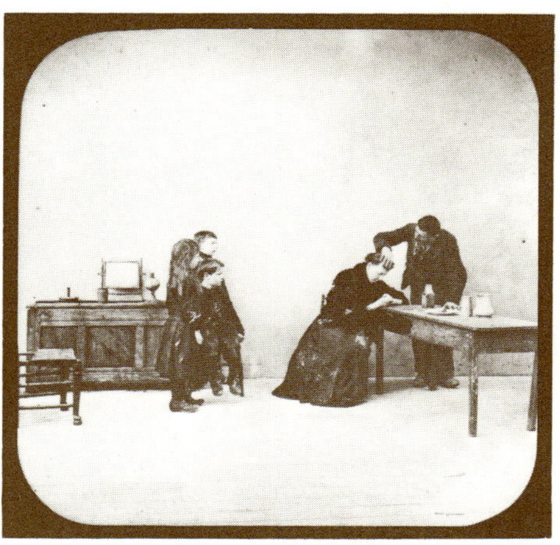

For in that wretched drunkard's breast
    There still was sense of shame.
"O God! this drink will drive me mad,
    I long to be set free;
Restore my wife—the pledge I'll try
    To save a wreck like me."

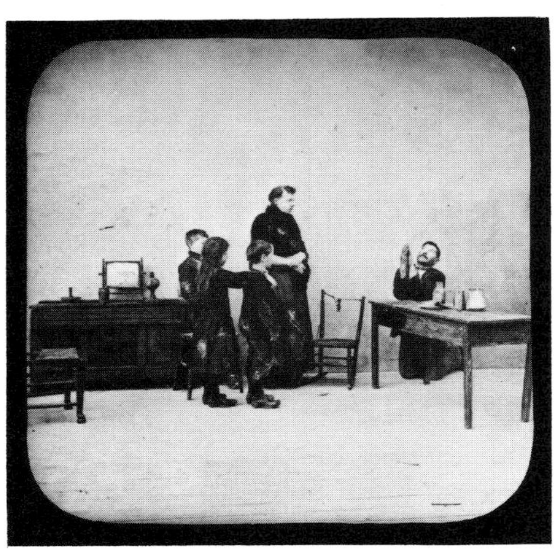

At such wondrous words she turn'd around
    Her husband's face to scan,
"Be brave, my lad," she faintly cried,
    "You yet will be a man."

[CHORUS]

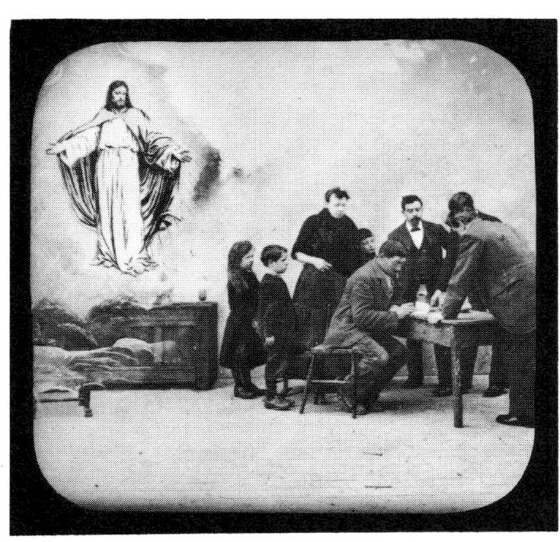

That good resolve was heard on high,
    And when the pledge was sign'd,
God heard the sigh, He saw the tear,
    And deep distress of mind.
He rais'd kind friends on ev'ry hand,
    His drooping heart to cheer,
And in Temptation's darkest hour
    God's strength'ning hand was near.
At His loving touch he look'd above
    His Father's face to scan,
"Dear Lord! keep near—no drink I'll fear,
    Once more I am a man."

[CHORUS]

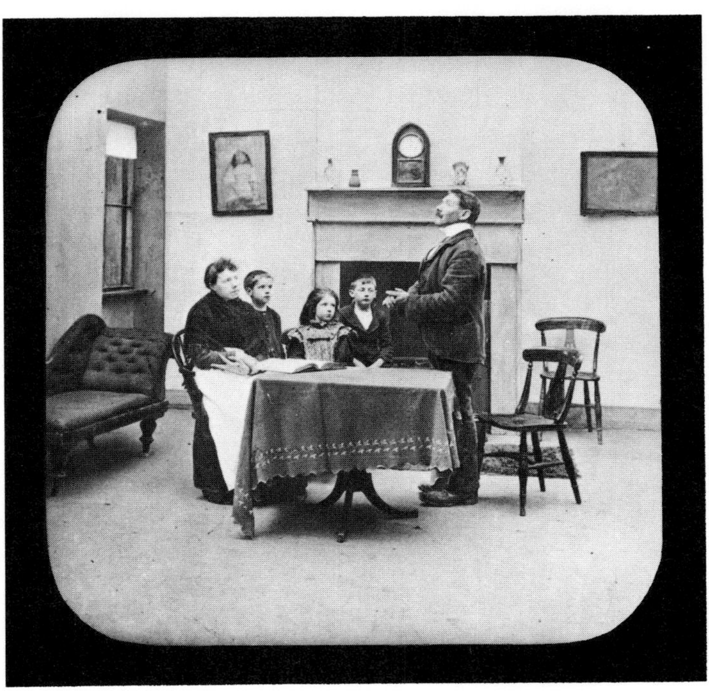

THE DRINK FIEND

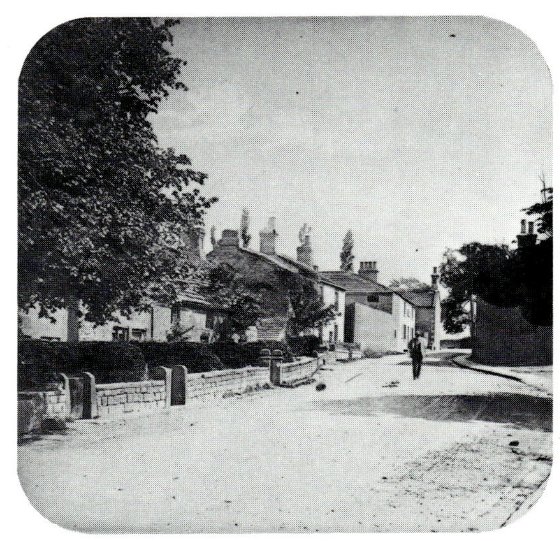

The cottage homes of England have been shewn
  To be among the gems of this fair land;
  And from the frozen to the torrid zone,
No better proofs of industry do stand.

How sweet for hind or artizan, when eve
Her sombre mantle o'er the earth has thrown,
To turn his steps towards home, and there receive
A loving welcome from hearts all his own.

The ruddy fire—clean hearth—and burnished stove—
The singing kettle filled from clearest springs—
The simple pictures on the walls above—
Make home the dearest of all earthly things.

And while around the table set for tea
They gather, can we wonder at the pride
Each member of that sweet community
Feels when he speaks about his "own fireside".

And such a picture is before us now,
And who would think that danger here can lurk?
But though the smiles light up each happy brow,
Yet even here the tempter is at work.

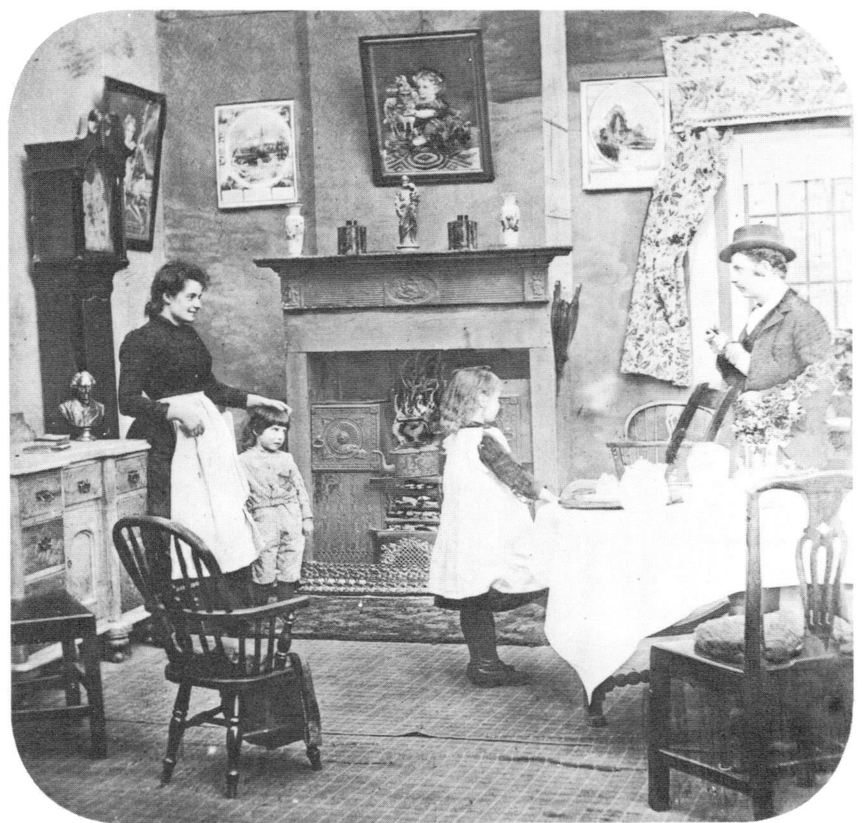

Elated by a rise in wages, he
A guest with him this evening home has brought,
To fire those loving hearts which soon will be
With every sin and every passion fraught.

The glass with fiery fluid filled is passed,
The shrinking wife "just wets her lips" at first,
And then more daring grown she sips, then drinks at last,
And thus acquires a never-dying thirst.

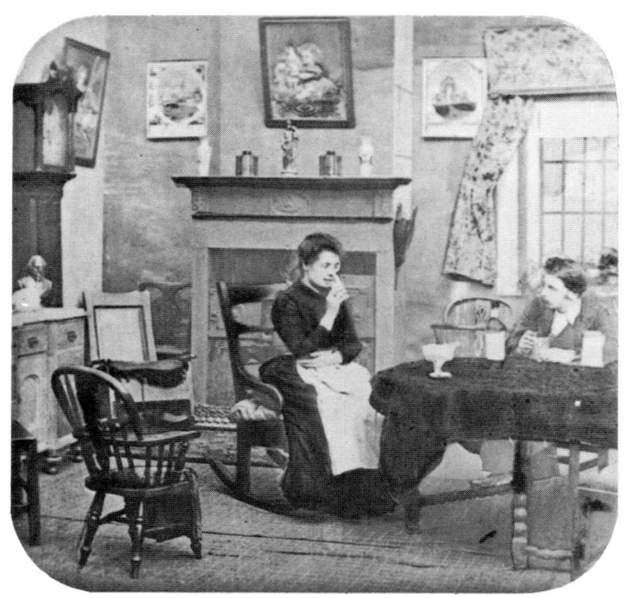

While he yet deeper drinks until at length—
His brain a whirling chaos in his head—
Turned now to feebleness his manly strength—
Is led by scarce more sober wife to bed.

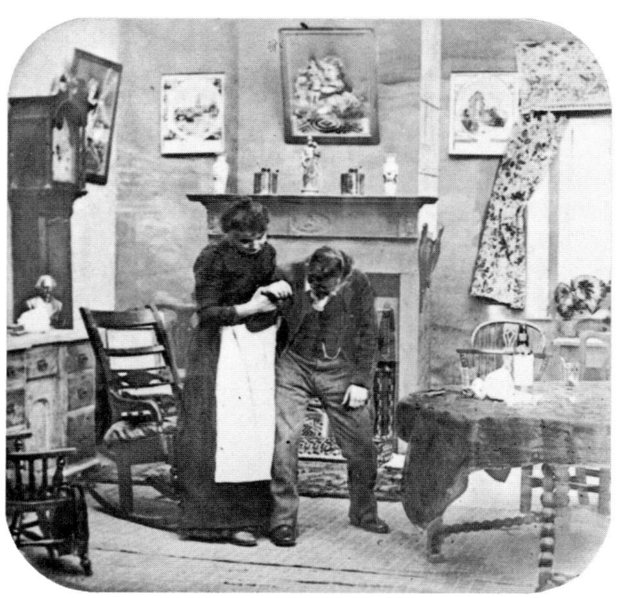

How changed the scene—where all around was fair,
Is now to us the picture of despair;
The cot that once for neatness might have vied
With any palace, now is shorn of pride.

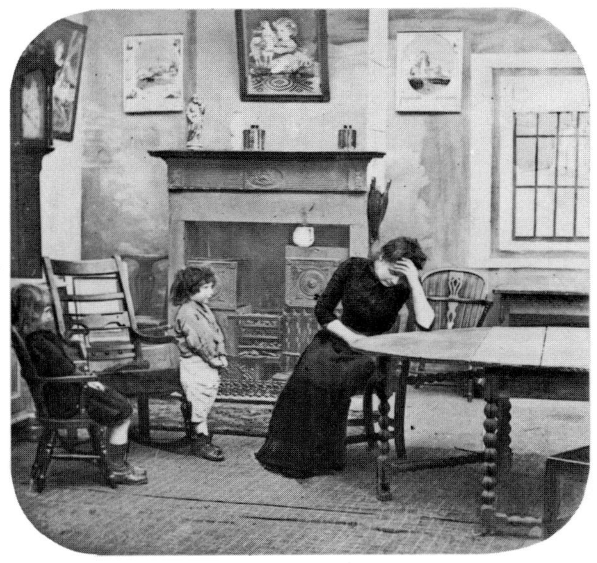

How changed from what it was of old—
The tidy hearth all cheerless now and cold—
The comfort that once reigned within has fled,
And misery set up her throne instead.

And why? has sickness visited that home,
And made it what it has become?
Alas! to poverty's most dismal brink,
They have been hastened on by drink.

We cannot banish evil from the earth—
And if we could what would our faith be worth?
'Tis ours the *privilege* to fight the foe,
And with the help of God to conquer too.

No pledge can e'er avail to keep from sin,
Unless God's grace be found to work within;
This man upon his own weak powers relied,
And soon was overwhelmned beneath the tide,

Careless he grew—neglectful too became—
And though reproof at first brought with it shame,
The last he soon forgot; the first but rankled in
His mind—and both he tried to drown in gin.

Discharged at last from labour, once his pride,
He sits and broods his cheerless hearth beside;
And frets and pines—and even something worse
Escapes his lips, that sounds much like a curse.

The children look with wonder in his face,
And try therein the mystery to trace—
Why father so much leisure has at home—
Why food so very scarce has now become.

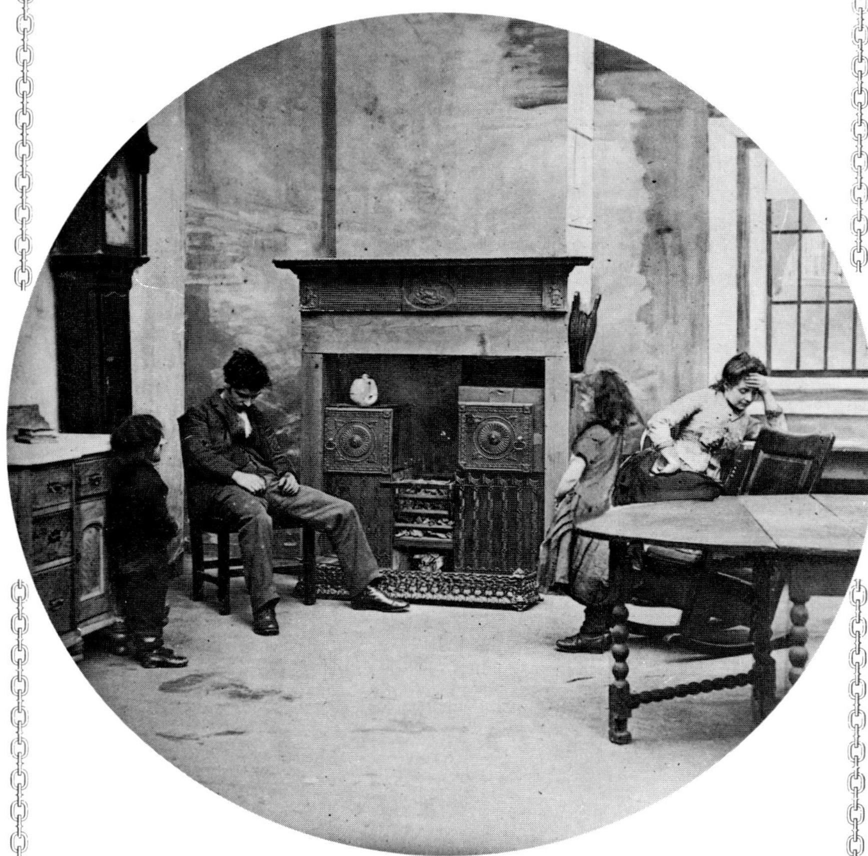

While he in degradation deeper sinks,
And deeper of potations strong he drinks;
No matter what his family's denied,
The thirst for drink must always be supplied.

The "poor man's banker"—by which dubious name
The pawnbroker is known—too oft became
The paymaster whence their supplies were drawn,
For many a household treasure held in pawn.

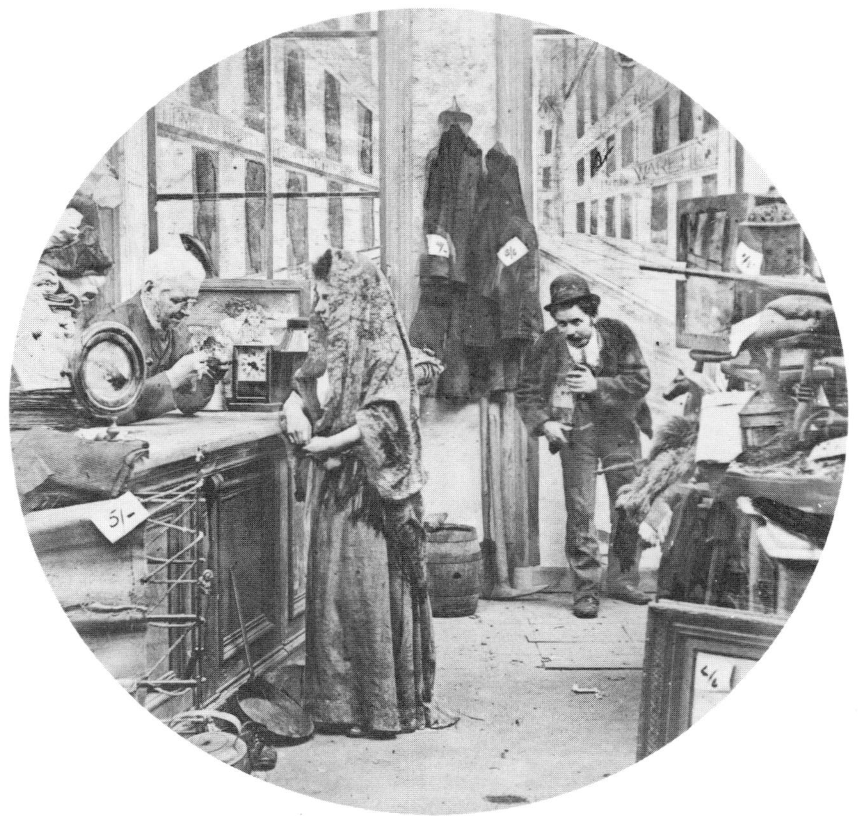

The landlord too was now upon the scent,
And soon put in a pressing claim for rent,
Which ere 'twas satisfied had left all bare,
The rooms adorned with so much love and care.

The useful drawers, long since despoiled
Of clothes, for which in hopeful days they toiled—
The table round which they were wont to meet,
Their daily bread in thankfulness to eat—

The beds—their comfort at the close of day—
The toys with which the children used to play—
The pictures too, and e'en the Sacred Book,
To which for comfort they had ceased to look.

All these and more from them are rudely torn,
And little left them, but the clothes now worn,
While they for solace to the bottle turn,
Whose vile contents their souls more deeply burn.

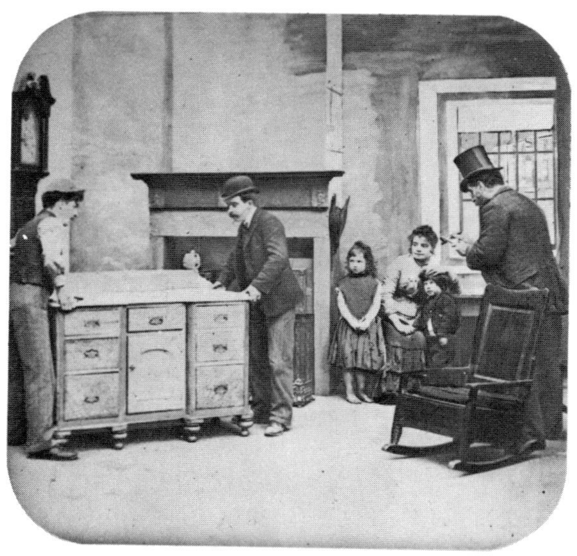

The children now are sent into the street,
To beg or steal from any one they meet—
Elicit sympathy with tales of grief,
Or with the unsuspecting play the thief.

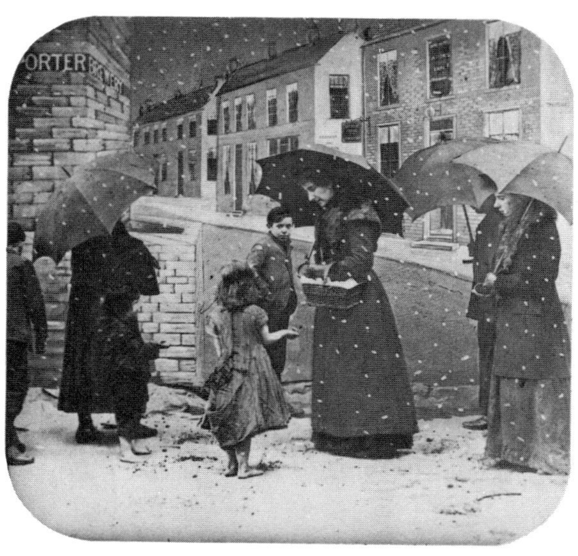

What ugly monsters does this drink produce,
When people give themselves to its abuse,
And in despair give up the faithful fight,
Against this growing sinful appetite.

The little child beneath its mother's shawl—
Which scarcely forms a covering at all—
Is shrunken for the want of needful food,
And sinking fast beneath the fatal flood.

The deadly work upon the child is done—
The scanty sands of life their course have run—
A parish coffin now confines the clay—
The precious soul to God has sped away.

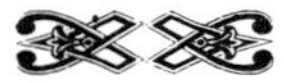

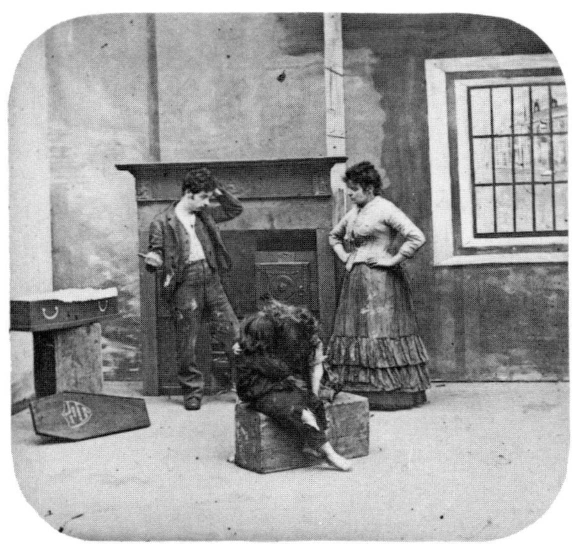

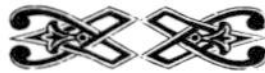

Still stupified by drink, the wretched pair,
Instead of taking blame for want of care,
Condole with, and themselves congratulate,
That it perhaps had shunned a harsher fate.

A lower depth of misery is here—
The wife and husband once to each so dear,
The one so manly, and the other pure,
Can scarce each other's presence now endure.

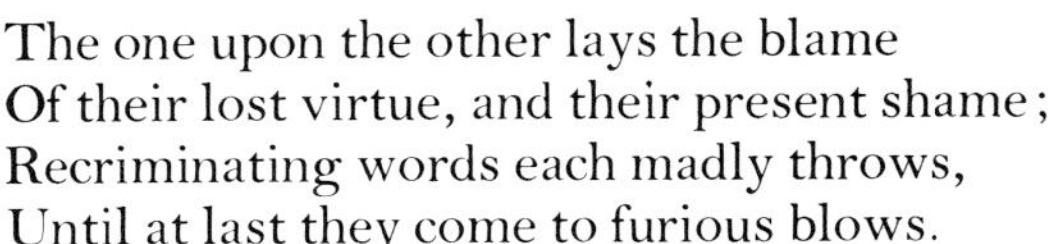

The one upon the other lays the blame
Of their lost virtue, and their present shame;
Recriminating words each madly throws,
Until at last they come to furious blows.

The last sad scenes of this sad tale is reached,
And was more powerful sermon ever preached?
Against the certain misery that is brought
By such a course—with every evil fraught.

The foe against which he would make no stand,
At last o'er him has got the upperhand,
And where he would not, he's compelled to go,
And what he would not, he is forced to do.

Impelled thus by the monster he did nurse,
And which has proved an everlasting curse,
He with a single blow crushed out the life
Of his once happy, but now wretched wife.

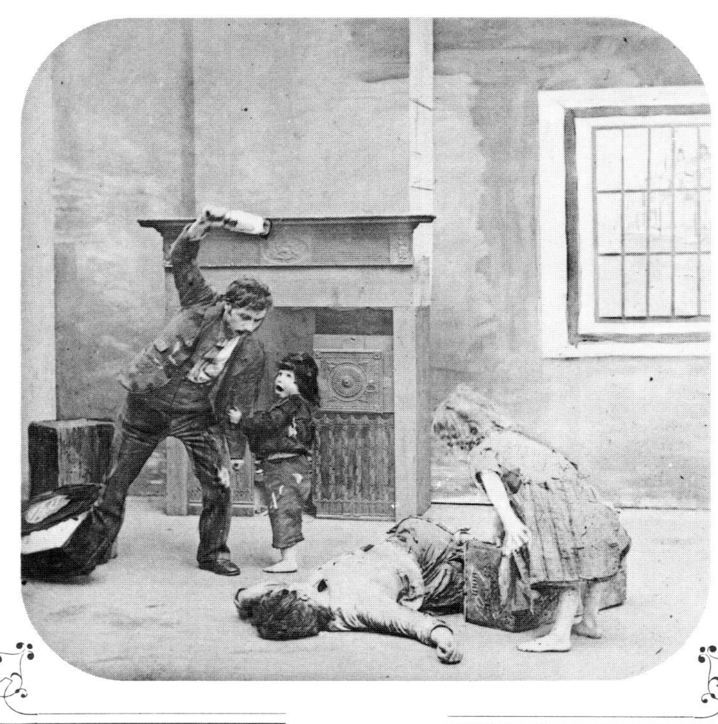

It surely is not justice to permit,
A man full liberty and power to fit
Himself for crime, and *only* when the same
Is consummated, to denounce and blame.

And now without a hope—in cell confined—
Diseased in body and without a mind—
Shielded from self—what brute in all the range
Of God's creation, with him now would change?

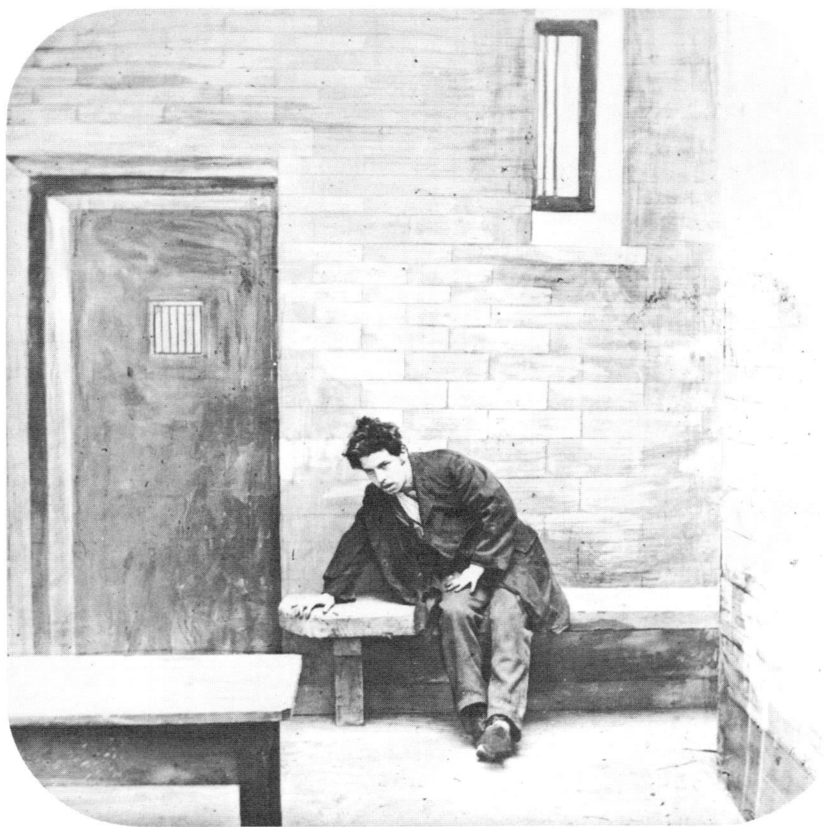

Oh! men and women, of this vice beware;
Your souls in peril are from this dread snare;
Remember Him, who once to deaden pain,
Was pressed to drink, and still was pressed in vain.

Then shun the tempting fiend—oh! be wise—
It is to most, the devil in disguise;
And, would you be secure, on God rely,
And you may then the Evil One defy.

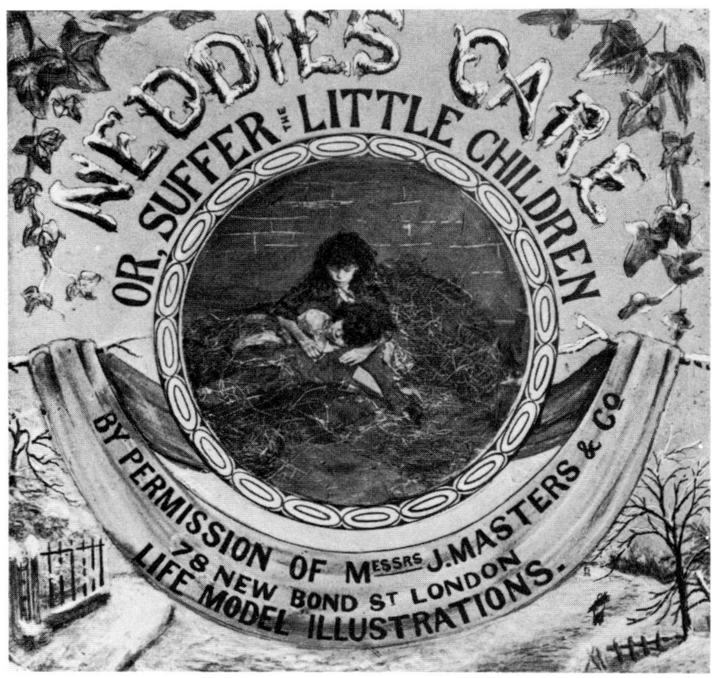

little girl, looking more like a bundle of rags than anything I know, stood peering through the railings of a large house in the outskirts of London. She was so small that no one seemed to notice her. The daylight was fading fast, and the wind came in mighty gusts round the corner of the street, blowing her long curly hair about her shoulders, and nearly blowing the breath out of her poor little body. There was already a quantity of snow on the ground. And when the shades of night set in, the cloudy sky again dissolved itself into snowflakes, and the poor girl, after remaining until it was quite dark, gathered herself up, and giving one more wistful glance from a pair of large blue eyes over the bars of the railing, hurried away across the street and disappeared at length down one of the worst looking alleys of the neighbourhood. But she had still further to go, and the snow lay thickly on the ground before she reached her home, – if home it could be called.

No one noticed her as she crept in, though the room was full of people, and she would probably have remained unobserved, had it not been that in crossing the floor she stumbled over the recumbent form of a sleeping man, who thereupon roused himself sufficiently to break out into a fierce succession of oaths. This attracted the attention of a group of evil-looking men who were crouching round one or two lighted sticks on what had once been a grate, and a gaunt-looking woman, stretching out her hand, seized the poor child roughly by the arm.

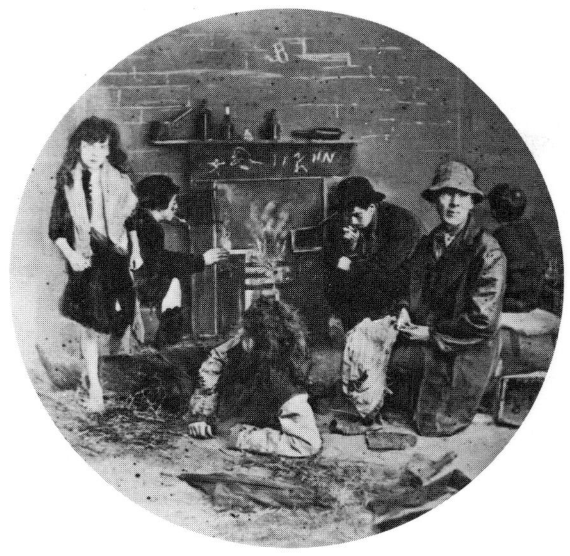

"What have you been up to all day? Where have you been, and what have you got?" she cried.

"There and back again, and I've got nothing," answered the child somewhat saucily and in a shrill little voice, and in no way disconcerted, she quickly shook the woman's hand off her arm and passed on. The woman shouted after her something about stopping her impudence. As, however, she did not attempt to follow her, the little girl took not the slightest notice of her, and going to the further corner of the room, sat composedly down on the floor, beside a poor little boy, who was evidently in the last stage of consumption.

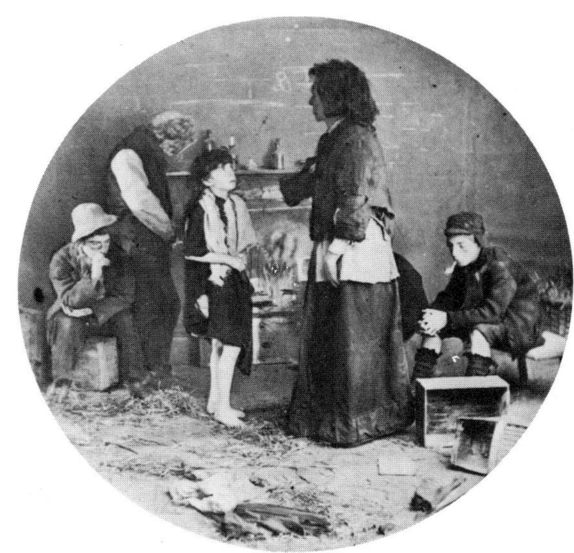

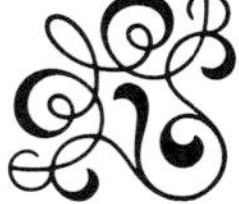

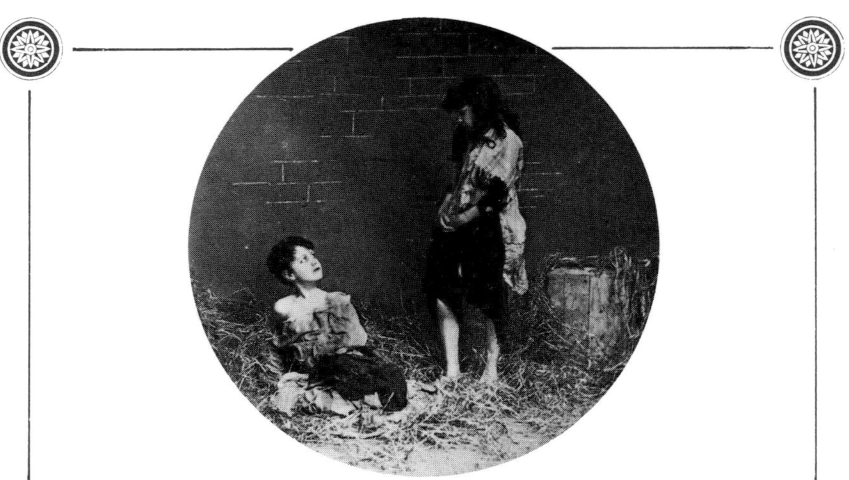

"Is it you, Neddie?" said the boy, opening his eyes, "You've been a long time gone."

"Yes, I know," replied the girl, "But hush! Dickey, I don't want that woman to hear. I've been *there* again."

"Have you, now? Oh, Neddie!"

"Yes, but Dickey, I couldn't get to speak to them, but I heard them singing, and saw after a bit, when it got dark, the shadows on the blinds."

"But, Neddie, I can't wait, I shall die if they don't come soon, I'm oh! so cold, and there's nothing to eat. I don't know as I could eat if I had it now, but it's the feeling of nothing in me that's so bad, and what with the cough."

"Oh, poor Dickey, poor, poor, Dickey; go to sleep dear, and I will make you warm if I can."

And so saying, the motherly little thing drew the weary head on her shoulder and wrapped her ragged shawl closer round the dying boy. She, poor child, was hungry too; food had not passed either of their lips that day; and when sleep came at last, Neddie would have slept till morning, had not Dickey's cough aroused them so often during the night, causing many an

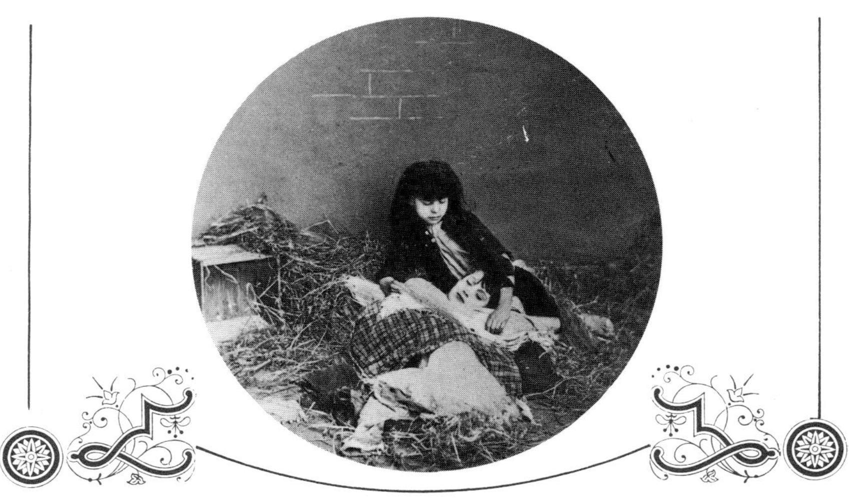

angry word from the other inmates of the room. But, from Neddie, only the murmuring sound of her motherly little voice, saying, "Poor Dickey, poor, poor little Dickey."

The following morning rose, with the snow still falling steadily, as it had done during the whole night. The snow made even that wretched part of London beautiful with its pure white covering. It was intensely cold, but it did not prevent the poor girl, ill-clad though she was, from turning out into the street. Neddie was up and out betimes, and doing a little business on her own account in the begging line. The passers by found her a great nuisance, and did not scruple to tell her so, as she followed them for several yards at a time, with her birdlike little chirp of "Only a penny, please give me a penny, Sir!" and though several hours were spent thus, no one seemed inclined to take pity on Neddie. Her clear voice grew gradually more desponding in its tones, till at last it had dwindled down into something like the true professional whine. The poor child was almost faint with hunger and cold; she had tasted no food for nearly forty-eight hours – there was no affectation about that.

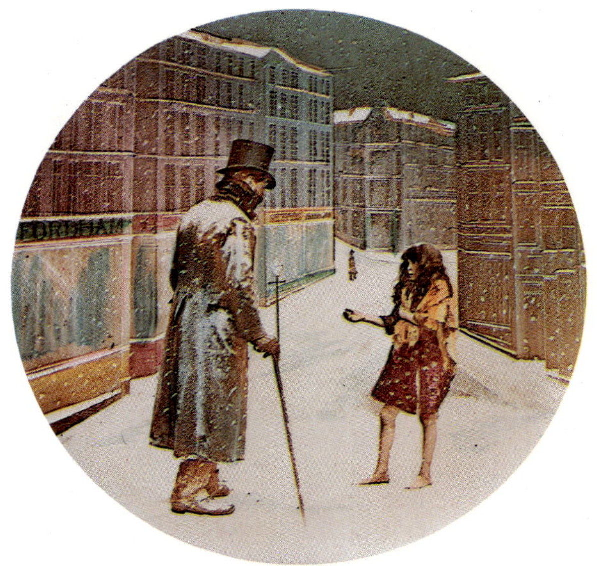

At length, she found herself once more close to the house with the iron railings, where she had waited so long the day before. In a short time Neddie saw a lady coming out of the gateway.

"If you please, 'M, will you," she began, but she stopped short when she saw the lady was one of the mission ladies.

"What were you going to say?" asked the lady, stopping before Neddie.

"Please 'M, I was going to say, 'please 'M, will you give me a penny,' but I ain't going to now," she added.

"Why aren't you going to, now, my child?" asked the lady.

"'Cause you are one of *them*," said Neddie, looking towards the house, "and I was going to say to one of *them*, please 'M, will you come to see my Dickey? he's very bad, he is."

"Who are you, and who is Dickey?" enquired the lady.

"Please, 'M, I'm Neddie, and Dickey's Dickey."

"Neddie!" said the lady, "why, that's a boy's name."

"No, please, 'M, it ain't, it's mine."

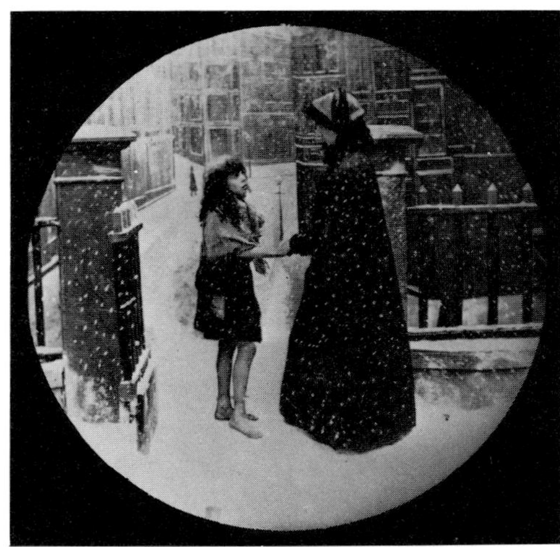

"Whereabouts does Dickey live?" she asked next, and on Neddie telling her, they immediately moved off together towards Stoke Alley. On their way Neddie told her how often she had waited outside the house with the iron railings. "I heard the singing," she said, "and saw little children as young as Dickey go in and out, so I waited patiently. I told Dickey I'd ask one of you to come and see him, as one did to widow Park's little granddaughter down in Fisher Court."

"You look cold and pinched with hunger, poor child; have you no warmer clothing to put on, no shoes and stockings?"

"Nothing but what I have on, and two days ago I had a bit of bread, so did Dickey, that's all, none since."

"Are your father and mother living?"

"Father died two years ago, he was raving mad, he was always drunk; had to keep out of his reach any way."

Poor child, she remembered her drunken father, her own mother she could not remember. She had only known a cruel, drunken stepmother; at an early age the children had been sent out into the streets to beg. Cuffs and kicks they got in plenty, but kindnesses were luxuries quite out of their reach, except what they received from each other, for each to each was more than all the world besides.

"Is your mother alive, then?" enquired the Mission lady.

"No, mother got drunk too when we begged enough pennies. One day she goes out, and don't come back; next day someone says there's been a splash from off London Bridge – that was mother!"

"Poor children, and how do you manage to live?"

"Sukey Brown took us in, and when I've begged enough pennies to keep Dickey and me from starving, I give her some. She's cross the days I don't get none."

"What's the matter with Dickey?"

"I don't know, good lady, he wastes and wastes, and don't get no better, and coughs day and night too."

"I am Miss Bell," replied the lady, "don't call me good lady, there is none good, save our Father in Heaven."

"Does your Father live there?" enquired Neddie.

"Dear child, have you never heard of your Father in heaven?"

"It's a mistake," said the poor girl. "My father was never there in his life, never went anywhere 'cept to the gin shop."

Alas, for our Christian land! that there should be any on whose ear the name of God has never fallen otherwise than as an oath, and who have never even so much as heard of a future life.

By this time the lady and Neddie had reached the miserable street, called Stoke Alley. The closeness of the atmosphere increased at every step. Here and there were groups of idle men, smoking the morning away, while barefooted children of all ages, and their wretched-looking mothers, swarmed the narrow footpath. Suddenly Neddie stopped, and looking up into her companion's face, said, "I say, don't be afraid, I'll take care of you, but if you've got a watch, I'd hide it if it was me."

"I'm not at all afraid," replied the Mission lady, and though many inquisitive glances were cast after the two, no one attempted to stay them, and they stopped at last at one of the most miserable and broken down looking houses. It was a cellar dwelling down a few broken steps. Neddie

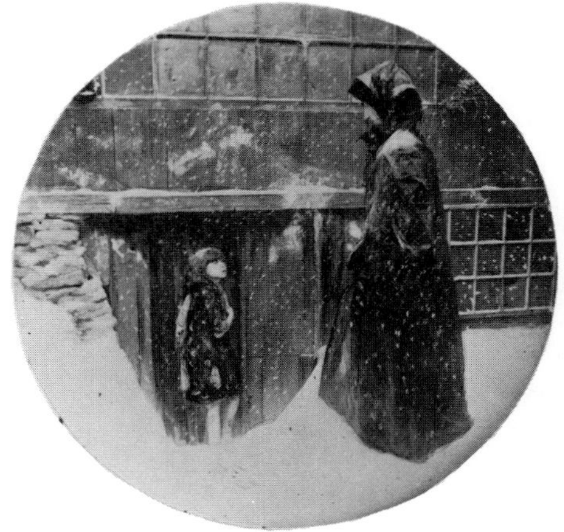

stood listening a moment outside the door. "Hark! that's my poor Dickey coughing," she said, and lifting the latch, they entered.

The room was quite empty, except for the poor boy, who lay there in sore need of aid. Neddie leaned over him and said, "She's come, Dickey, boy, look up, dear, and speak," but after that last fit of coughing, poor Dickey lay back quite exhausted, with his eyes closed.

"Something must be done at once," said the lady, and taking a pencil out of her pocket, she wrote a few words, and giving the paper to Neddie, said, "Go back at once to the house I came out of; ask for Miss Gray; give her this, and she will tell you what to do next."

"Shall you be here when I come back?"

"Yes, yes, only you must be quick."

Neddie waited for no more, but set off running as fast as her poor legs would carry her.

As soon as she was gone, the kind lady, gently raising the boy, wrapped him up as well as she could, then sitting down on the ground, laid his head on her lap. After a while, Dickey ceased shivering and opened his eyes. "Who is it?" he asked.

"I am from the 'Children's Home', and am come to try and make you better."

"I'm so tired," he murmured, and the poor child, worn out with coughing, dropped off to sleep almost as he spoke, and the time went by, and still Dickey slept on, supported by that young and carefully nurtured lady, who, leaving all the pleasures of life, except the pleasure of doing good work, sat there in the very centre of sin and wickedness, such as haunt the worst parts of London in the blackest form, and yet she was not afraid, but felt as safe there as in her own peaceful home. Miss Gray and Neddie came at last, carrying a basket and shawl.

Dickey woke up as they came in, and Miss Gray, taking from the basket a vessel containing warm beef tea and pieces of bread, soaked a morsel in the broth and put it into Dickey's mouth. After a few mouthfuls, which he swallowed eagerly, he raised himself up, and looking round, said faintly, "Neddie have some too."

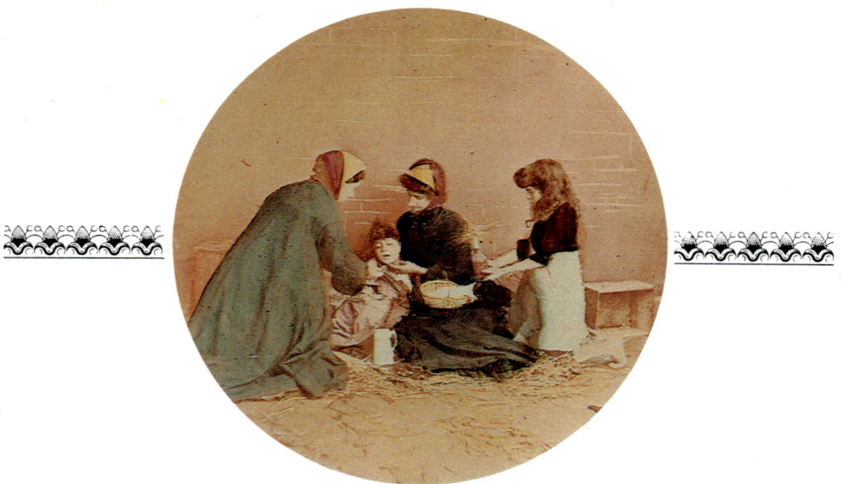

"Yes, Neddie," said Miss Gray, "You will eat now, won't you?" and she gave the starving child a large slice of bread. "Poor child, you are famished," and, turning to her co-worker, she added, "Yet she wouldn't touch a morsel till her brother had had some."

The Mission ladies then consulted together a moment on what was best to be done, and they decided on taking the boy back with them at once, and that someone should see Sukey Brown and explain how matters stood. Miss Bell then raised the poor boy, and after wrapping him in a warm

woollen shawl which Miss Gray had brought for the purpose, and covering
him entirely with it, she carried him into the open-air. He was so very thin
and light that the ladies found their task not difficult, and carrying him in
turn they brought him to the "Home for Destitute Children". It was not
till Dickey was laid on one of the white beds in the "Home" that they
unwound him from his shawl, and the look of astonishment and delight he
gave well repaid the ladies and Neddie for their united efforts in getting him
there. After seeing Dickey washed and cared for, Miss Bell prepared to lead
Neddie away, but to this she strongly objected. "I can't leave him," she
said, "He's such a little fellow; it would never do for him to be left."

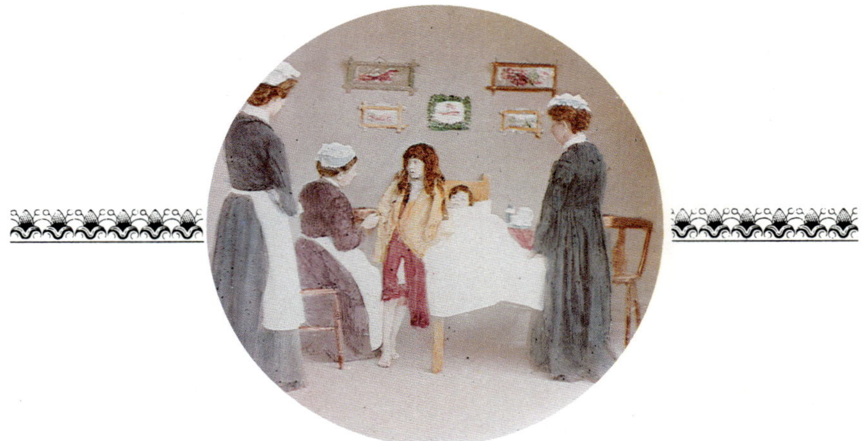

   "My dear, he won't be left," answered both ladies. "He shall be properly
attended to."
   "Oh! do let me stay with him," said Neddie. "He's all I have, you
know, and I wouldn't have him left alone, was it ever so."
   "Not to-night, my dear, but to-morrow you shall stay with him, he
is tired now and so are you, and a good night's rest is the best thing for
you both."
   "Then ain't I going back to-morrow? whatever will Sukey Brown
say?"
   "No, you are never going back to her again, I hope, and you need not
trouble about what she will say, we have arranged it with her; but now,
my child, you must go to bed; Miss Gray will show you the way, and now
good night; may God bless you!"
   "I say, she didn't ought to have said that," remarked Neddie, as soon
as they got outside the door.
   "Said what, Neddie?"
   "Well, I didn't think such as her would have said it, you know, that
about the bad words, 'God bless you!'. Father used to swear awful when he
came from the gin shop, and Sukey Brown and all of them swore a lot, but
I didn't expect to hear anything of that kind here."
   Oh! Neddie, child, you have much to learn, but you are in the right
hands to learn it; may Heaven prosper the good work of these noble
Institutions!

The next morning Neddie was relieved to find that Dickey was much better than usual. She found him sitting up in bed with his breakfast before him. He was very weak, poor little fellow, and very glad of Neddie's help in raising the teacup to his lips, and feeding him with the white bread and butter, so fresh and clean, and different to anything he ever remembered before. Poor children, they had seen better days during their own mother's life; but all was forgotten in the misery that followed after her death. They had lived so long in want and misery, that this seemed quite a new life to both these little ones. Warmly clad in the neat dress provided for the children in the Home, Neddie looked quite a different child, and though Dickey was too far gone for there to be any real hope of recovery, yet the tender care bestowed on him caused him to rally for a time.

Neddie was sent to the school of the Institution, and got on well with her lessons. Just at first her school-fellows were inclined to laugh at her old-fashioned ways and strange name, but as time went on, quaint little Neddie became a general favourite. On enquiry, Dickey was found to be two years older than Neddie. Neddie·was only eight years of age, but from her manner anyone would have supposed her to be Dickey's senior by several years. Poor Dickey, he was so patient and uncomplaining! Miss Bell, who from the first had watched him with more than ordinary care, spent many a happy half hour by the sick boy's bed, teaching him in sweet simple language, which he could without difficulty understand, the glorious story of the Saviour's cross, and helping him to bear his own. Both of the children were indeed grateful for the kindnesses they received, and were always trying in their simple fashion to devise some means of repaying them.

One day she was missing; the ladies were seriously alarmed, and it was a relief felt by all when evening came and Neddie with it, looking tired, but as completely self-possessed as ever. She said not a word, but with an air of triumph took off her bonnet and cloak, and approached Miss Bell and poured a heap of pennies into her lap.

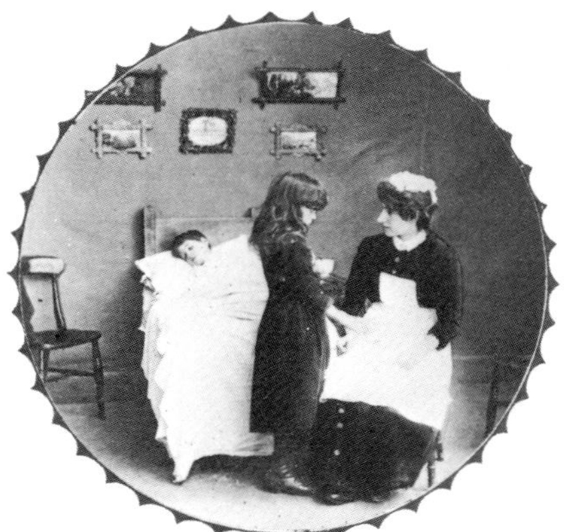

"There," said the child, "I've been at it all day, and gathered the flowers this morning; I could not carry them all at once, but I'll go again to-morrow with the rest."

"You haven't been selling our snowdrops, have you?" said Miss Bell. "Oh, Neddie?" Then looking at the disappointed expression on Miss Bell's face, the child seemed to take in for the first time that something was amiss.

"My child, you should not have taken the flowers; we do not grow the flowers for sale, but to place in the rooms of the sick; however, never mind, my dear, only this must never happen again, nor must you go out without leave."

Poor Neddie hid her face in Miss Bell's lap and sobbed out, "I thought you'd be so pleased; it was me and Dickey's way of saying thank you!"

"I daresay, my dear," said Miss Bell, gently stroking her head, "you meant it as a little thankoffering. Come, cheer up, Neddie, my child, we are not angry with you at all – only rather sorry for the loss of our flowers, they are rather scarce at this season, and we prize them very much."

It was the custom at this Institution for the relations of the orphans to visit them on the first Sunday of every month.

"There's no one to come and see Dickey and me," said Neddie, "unless –"

"Unless what, poor Neddie dear?" replied Miss Bell.

"Unless – Miss Bell! are brothers and sisters relations?"

"Why, yes dear, most certainly they are."

"Oh, then it's all right," said Neddie, "and Dickey's got a relation going to see him to-day; that's me! Oh, Miss Bell, won't you let me have my bonnet and cloak," said Neddie.

"Why? what do you want them for? you aren't going out again?"

"No, Miss Bell, but oh, please, I'm a relation, and if I don't wear my bonnet and cloak I shan't look like one."

In a few minutes Neddie made her appearance, attired in full walking trim. It was with the greatest difficulty that Miss Bell prevented herself from laughing, and at the same moment Miss Gray entered the room holding up a bunch of violets.

"Why, Neddie! where are you going?"

"I'm Dickey's relation," replied Neddie. "I'm going to visit him; do I look like a relation?"

"Very like one, indeed, Neddie," and the ladies exchanged smiles. "Should you like to take him some flowers?"

"Oh, if you please, Miss Gray – oh, thank you, Dickey will be pleased."

Little unselfish creature, all her thoughts day and night were on Dickey. It was amusing to see how demurely she walked into the ward, and sat gravely down on the chair by Dickey's bed, just as she had seen other relations do before. She put the violets into his hand, saying, "Miss Bell and Miss Gray sent them for you."

"Beautiful!" said the boy, as his thin fingers closed around them. Suddenly Neddie cried, "Oh, look Dickey, look through the window at the sky! see, over there, blue like the violets; but oh, how bright and pink on this side!"

Then remembering a beautiful hymn she had been taught to sing, she sat down on the pillow beside him, and putting her arms around him, she sang that beautiful hymn which I will ask you to join in singing:

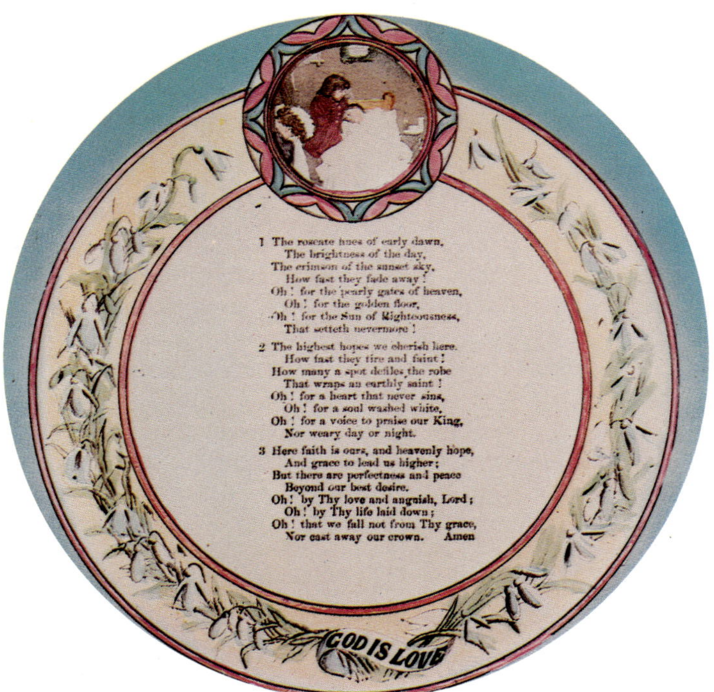

The sweet notes died softly away, and for a few minutes after Neddie stopped singing, no one spoke. The ladies could not restrain their tears; they never forgot the impression left on their minds that golden spring evening, and the touching words fell sweetly on the many hearts of those who afterwards never heard them without thinking of Dickey's relation, as she sang them to the dying boy.

If there had been no institution of this kind, what would have become of these two little waifs? How different was their lot now that they had been found.

The right Hon. the late Earl Cairns, says: "I cannot but think that if the nature of the work which is being done by these Homes were more widely known and better understood, these institutions would never have to experience, as they now do, the keen pressure of financial difficulty. Homes like these which assist without distinction children of all denominations and of none, have a strong claim for support upon us all – both as citizens and as Christians."

The Rev. C. H. Spurgeon says: "I believe that the work carried on by Dr. Barnardo meets a great necessity of London life. Undoubtedly great poverty is being relieved, and the worst forms of vice are being prevented in the cases of hundreds of children, who would either starve or grow up to be the terror of society."

To return to our story. The first balmy days of spring seemed to bring to Dickey fresh life, and with the usual changeableness of the disease he was able to sit up an hour some days, taking great interest in the faint glimpses of spring, that could be seen from the windows of the Home. Neddie was of course overjoyed at the improvement, but those who knew better shook their heads and said to themselves that it was but the momentary flaring up of the little flame, so soon to be put out.

"I never saw anything like it before," Dickey said, as one day Miss Bell sat with him in the front of the window, and pointed out to him the tiny green leaves on the few trees in the garden below.

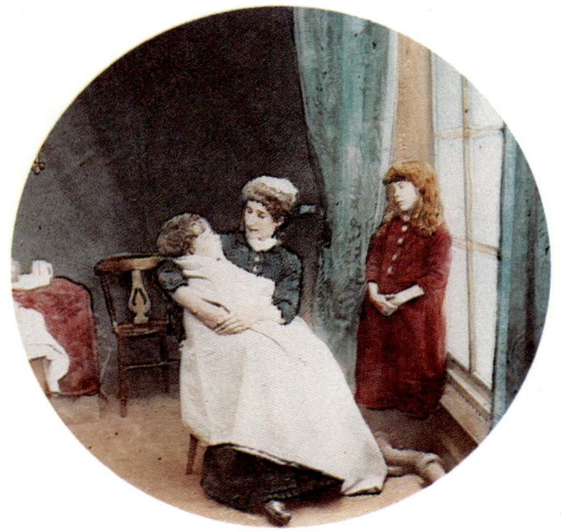

"No, poor child, how could you?" she answered, "I cannot bear to think of those dreary days for you in that miserable Stoke Alley."

"I wonder," said Dickey, "if it will be a blue sky like it is now when I die!"

"Hush, Dickey dear," said Neddie, "you aren't going to die yet awhile. I dare say I shall die first; I'd like to, I know."

"Why, Neddie?" asked Miss Bell.

"I'd like to know all about it against Dickey's turn; I shouldn't like him to go alone first."

"But, Neddie! you forget, 'Though I walk through the valley of the shadow of death, I will fear no evil, for Thou art with me;' so you see he would not be alone."

"No, Miss Bell, but anyhow I'd like to be there to meet Dickey."

"Do you think, Miss Bell, that it will be as beautiful again from here to heaven as it was from Stoke Alley to here?" asked Dickey, raising his eyes to hers with that expression they so often wore now, of "the light from otherwhere".

"Yes, indeed, Dickey, and very far more than that," answered Miss Bell; "but here comes nurse to see that Dickey does not sit up too long."

As she placed him in his bed again, the thought struck her that notwithstanding his apparent improvement, the time was very near now for his little spirit to be set free, and though she feared the shock for Neddie, she felt how necessary it was that she should know what all in the house, except herself, knew too well.

"Poor Neddie," said she, "she will feel it dreadfully, it's pitiful to see her so pleased because she thinks he is better."

As she spoke, she heard a violent ring at the door, and then hasty footsteps coming up the stairs. Knowing that something uncommon had happened, they were hurrying out of the room when they were met by the cry,

"Oh the poor little Neddie! run over! killed! oh come, come!" They waited for no more, but hurried on.

"My poor darling!" cried Miss Bell, and a low groan broke from her lips as she caught sight of what was to all appearance the little dead face of Neddie as she was carried by two men on a stretcher. They carried her in

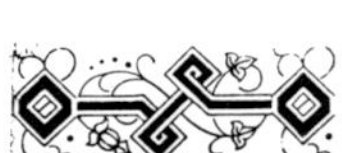
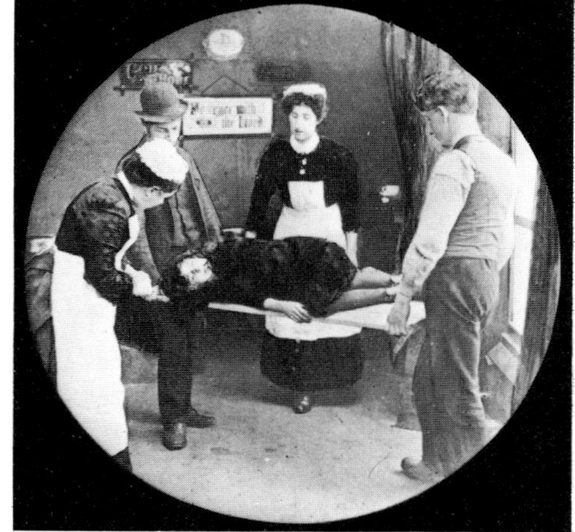
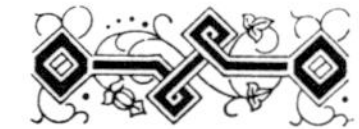

and laid her down on one of the little white beds in a vacant ward, and did all they could for her. The doctor was not long in coming, for the lady to whom the carriage belonged, which had run her over, sent it at once to fetch him. All this time Neddie lay without stirring in a death-like swoon. Whether she would recover the doctor felt unable, as yet, to give a decided opinion, for though only her arm was actually broken yet the other injuries were many and very serious.

This is how the accident happened. It seems the children, attended by their teachers, were just crossing the street, when a carriage came suddenly round a corner, and the next moment had knocked down poor Neddie, and the wheels had passed over her. Trying to suddenly stop the horses, had only added to the fearful mischief that was done. It was not till the middle of the night that Neddie first showed signs of returning life. She began to move a little, and suddenly opened her eyes.

"Where am I?" she raved, "is it Neddie? but Neddie isn't ill – then it must be Dickey, but Dickey's arm isn't bad, nor his back – O! Miss Bell! Who is it? poor little one!" All through the long weary hours she moaned on. The fever did not abate till far on in the day, when she fell into a troubled sleep. Miss Bell was near when poor Neddie awoke, and she saw with thankfulness that the child was conscious.

"Have I been ill, Miss Bell?" said Neddie.

"Yes, dear, you have hurt your arm; don't try to move it."

"I can't remember – Where's Dickey – What does it all mean?"

"Don't try to think, dear, but keep quiet," said Miss Gray, who had just entered the room, "you will be much better if you keep quiet."

Neddie lay still with her eyes closed, and they thought she was going to sleep again, but in a minute or two she raised herself and spoke again in a low voice,

"Miss Bell, am I going to die?"

"Darling, I hope now you are going to get well; but you must lie still and not talk."

"Oh, but Miss Bell, I must talk! I can't die yet, Miss Bell – I'm frightened – I can't think," she cried, "I don't remember, but I can't go alone – Oh! Miss Bell, do say, you know, about the shadow, and not afraid! oh, do! say it!"

Then Miss Bell repeated softly: "Though I walk through the valley of the shadow of death, I will fear no evil, for Thou art with me, Thy rod and Thy staff they comfort me."

The child grew quieter, "Go on," she said, and lay back listening.

"Suffer the little children to come unto Me and forbid them not, for of such is the kingdom of heaven."

"I like that," whispered Neddie, "I'm not afraid now," and Miss Bell continued in a sweet low voice: "Come unto Me all ye that labour and are heavy laden, and I will give you rest." She then sang:

"I heard the voice of Jesus say, come unto Me and rest." The soft music of her voice lulled the child to sleep again.

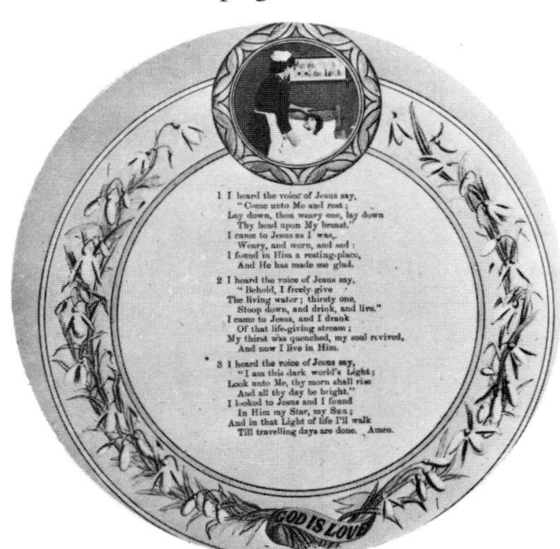

It became necessary, on Dickey's repeated enquiries for Neddie, to break the news to him. Poor Dickey, he begged so hard to be allowed to see her that they carried him to her room. They chose a time when the little girl was peacefully sleeping, and he was removed again from the room when she showed signs of returning consciousness. Those were weary days for all, with Dickey, patient Dickey, slowly but surely fading away, and Neddie so ill, that it was feared her recovery was doubtful. The lady whose carriage had been the cause of the accident was greatly distressed. Not a day passed but she came to the Home laden with delicacies for them both, and the children grew fond of her, and looked forward to her visits from day to day. They all knew there was no hope for Dickey, but it was a severe shock when the doctor told them on one of his visits that little Neddie also was beyond the aid of human skill. The internal injuries she had received were of a far more serious nature than had at first been supposed, and left no chance of recovery.

"It was possible," the doctors said, "that she might linger on a week or two, or perhaps in a few hours the end might come."

It was decided that the dear child should be told how near she was to the "Golden City". But it happened that Neddie herself began the conversation. Miss Bell and Miss Gray were watching by the side of the little white bed, when Neddie suddenly raised herself in bed and spoke thus: "Miss Bell! oh! please, won't you take me to see my poor boy? He'll think me very bad, and will fret if I don't go. I won't cry out, let it hurt me ever so!"

"No dear; the doctor would not like you to be moved. But Dickey has been brought in to see you while you were asleep; we did not like him to see you while you were suffering so much, it would do him harm."

Neddie lay a long time without speaking, but the ladies saw by her face that the ever-busy little brain was hard at work.

"What is it?" asked Miss Bell, "don't worry yourself, Neddie dear, with thinking."

"It doesn't worry me, Miss Bell, I must think; I'm not afraid now, and you will take care of Dickey, won't you?"

"Yes, darling, we will while he needs help," replied the ladies.

"I'm not going to get well, am I Miss Bell? Please I want to know for sure."

Miss Bell knelt down beside the child and put her arm around her. "Darling," she said, "the pain will soon be over; it will be only like falling asleep to wake again in Paradise."

"You'll mind how you tell poor Dickey?" was all Neddie said, and then she slumbered again. And so, after all, Neddie would have that wish of hers granted, which she had expressed such a short time before: "Anyhow, I'd like to be there to meet my Dickey. I shouldn't like him to go alone first."

The following was one of those bright warm days that remind us that summer is close at hand. The heat was almost oppressive, and poor dear little Neddie, whose sufferings during the morning were very severe, felt it very much, yet, through the keenest pains, she remained patient and gentle.

Towards evening, she suddenly became quiet, and told those around her that the pain was all gone. They knew what that meant. The doctor was sent for at once.

"Can there possibly be any risk now for her to see her brother?" Miss Bell asked him.

"It is the only wish she has left, and I cannot bear for her to die without having it gratified, and, as regards Dickey, I am confident it will do him more harm than good to be prevented from seeing her."

"Now that he will not be upset by seeing her sufferings, I see no reason against it," the doctor replied.

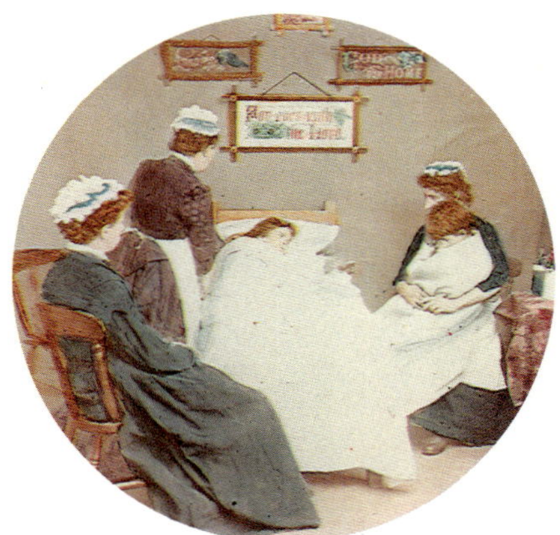

Miss Bell whispered to Neddie, to prepare her for the interview, while Dickey was carried to her room. Miss Bell sat down by the bedside with the boy in her arms, and Neddie put out one tiny hand towards them. It was so sad and touching to see them that the nurses could not restrain their tears.

"Poor, dear little Dickey," she murmured, "it doesn't hurt, dear," for the boy was crying silently.

Then she turned her eyes to Miss Bell, and whispered, "I'm so glad to go first, now, I can tell him what it's like against his turn."

It was a long speech for her to make, and a very sweet one, for it showed that her devotion to Dickey was so great that it swallowed up all thought of self, even in her dying hour.

"Please, Jesus Christ," they heard her say, "let me always be near my Dickey." Then, after a moment, "it's like going to sleep, Dickey, dear, it doesn't hurt."

These were the last words she said, and then she passed away so quietly and peacefully, with such a calm, happy smile on her face, that it seemed in very truth, "falling asleep".

"For so He giveth His beloved rest."

In the churchyard near the Home, side by side, are two tiny graves. At the head of them both, casting its shadow equally on each, stands one pure white marble cross, erected by the lady whose carriage was the cause of poor Neddie's death. On it is engraved:

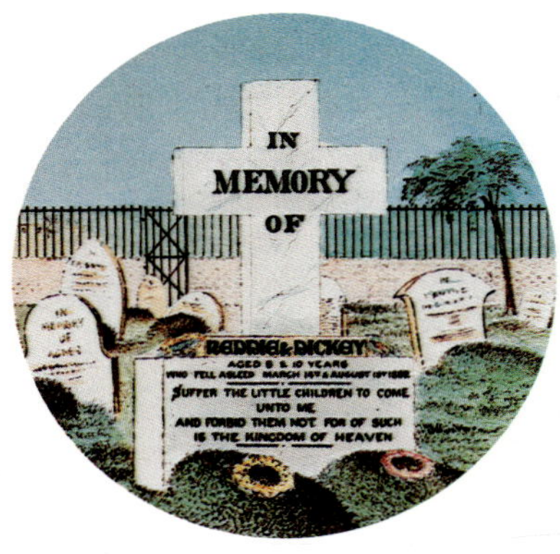

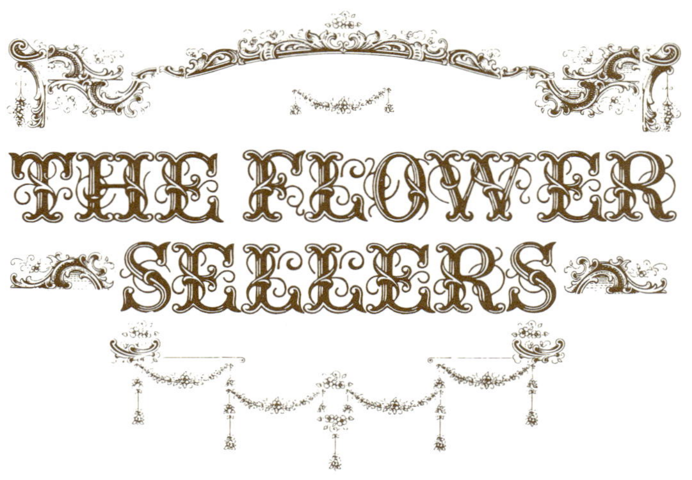

THE FLOWER SELLERS

In the outskirts of a city stood a spacious house of stone
With a garden fair surrounded; there John Emlyn lived alone;
    He was a studious, silent man,
    Whose days and years eventless ran.

Few in that great city knew him – none to love him were inclined –
Science and his books were dearer to his heart than humankind;
    Yet not ungentle was that heart,
    Although he lived from men apart.

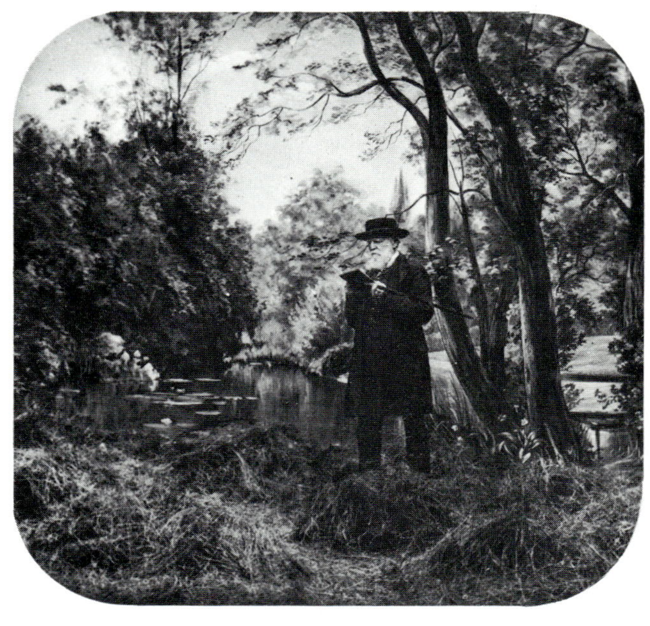

Taking once his daily ramble, from the fields his steps he turned
Towards the city streets so busy, where the poor their living earned;
        There he saw two bright-eyed children stand,
        Each with a bouquet in the hand.

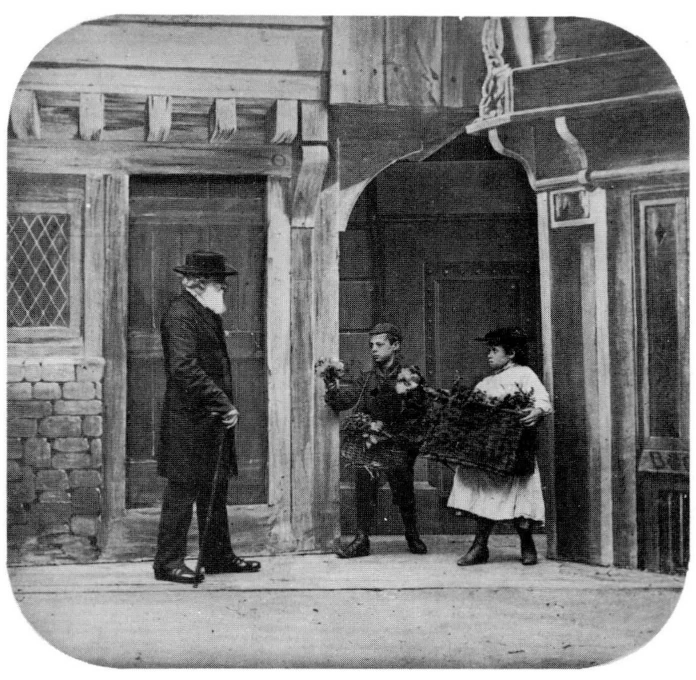

Lifting up her eyes so bonny to his grave and thoughtful brow
"Buy my flowers," said little Annie, "sir, the price is very low
        They're gathered fresh this very day,
        And each one scented; but, sir, pray."

Emlyn stopped and looked upon her, on the boy, and kindly smiled
Said, his hand within his pocket, "Who are you, my pretty child?
        Your parents – what is their employ?
        And you – are you her brother, boy?"

Then the merry faces clouded. "Sir," the boy said, "they are dead
Both our father and our mother; so we have to earn our bread."
        "What!" said he, "have you not a friend
        Upon whose care you may depend?"

"No," said Jack, "we've no relations; and on Mother's funeral day
People said that to the workhouse we should go without delay.
        But then, you see, we'd promised her
        We never would go near it, sir.

" 'Jack,' she said, 'take care of Annie – you're getting big and strong
Try, my boy, to earn a living; you will be a man ere long.
            So say your prayers and do your best,
            And God will help you when I'm at rest.'

"So we two we live together, and we do as mother said.
'Tis a little hard, and often Sis and I have wanted bread;
            But still 'tis better than to go
            Into that place she hated so."

Emlyn took from each a nosegay, added to the price a crown.
Made the children's brown eyes sparkle, then he turned and left the town
            And he forgot those children soon –
            His thoughts were far in sun and moon.

Summer came. 'Twas hot and sultry: fever followed in its train –
Seized on little brown-eyed Annie, and in weariness and pain
            She lay upon her garret floor:
            It seemed that she would rise no more.

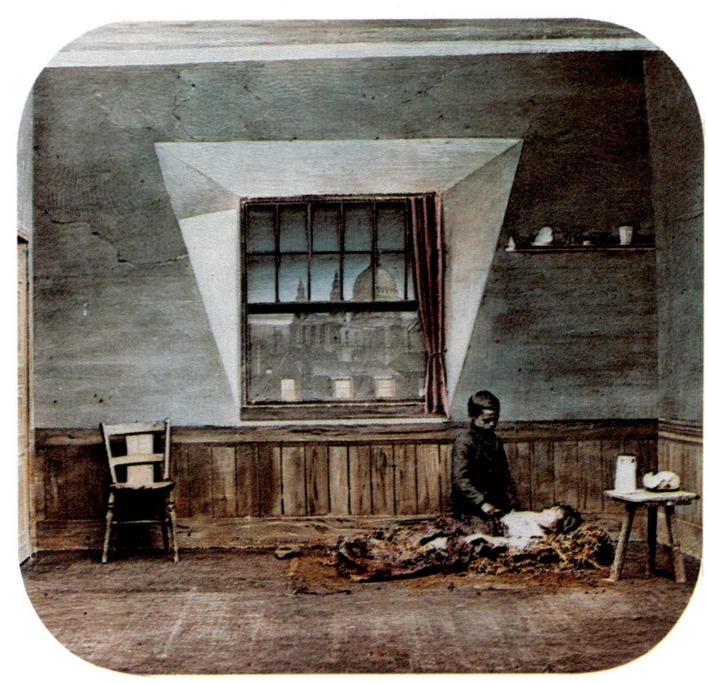

Straw she lay on – no soft pillow had she for her aching head;
By her stood a jug of water and a dry stale piece of bread.
            It was the best that Jack could give,
            And oft he thought "She cannot live."

One bright evening she seemed weaker than she'd ever been before;
Jack, with tearful eyes, beside her knelt upon the dusty floor.
        "Eat, Annie! Just a little slice!"
        "I can't, Jack! I want something nice!"

"Jack, you gave me once an orange – 'twas not very long ago –
Could you get me, think, another? I could suck the juice, I know;
        Or any fruit that's ripe and sweet,
        Like plums or peaches, I could eat."

Nothing could he say in answer – poor, brave, faithful-hearted Jack –
In his throat a sob was rising though he tried to gulp it back;
        For all his coppers had that day
        For rent been duly paid away.

Then a sudden thought came o'er him, and he dashed the tears aside;
"Annie, darling, I will bring you some nice fruit at once!" He cried.
        "But how? where will you get it, Jack?"
        "Oh! Never mind; I'll soon come back."

Down the stairs he dashed, and scampered fast through many a narrow street;
Onward still where streets were wider and the air was pure and sweet,
        And as he hastened on apace
        All dark and sullen grew his face.

"Why be honest?" Said the tempter, "is there anyone who cares?
God himself will take no notice – does He listen to your prayers?
        So help yourself, for you will find
        None else to help you are inclined."

Soon he reached the city's confines, where the houses were but few,
Each in its own garden standing, there were fruit trees there, he knew;
        One wall, upon the sunny side,
        Had peaches trained – and there he hied.

Dew was falling, light was waning; up and down the quiet road
Looked he, but he saw no figure – there was none to see but God;
        And God, though Jack His law might break
        He thought, would scarcely notice take.

Jack was young and lithe and active: 'twas not hard to scale the wall,
Fill his pockets with ripe peaches, then descend without a fall;
        And then he fled, as sinners do,
        With trembling haste, though none pursue.

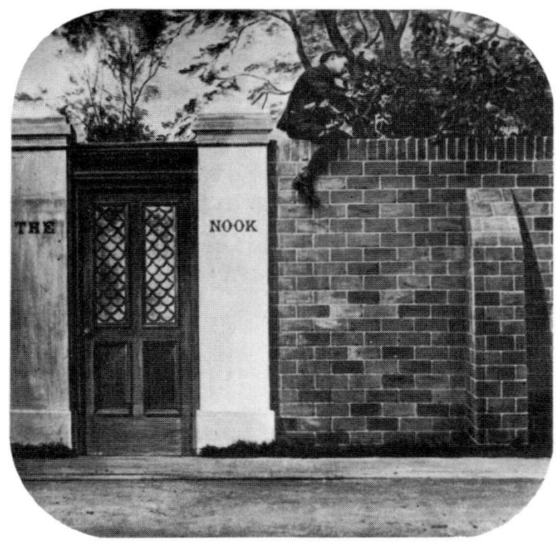

Short his flight was: scarce the ending of the garden wall was gained
When he slipped, and on the pavement there he lay with ankle sprained –
      A bit of orange peel that day
      Had stopped him in destruction's way.

Someone walking in that garden heard the smothered cry of pain
Forced from Jack's lips as he slowly rose and tried to walk again,
      And quickly he came out to see
      What creature was in agony.

Sitting there upon the pavement, white with pain, a boy he found;
Peaches fallen from his pocket lay beside him on the ground.
      "You've hurt yourself, I fear, my lad;
      What! Sprained your ankle? That is bad."

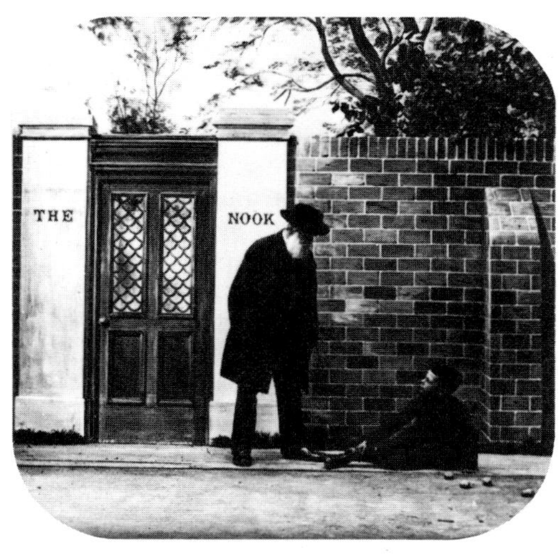

"Yes, I'm hurt; but I deserve it. I don't think you'll pity me
When you hear that I've been stealing all these peaches from the tree
          That grows beside your garden wall;
          And now I'm punished by this fall."

"Stealing, boy! For that I'm sorry" – "So am I, sir, now 'tis done;
But, you see, 'twas for my sister – she is so ill, and friends we've none,
          And I can't give her anything
          But bread that she can't eat, poor thing.

"You'll of course to prison send me, and no doubt 'twill serve me right;
So I've made things worse for Annie, doing what I've done to-night:
          With me in gaol, alone she'll lie
          With none to help, and soon must die."

"If the tale that you have told me," said the gentleman, "be true,
I may promise to forgive you; there is some excuse for you;
          I never heard a harder case –
          But surely, boy, I know your face?"

Jack looked up – "And I know you, sir; you gave Sis and me five bob.
Wish I'd known it was your garden; I'd have never come to rob
          Your fruit-tree – quite ashamed I feel –
          Things turn out wrong when people steal."

"Boy," he cried, "if you're a sinner, I am a far greater one;
Had I sought you out and helped you, this would never have been done.
          Poor child! neglected all this time,
          Till want has driven you to crime.

"I have loved the stars above me and the stones beneath my feet
Better than the hearts around me that with love and sorrow beat;
          To-day this selfish life shall end,
          And men shall find in me a friend.

"Cheer up, lad! Your childhood's troubles from this day are past and gone –
You and Annie a protector now shall have to lean upon:
          Come, both of you, and live with me –
          I will your second father be."

Emlyn kept his word; and Annie did not die, but lived and grew:
Grew and blossomed like the peach-tree that so well her brother knew;
          And Jack an upright man became,
          Whose friendship no one blushed to claim.

Not alone had these two orphans cause good Emlyn's name to bless:
Multitudes of tried and troubled succoured he in their distress;
    And many, many children knew
    And loved him well, besides these two;

So he lives, by all beloved, in the winter of his days.
In the house that was so lonely merry happy childhood plays,
    For Jack's young daughter, Annie's son,
    About its spacious chambers run.

Yet at times his heart is heavy, when they sit upon his knee,
And a look upon their faces of those children he can see –
    Those two who once, in bygone hours,
    Stood in the city selling flowers.

Then to him the past is present: Annie lies without relief
Sick in that poor wretched garret, want again makes Jack a thief;
    Then Emlyn sighs, and hastes to find
    Some soul to whom he may be kind.

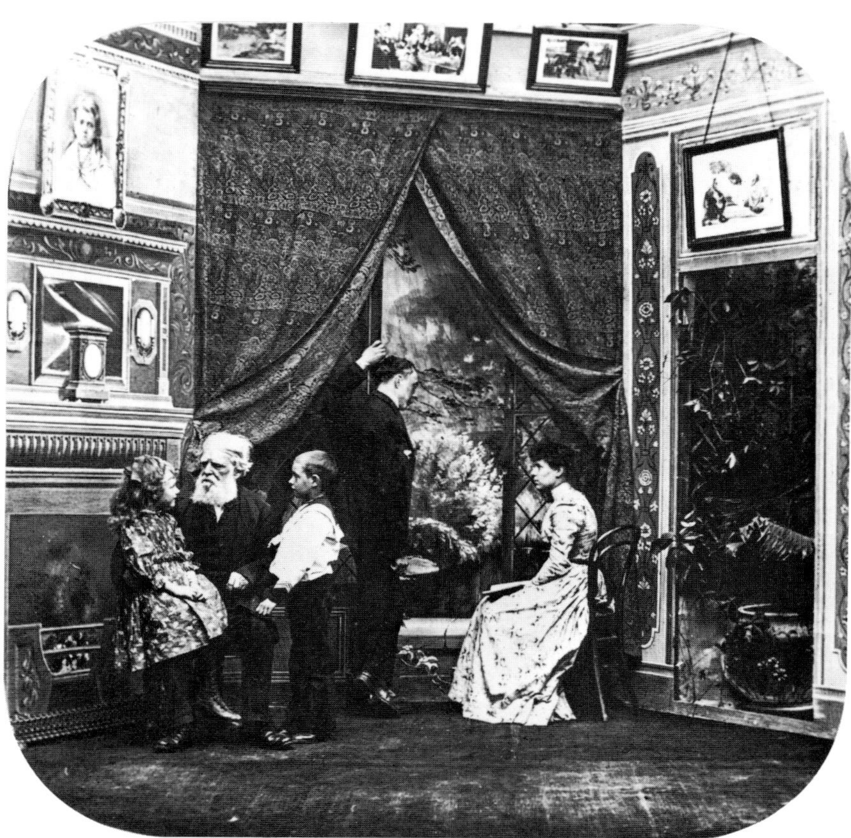

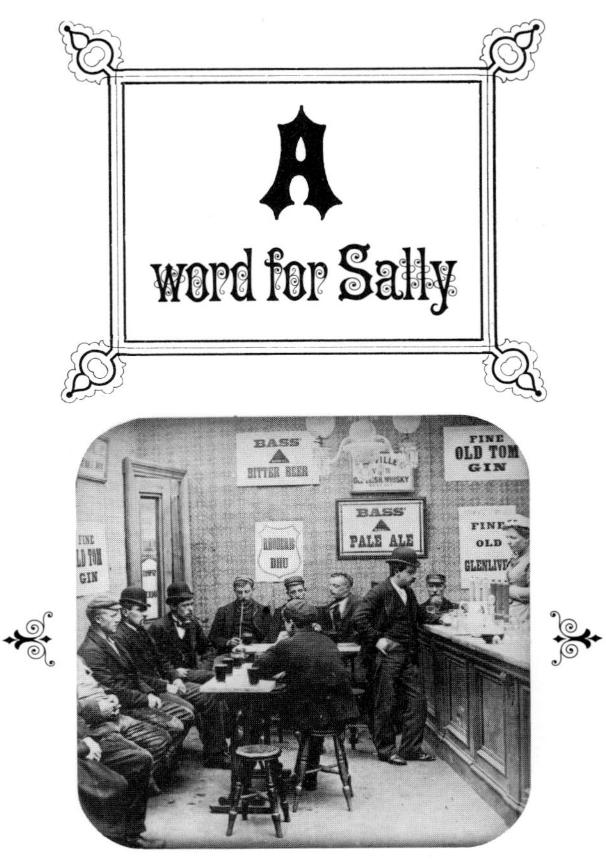

The day is done, and the work is over,
   And sober men to their homes are gone;
   But not so John; of home no lover,
He hastens away to the bar of the "Crown".

For his cottage is bare, and his wife is gloomy;
But there he sits by a blazing fire;
The company's gay, the place is roomy;
And the landlady who can fail to admire?

Surprised at her splendour, John stares a full minute;
She has rings on her hands, and silken gown,
And a brooch of gold, with gems flashing in it;
Who so fine as the publican's wife at the "Crown"?

Her face is all smiles, her words like honey,
She is ready to do any customer's will;
And John half forgets how much of his money
Has gone her husband's coffers to fill.

"She's a grand one, she is," says John, "I'm thinking
If my wife were only a woman like her,
I shouldn't be sitting in this tap-room drinking;
From 'home, sweet home' I never should stir".

*   *   *

At home poor Sally sits lonely and weary,
Shabby and thin, a real drunkard's wife;
And longs for the end of a life so dreary,
So full of pain, and care, and strife.

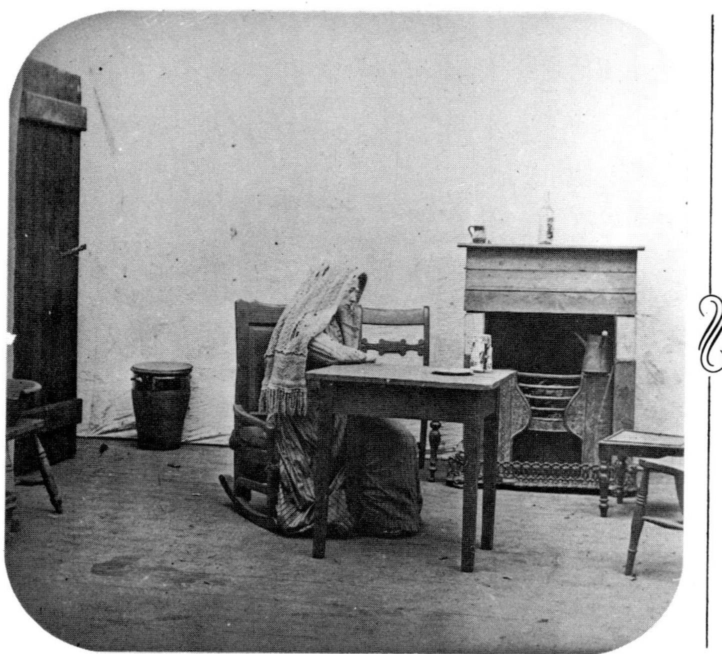

There's a cold North wind, and the snow is lying
Deep on the ground, and the window pane
Sparkles with frost, but her fire is dying,
And she has not a coal to light it again.

*   *   *

Ah, John! why surely you must be forgetting
The years long past – those evenings in June,
When with Sally you walked till the sun was setting –
And the tender talks 'neath the harvest moon.

86

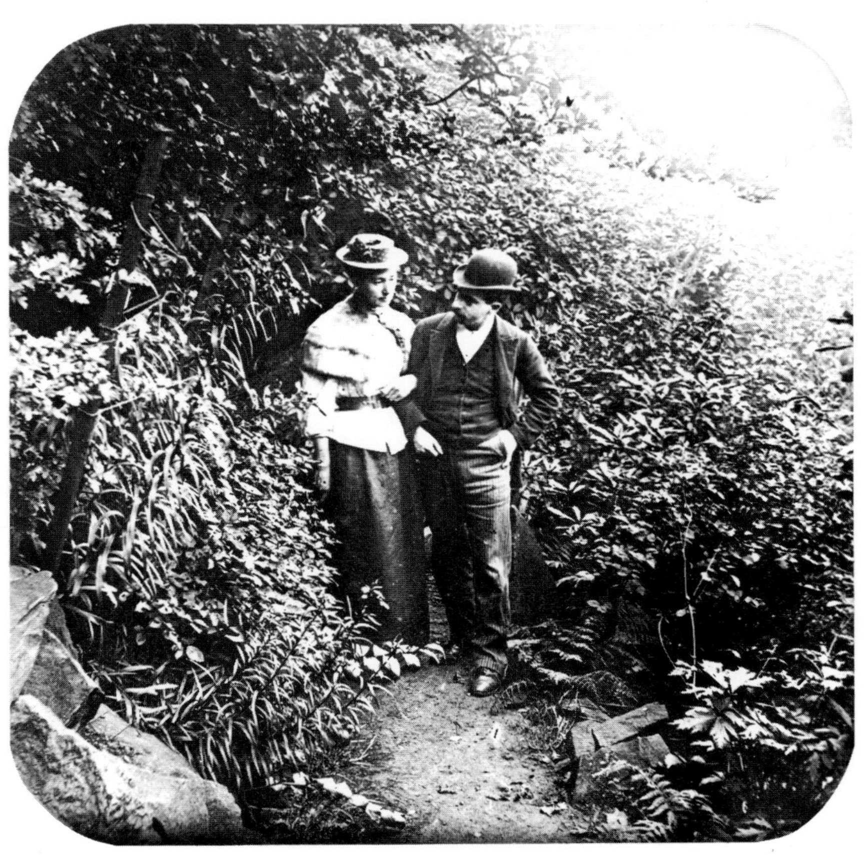

"The grandest girl that stepped" you thought her,
The brown sunny locks curling over her brow,
And her eyes, like stars mirrored in the deep water,
Look'd brighter than landlady's jewels do now!

If her beauty is spoil'd by hunger and weeping,
If her gown is just fit for scrubbing the floor,
'Tis the fruit of your unkindness she's reaping;
Why don't you keep out of the publican's door?

Do you say she is sharp, and given to scolding?
It was not so in the days gone by;
For when the cradle your first born was holding,
How kind was the glance of his mother's eye!

*   *   *

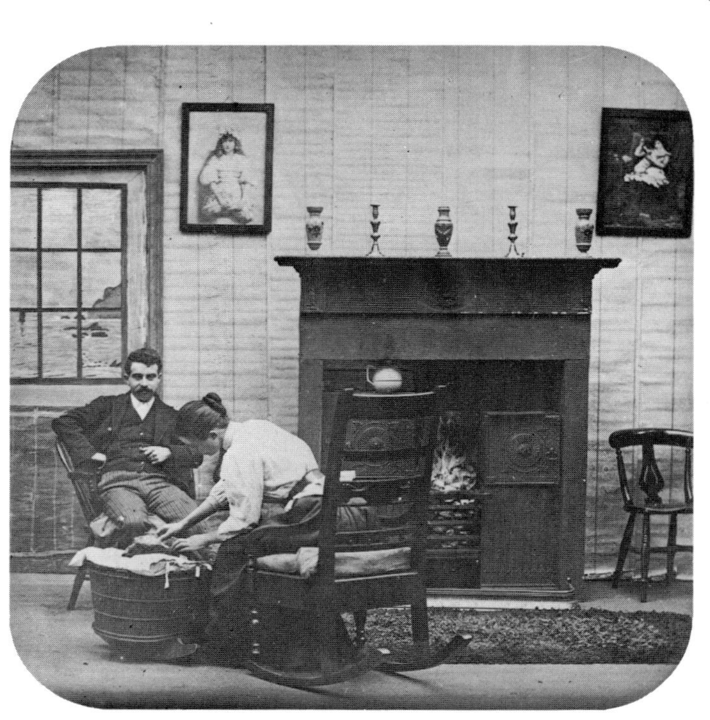

But her wrongs the saintliest soul would embitter;
How *can* she be gentle, how *can* she look sweet,
When she sees on the neck of the landlady glitter
The gold that should make her own little ones neat?

Yet the best of each scanty meal is for "father";
For the drunkard before his babe must be fed;
And as for herself she pretends she would rather
Her own hunger quench with weak tea and bread.

*   *   *

Can you wonder that such results will follow?
That half-fed lips speak fretfully?
Nor smiles relax those cheeks so hollow,
Nourished only on bread and tea?

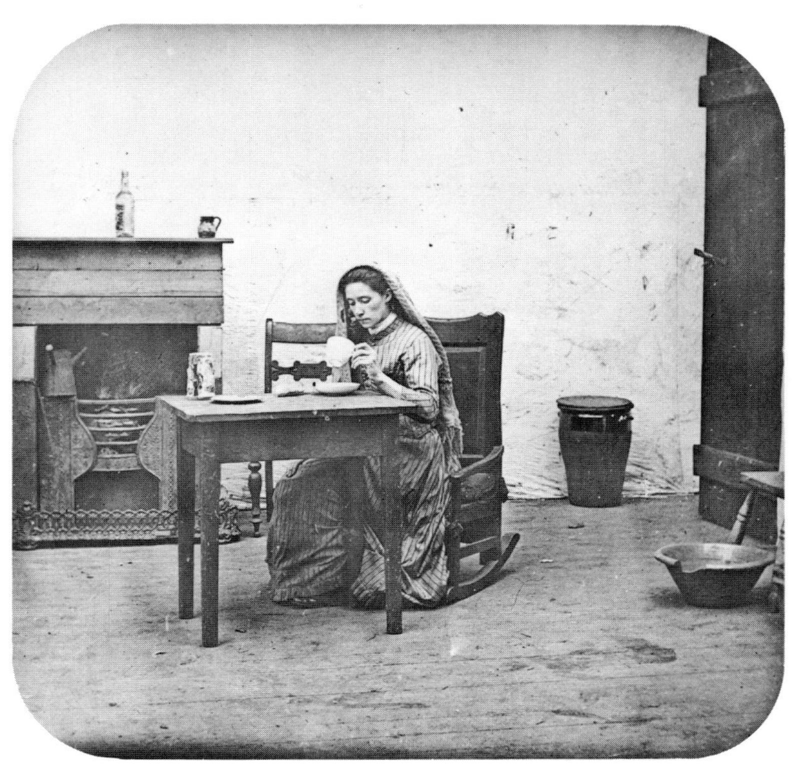

But you go and put in her hand every shilling
You pay to the publican's wife at the "Crown",
And soon you will see those hollow cheeks filling,
And their roses will bloom as in days that are gone.

And she'll hush the sharp word, when she sees it adorning
Your breast, that little cerulean badge;
She'll sing like a bird, and smile like the morning,
When you've signed and are keeping the temperance pledge.

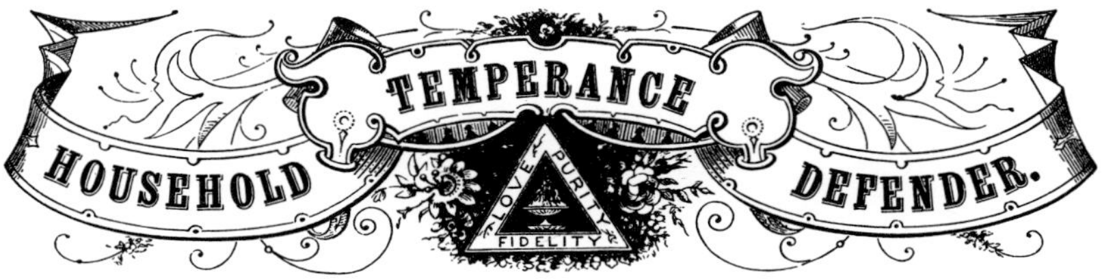

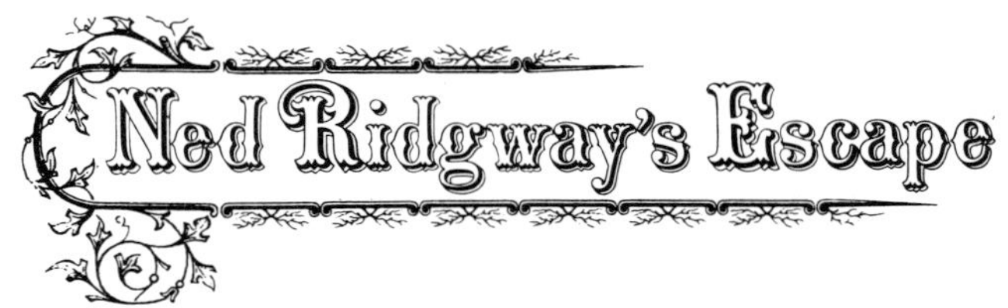

I welcome you kindly, Jack! I do from 'eart of 'earts—
My jolly old chum come back from far and furrin parts.
God knows there was tear-drops riz—you couldn't but twig 'em stand—
At the sight of your dear old phiz, and the touch of your kind old hand.
I know what a friend is worth, and I tells you straight and true,
There's hardly a thing on earth I'd ever refuse to you.
Are you short of a five pun note? old feller, it's yourn—why not?
D'ye fancy you'd like my coat? I'll peel on the werry spot.
But you collars my arm, old pal, and you says, say you, just so,
"We'll drink at six at the 'Jolly Bricks';" and the answer I make is "No."

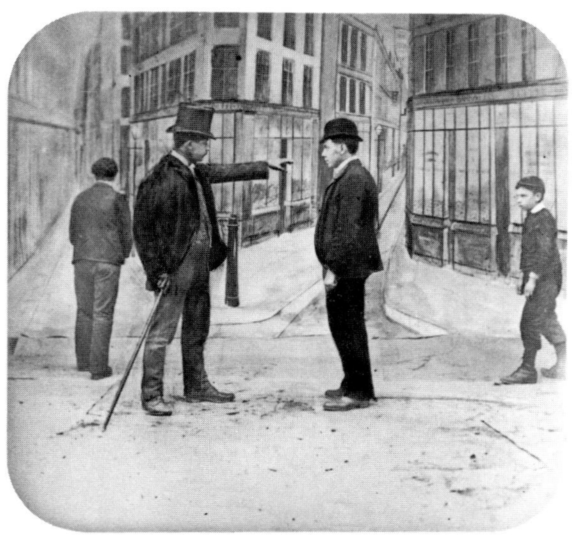

Don't think as I acts unkind,—"A drink" was the thing you said;
I'm ready enough, you'll find, if you'll make it "a eat" instead.
There's a nice little shop below—you've only to say the word
(Though I wittled an hour ago) and I goes with you like a bird.
Soup, on trays, hot or cold—I'm ready to gorge and stuff;
As far as a chap can hold, I'll never cry "hold! enough."
But you're on for a drink instead, and you takes my arm in tow;
And I sighs and I shakes my head, and the answer I make is "No!"
The answer I make is "No!" Do you ax for the reason, Jack?—
I've climbed out well from the pit of hell, and I ain't a-goin back.

Take stock of your friend, old chap!—how's that for a chain and ring?
This hat has a tidy nap; this coat is about the thing.
Not shabby, I guess, not quite—not bad for a workin' man;
Well, putting it straight and right, I'm nothin' to Mary Ann
Rigged out in her Sunday gownd, and setting to pour the tea,
With flounces and bows all round, her's one as you ought to see.
And the kids, with their 'air in curl, and their noses nicely blowed—
They isn't the boys and gurl you's meeting on every road.
A-taking our Sunday tea (a hegg and a crumpet 'ot),
The misses and me, and the youngsters three, is rayther a likely lot.

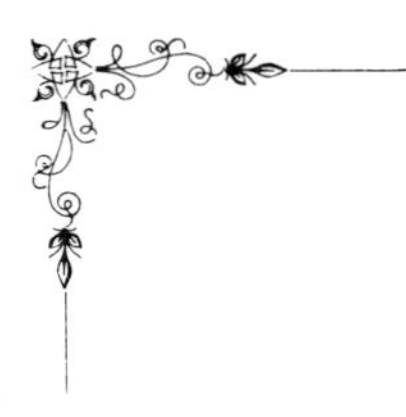

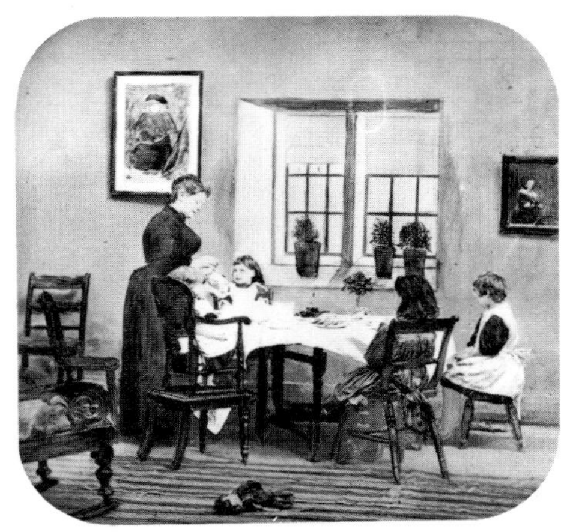

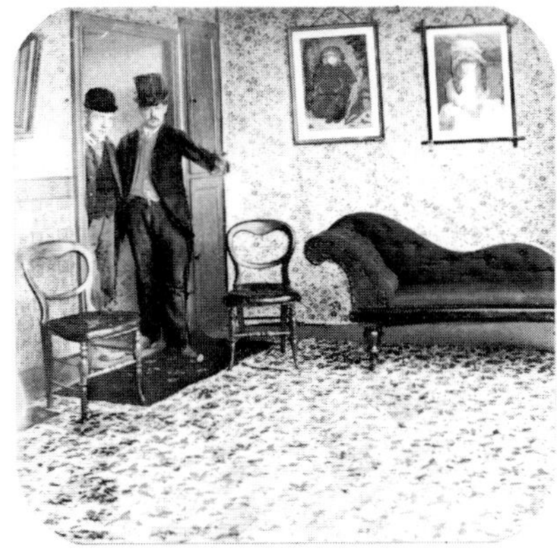

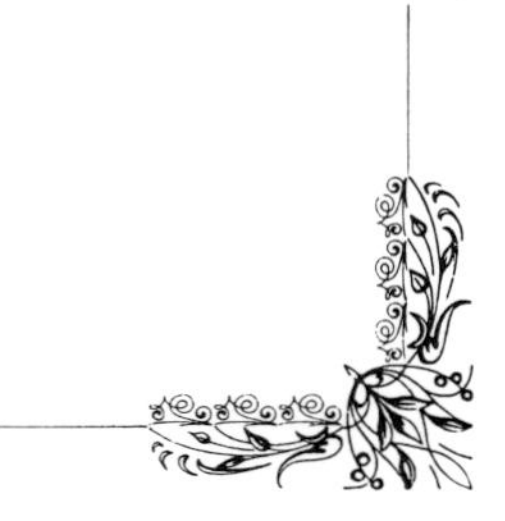

And isn't the parlour snug? I tell yer it's reg'lar neat;—
With a carpet like that and a rug, a fellow must mind his feet.
And tables and chairs like those are as common as mud in town—
Though, of course, in your working clo'es, you're shy about sitting down.
The paper is mauve and gold, you trust my missus's taste;
And the 'ole effect, I am told, is reckoned uncommon chaste.
That chap in the picture there, a-smiling so bland and free—
You wouldn't have guessed, I swear, that affable cove was *me*.
The kitchen—that ain't so grand, but it's quite in the cosy line;
And, blowing my cloud, I'm reg'lar proud of this snug little nest of mine.

Now listen the best you can: not two years since—not quite—
A beast as was born a man crep' out of his den at night.
His heart-broken wife lay sick, she laid on the floor for bed,—
The house had barely a stick, and never a crust of bread.
His cheeks were ghastly white, his tatters were foul with dirt,
And his clothes were buttoned tight, for he hadn't got no shirt.
A horrible coiling snake was writhing his heart within;
And he prayed, "For dear God's sake, one penny to buy me gin."
He stole for the devilish drink, for nobody heard his plea,
And that felon pale as they dragged to gaol, old feller—'twas me! 'twas me!

So that is my story, mate, and you know as the story's true;
I've tipped it you fair and straight, with never no flam all through.
Look here—look over the way—look round on every hand;
Poor devils! they stand to-day, as you might have seen *me* stand,
By thousands, as God can tell, they's treading the sloping track
As leads to the pit of hell—but few on 'em treads it back.
And you points to the "Jolly Bricks," and you says, says you, just so.
"Old feller, we'll drink at six," and the answer I make is "No!"
The answer I make is "No!" can you doubt of the reason ,Jack?
I've got well quit of the flaming pit, and I ain't a-going back.

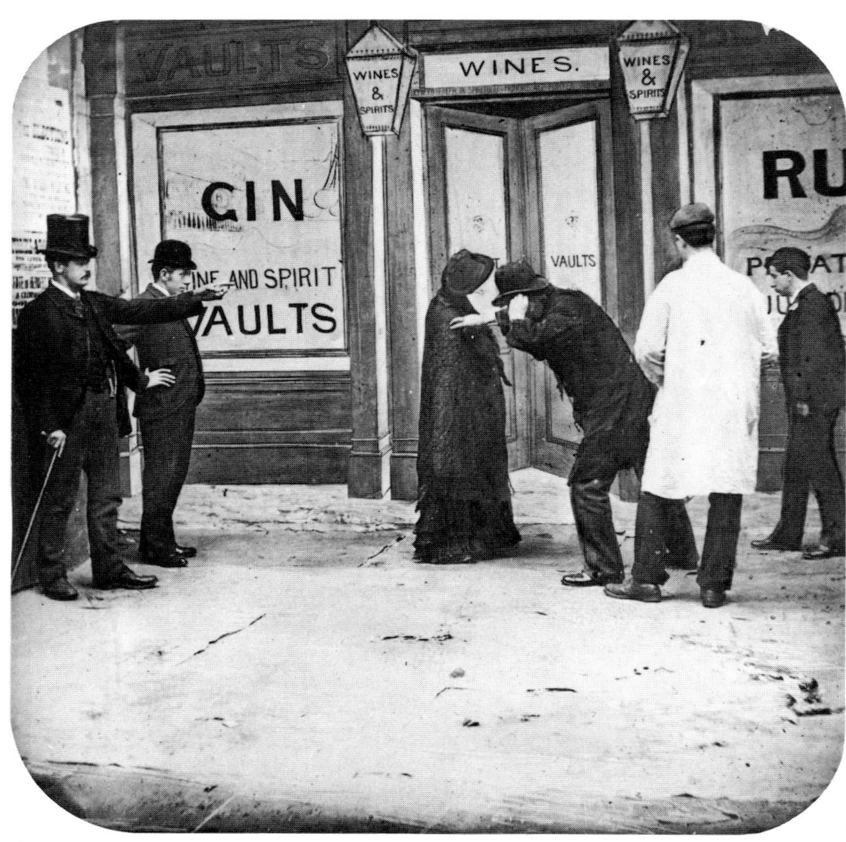

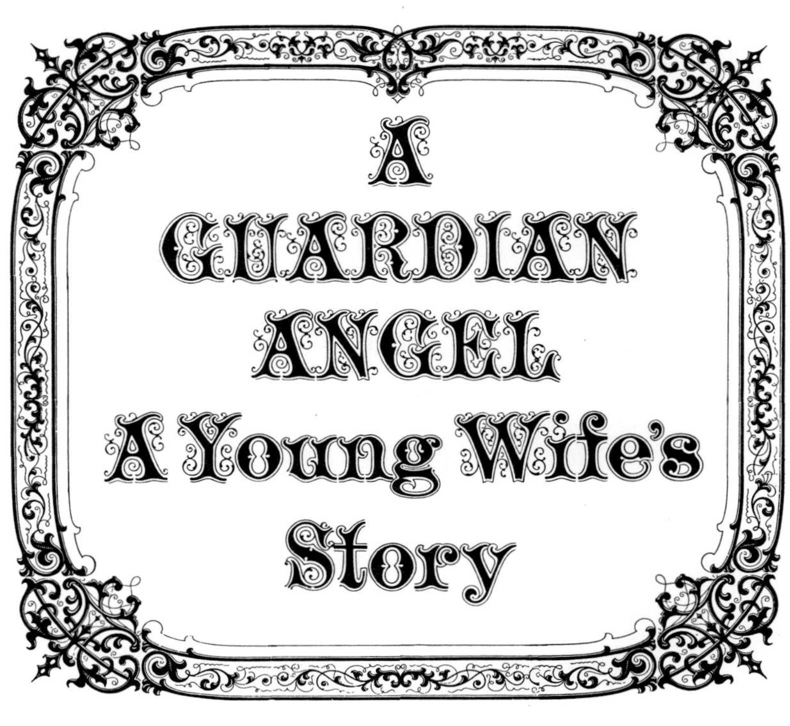

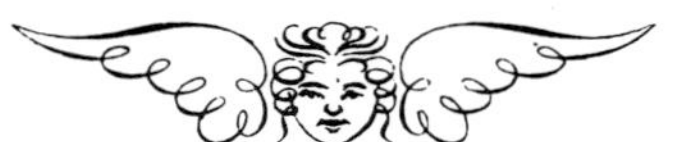

"And so you advise moderation? You say I am not looking well?
You may as well tell me to cure myself by a moderate leap into hell!
Strong words for a woman? I know it, but mine's been a strong disease,
And when you're just pulled from a blazing pile, you can't all proprieties please.

"But there's one way of looking better, and the same way of feeling worse,
Of the outward semblance of gaiety, and the inward gnawing of curse;
And if for the vow I've taken, I must pay by dying this night,
There would be the ministering angels, who always succour the right.

"My eye may look leaden and joyless, but not from a recent stain,
For the guilty past of a sinner in the flesh for long will remain;
And because there's a chance that my struggle—the battle in which I fell—
May came home to the life of another, my story to you I'll tell.—

"I married when barely a woman, a child in what wives should be;
We prospered, and yet in true riches few were so poor as we;
All went well while the novelty lasted; the plucked flower is scarce cast aside
While the dew of the morn is upon it; but few see the eventide.

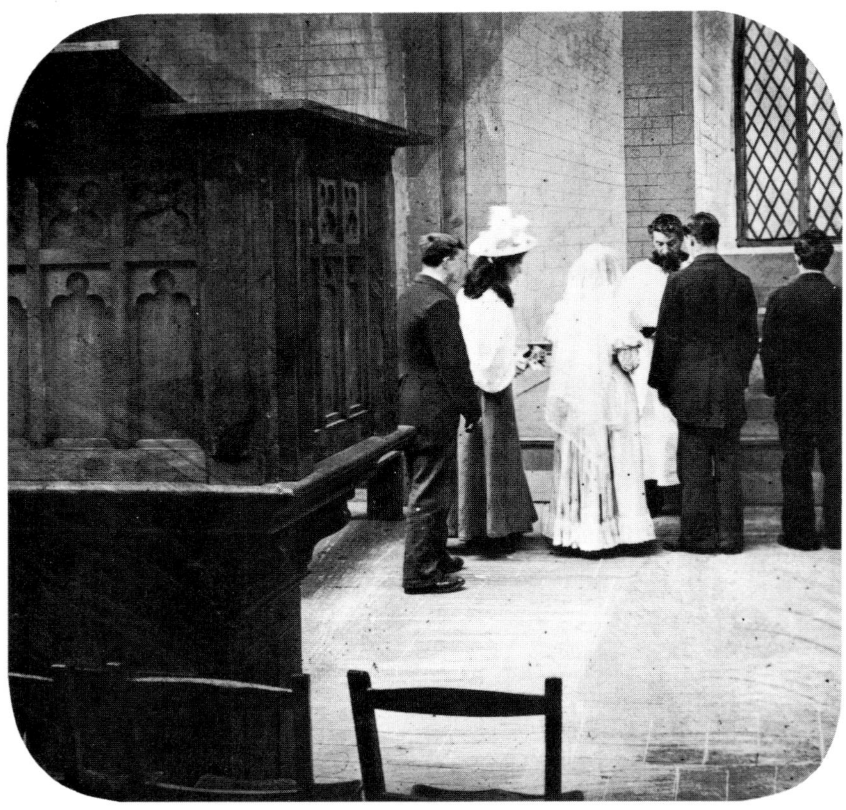

"But social ambition, and pleasure, and the giddy unrest of the crowd
Were the rapids that carried our lives down, the idols to which we bowed;
And when three little weaklings we buried, and my health did nothing but ail,
Disappointment begat indifference and Jack's love began to fail.

"By a dozen ways daily I knew it, as only a wife could know,
For we kept up the hollow pretensions, the outside glitter and show,
But the hollowest sham about it was an injured wife's false smile,
Made to blind the eye of suspicion, while her heart was bleeding the while.

"One night at an evening party, full of revel and sad excess,
I was overcome by some brandy. Alas! that I must confess
That I, a delicate woman, who could scarcely touch any food,
Was that night known as inebriate and had stained my womanhood.

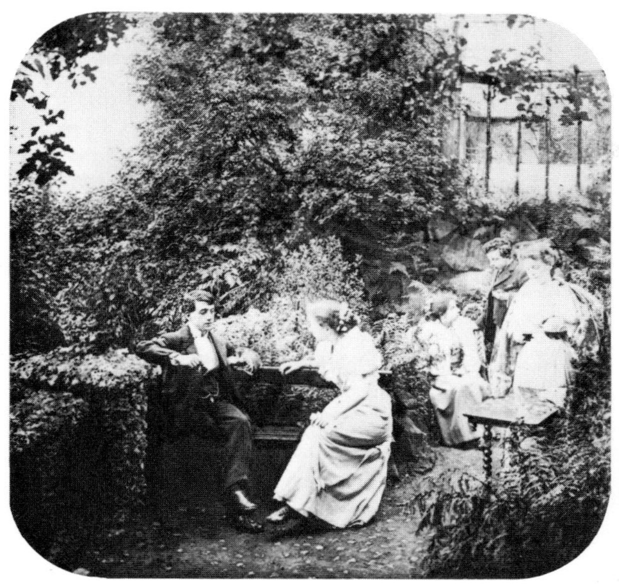

"And oh, the scorn of my husband! the bitter unmeasured scorn—
When we met alone together on the following weary morn.
Such a heap of dreadful reproaches, beneath which all hope sank,
And from then his words were verified, he had a wife who drank.

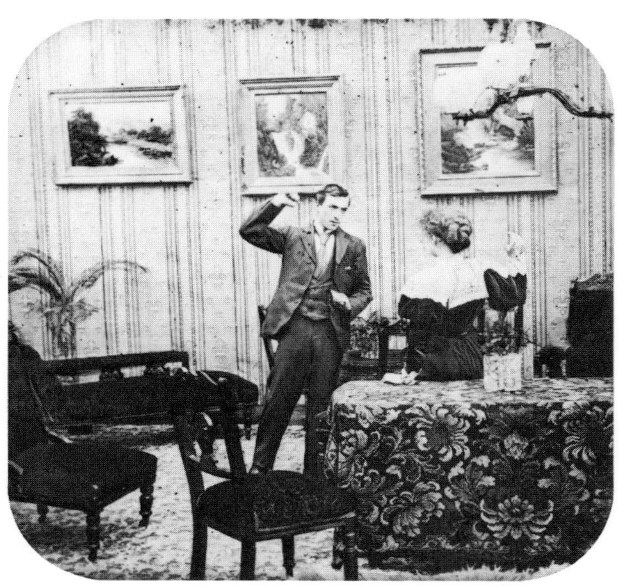

"Ah, don't look in that way at me, and make your garments shrink!
It's neglect that brought me to it, it's contempt that made me sink;
If a dog or a bird is in peril, there's a womanly hue and cry,
But a sister whose soul is in danger—spurn her, and pass her by!

"I know I am wrong in excusing what was weak and sinful and vile,
But at times I practised abstention to try to regain Jack's smile,
For I craved for his love and sympathy more than I craved for wine,
But he came and went like a stranger, and never gave me a sign.

"And once, when I pleaded my weakness and hunger of heart for his aid,
He turned on his heel with impatience, and a sneer at my penitence made;
Then I waited for night and the darkness, with my mind on a purpose set
By which I could gain deliverance, and all my troubles forget.

"Some two or three miles from our suburb, the trains that bring people from town
Run awhile through a straight narrow cutting, with banks on each side,
          sloping down
To the edge of the rails very sharply; no houses at all are at hand,
And the sides of the gorge you may sit on, but a goat would be puzzled to stand.

"I found a small gap in the hedge-row at the top of the outer climb;
And then I slipped down on the inside, within just a minute of time
That the train, in which he would sit smoking, would be up and thundering by,
And soon 'twould be known at the station that a woman had chosen to die.

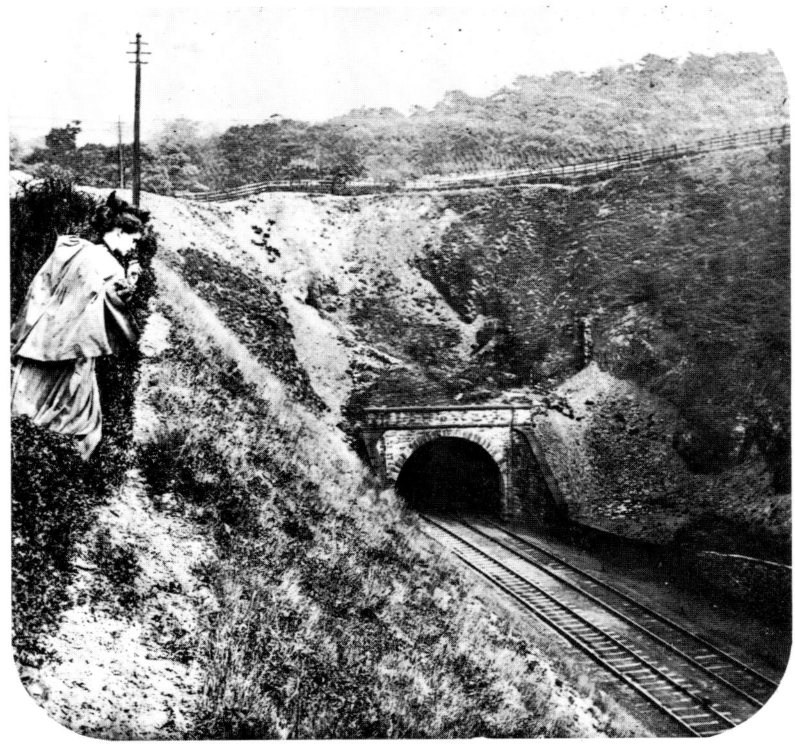

"She was coming! her red lights grew redder, like a wolf's eyes in search of
            his prey!
Already I let go of a furze-stem that kept me from slipping half way;
My footsteps began a quick tremble, resolve not an instant fails,
When I'm seized by my skirts! there's a struggle! and two women roll down on
            the rails
"Just clearing the guard's van by two feet, my saviour and I in embrace;
And I saw close to mine in the dim light the wistful familiar face
Of Lizzie, my housemaid, a treasure, a girl who'd been with me for years,
As she said, 'Thank God, you are saved, ma'am!' and I felt the rain of her tears.

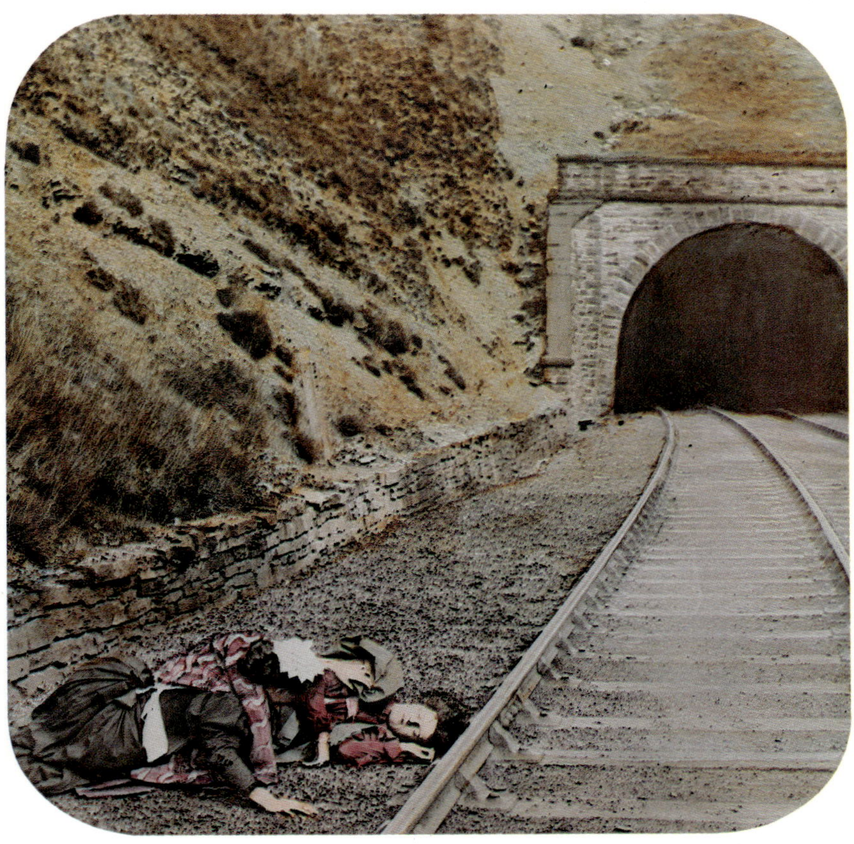

"A revulsion of feeling came o'er me, I breathed as one barely escaped
From some gulf of perdition, whose black jaws to swallow me wholly had gaped;
'Oh Lizzie! I'm saved from myself, I'm unworthy of love like this!'
And then, once more, after many a day, I knew the warmth of a kiss.

"We got home with little observance, for if ever a fog did fall
One fell that night, and, what's stranger, Jack was not in that train after all!
And Lizzie, whose brave soul was beaming in her true and steadfast eyes,
Breathed new hope and faith within her like a herald from Paradise.

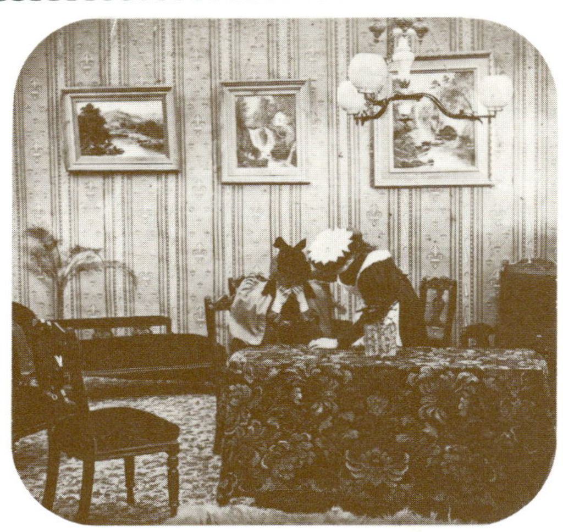

"You may say, 'She was only a servant; would you confidant make of her?
And call her a guardian angel, and judgement to her defer?'
I have only one answer to make you; just turn to salvation's plan —
'Twas in the form of a servant He chose to come, Who suffered and died for man.

"And I never did see, till she showed me, that the highest motive of life
Is goodness for sake of goodness, and not for husband and wife;
And having the kingdom of heaven within, we possess the essence of bliss,
And all things else, that are fit for us, in time shall be added to this.

"And what of my Jack? Why he wears for me a smile as he did of yore;
But hark! here he comes; he is early now, and I need not tell you more;
And if, as you make your departure, you see Lizzie about on the stairs,
You can't say you have met on my threshold 'an angel unawares'."

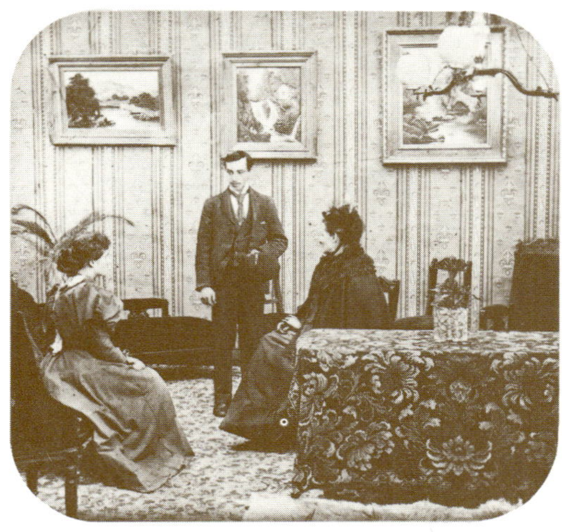

IN FLOWER ALLEY

This is a little story,
    Of nothing . . . you may say,
Yet it filled my heart with sunshine
    One dull, dark winter day.
And if it cheers another who is sad, as I was then,
It's worth my while to tell it, to women—or to men!

    *   *   *

I'd done a deal of fretting:
    For when your husband's ill
And in Hospital, it damps you!
    Try and take it how you will.
A lady gave me sewing. She was *very* good to me.
But the day I took the work home, I was low as low could be.

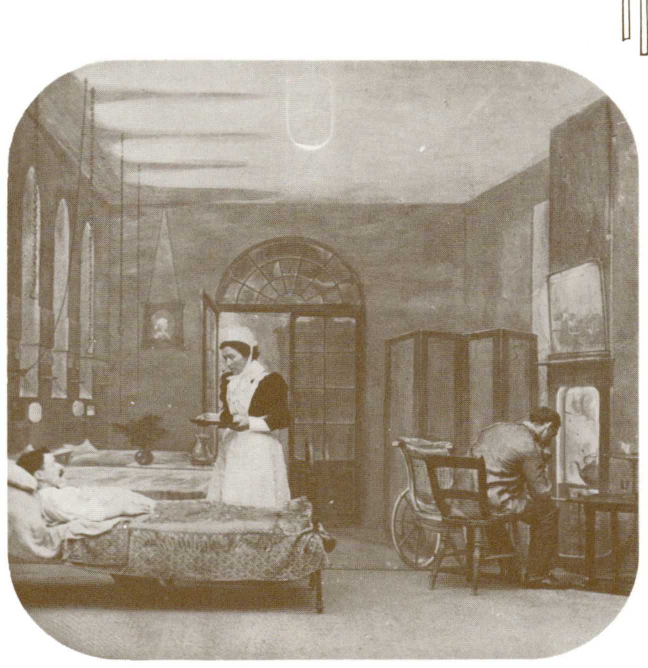

We were living in Flower Alley
　　(That hadn't a flower to show!)
And the fog hung cold as grave-clothes.
　　And though it's years ago,
I can feel its chill upon me as I hurried down the street,
Knowing I'd left my children with scarce a crumb to eat.

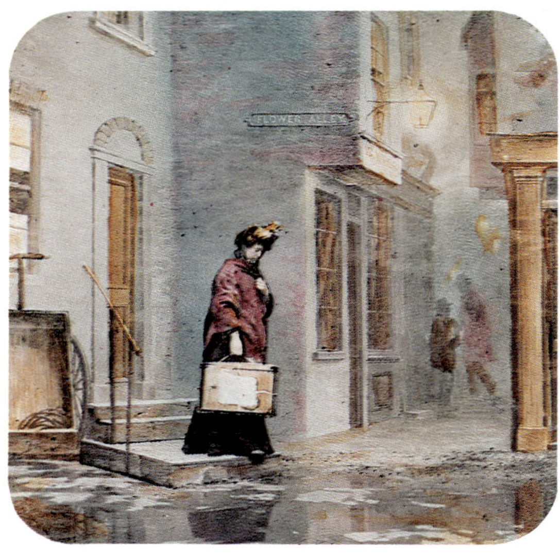

I was worrying about them
　　When I reached the lady's door.
'Twas a splendid house she lived in.
　　I hadn't been there before.
I was asked to wait in a passage: and I sat down in a chair,
With a sort of arch before me—as it might be, over there!

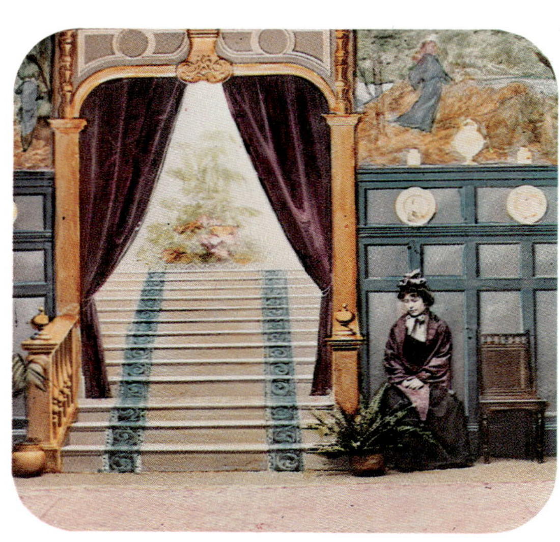

And through the arch was a staircase,
    All flooded in golden light.
And as I sat there, waiting,
    I saw the prettiest sight
You ever could imagine. Three children came down the stairs.
I've seen cherub heads in pictures, but never none sweeter than theirs.

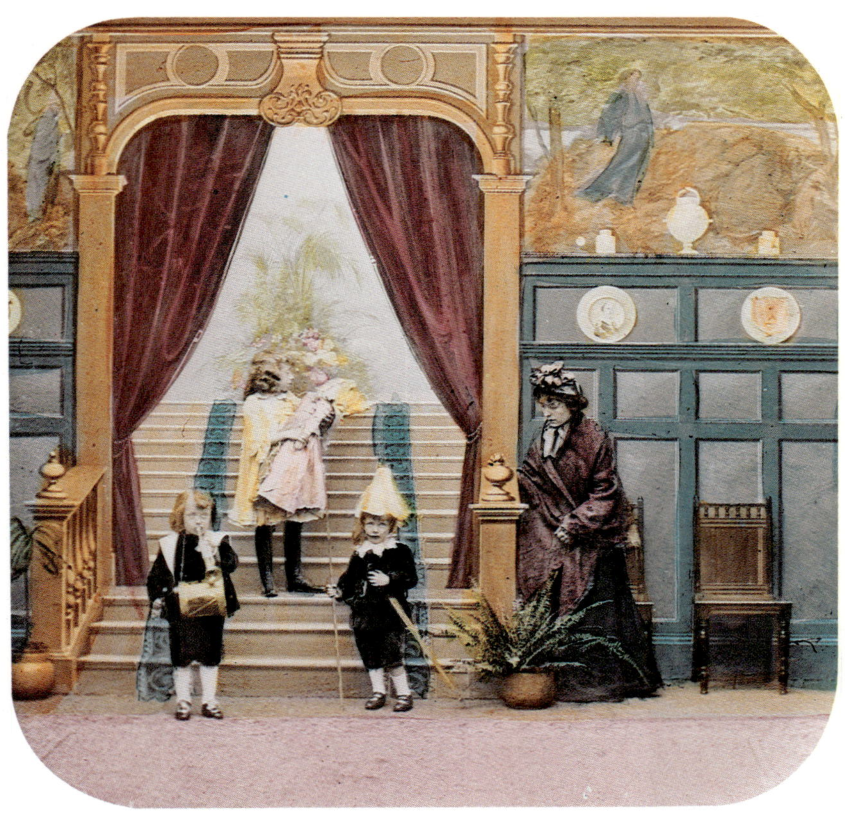

Such darling rosy faces!
    Such hair! all wave and shine.
All dresses of lace and velvet,
    So rich! and dainty! and fine!
Three. Just the same as my children! A girl and two little boys.
Laughing . . . and stepping careful . . . with their arms full of lovely toys.

The little girl held a dolly,
    As big as herself, very near!
And a boy just the size of Harry,
    Had a helmet! and sword! and spear!
And the other boy had a trumpet! and a Noah's Ark! and a drum!
"Let us go and show them to mother!"—they said, as I watched them come.

And they passed down the great wide staircase,
       All three! And I saw them no more.
     Though the chime of their happy laughter
       Followed me out at the door.
It's pleasant now to recall it. But *that* day, in my distress,
It filled my breast with a passion of envy and bitterness.

     For I thought of my wretched young ones
       Waiting for me in the gloom,
     By the farthing dip, where I'd left them
       In our poor living-room.
Tired: and maybe, crying: in the dreary evening shades.
And the laughter of those rich children stabbed me like dagger blades.

     I'd never coveted money,
       But I grudged and coveted then.
     It made me mad to be thinking,
       That the children of working-men,
Were to have life's tears and sadness, and the others have all the joys,
"It's easy for *them* to be laughing, with their clothes, and their beautiful toys!"

     Thinks I, as I reached our Alley,
       Squalid, and dismal, and wet.
     And trailed up our steps, and stood . . . rooted!
       By a sound I shall never forget.
Peals of the merriest laughter that ever rang out on the air!
Peal after peal! Sweet as music! . . . where did it come from? Where?

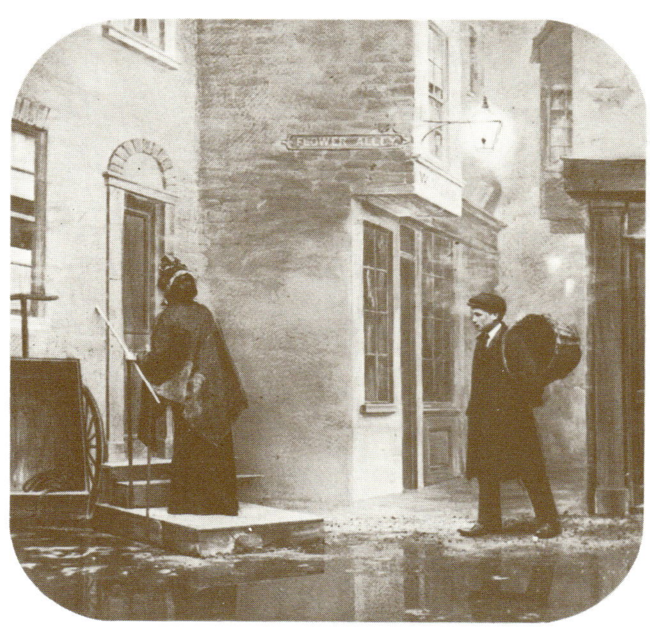

Never from my poor children!
    I gasped . . . and I opened the door . . .
There were my three youngsters,
    Sitting down on the floor.
Sitting and shouting together, in the guttering candle flame,
Laughing their little heads off, over some wonderful game.

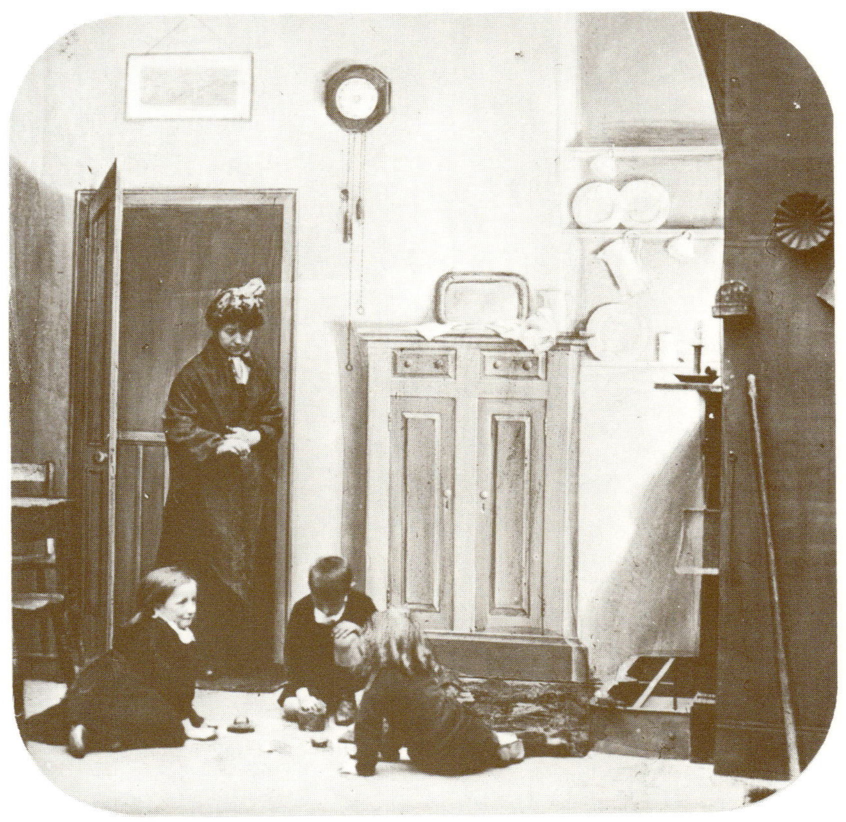

There they were. POOR OF THE POOREST.
    Bubbling with laughter and fun!
"Let's go an' show 'em to mother," says Dickie,
    Just as the rich ones had done!
And they brought me their toys and treasures . . . Some bits of orange peel!
And bits of a broken tea-pot! And an empty cotton-reel!

And an oyster shell! And a hairpin!
    And an old boot, burst to shreds!
They were playing at shop, they told me.
    Oh blessings on their young heads!
They didn't know why I was crying: why I kissed them so warm and fast.
But the fog had turned to sunshine, and my bitterness was past.

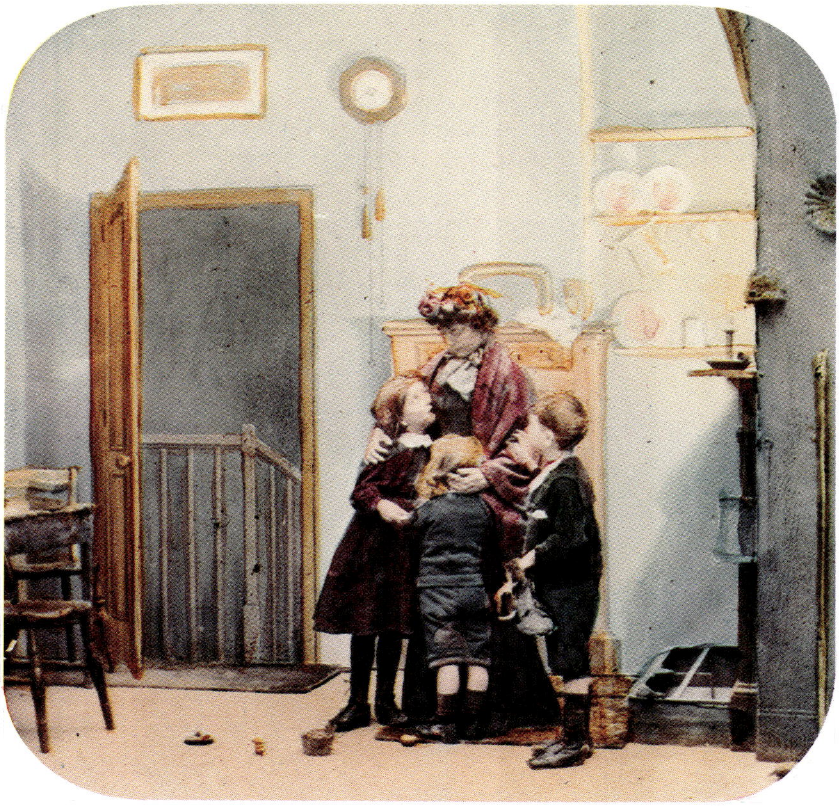

Friends! the world worships money,
   And sells for it Peace and Health.
But Happiness, thank Heaven,
   Has nothing to do with wealth.

It's God's free gift, like summer,
   For the rich, and the poor, to find.
And all the money that's minted
   Won't buy a contented mind!
And all the money that's minted will never hold or sway
The happy-hearted laughter where little children play.

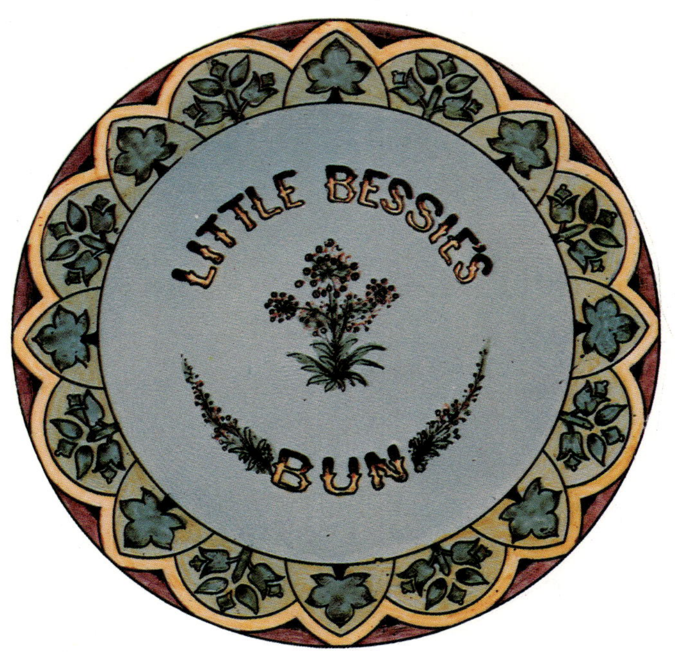

John Varley quietly made his way, as oft he'd done before,
Straight from his work to Barton Arms, where ale was kept in store;
Its baneful power had not as yet quite hardened this man's heart,
But still he'd have his fling sometimes, though pleasure brought its smart.

It happened on this self-same day, and in this very street,
His little daughter Bessie came, expecting him to meet;
"O daddy," quoth the simple child, "give me a penny, pray,
I want to buy a bun with it, and then I'll go and play."

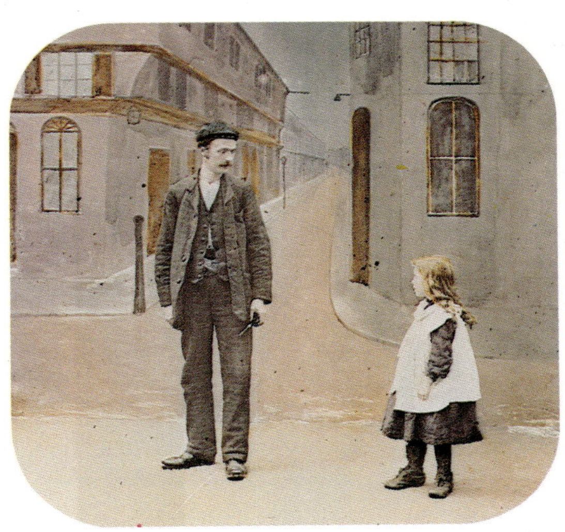

A father's feeling sprang at once within John Varley's breast,
And sore he grieved to see his child so thin and poorly dress'd;
"What I would now spend in that house I'll give," thought he, "to her
Many's the sixpence I have drunk—I'm sure that's only fair."

"Here, lassie, here's a penny. Look, a penny six times o'er,"
And quick he dropped the little coin into her pinafore;
"Thank you, dear dad," then off with eyes quite full of joy she ran,
While John e'en now began to feel himself a better man.

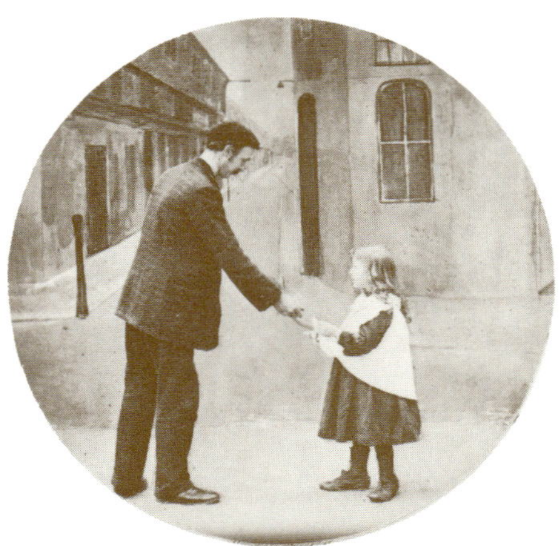

"They'll not expect me yet, I'm sure, an hour or so at home,
I'll go and have a quiet walk, and in the country roam;"
So off he turned and wisely left temptation far behind,
And in sweet Nature's lovely path found much to calm his mind.

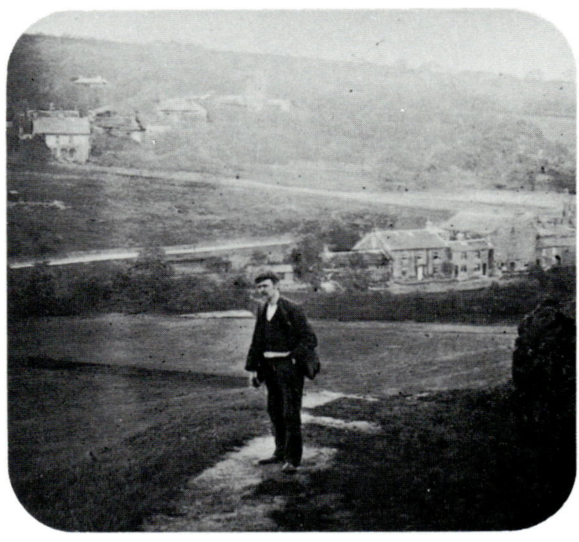

The fields, he thought, ne'er looked so fair, the birds ne'er sang so sweet,
And oft he wished his wife was there to enjoy this country treat;
And then his mind would backward turn and fill him with delight,
To think how Bessie look'd, who'd got the silver bright.

Much more than this John thought and felt, as homeward now he went,
His mind being free and clear enough when not on liquor bent;
'Twere well if thousands more would choose a walk through country fair,
Instead of filling in a vault the noisy drunkard's chair.

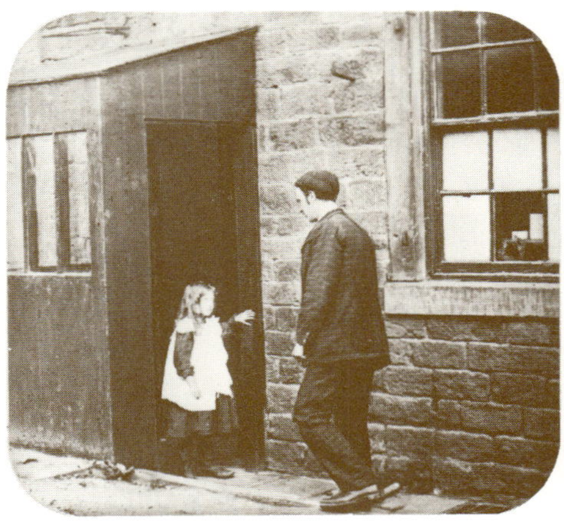

"Come, father, come," poor Bessie cried, as John his door just reach'd,
"You're just in time, and mother's got us such a pretty feast;
The shopman gave me heaps of buns all for that silver thing,
And tea will soon be ready now—I've heard the kettle sing."

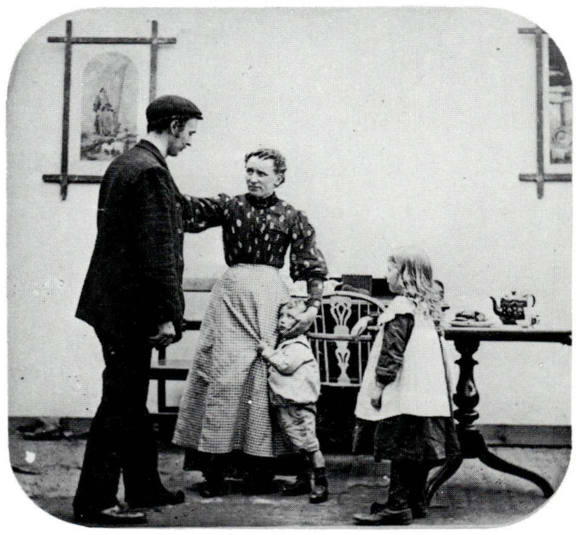

Then came his wife, with little Tom, and kindly him address'd;
"Come, daddy, sit you down a bit, you surely want a rest;
But what is now the matter, man? You seem half right, half wrong;
I wish those folks at Barton Arms you'd never mix among.

"I've scolded Bessie well, the puss, for all that money spent
In foolish buns, but, little thing, 'twas done with best intent;
She said when you came home again how fine and pleas'd you'd be
To see, instead of only bread, nice currant buns for tea."

"Look here," John said, with brimful eyes and penitential tone,
"Scold not the girl—she's done what's right—the money was her own;
This very afternoon I gave our little Bessie, dear,
The money that I meant to spend upon myself in beer.

"To please my precious self for long I've grudged not many a pound,
Besides the time that's wasted, and will never more come round;
But 'good for evil' you've returned, your sixpence shared with me;
Oh! may I then in future time more generous to you be.

"Most cruel man, how long have I to selfishness inclined!
And given myself to baneful drinks, which do in fetters bind.
God bless our little girl," he said, "my turning-point she's been,
For never in Barton Arms will I again be seen."

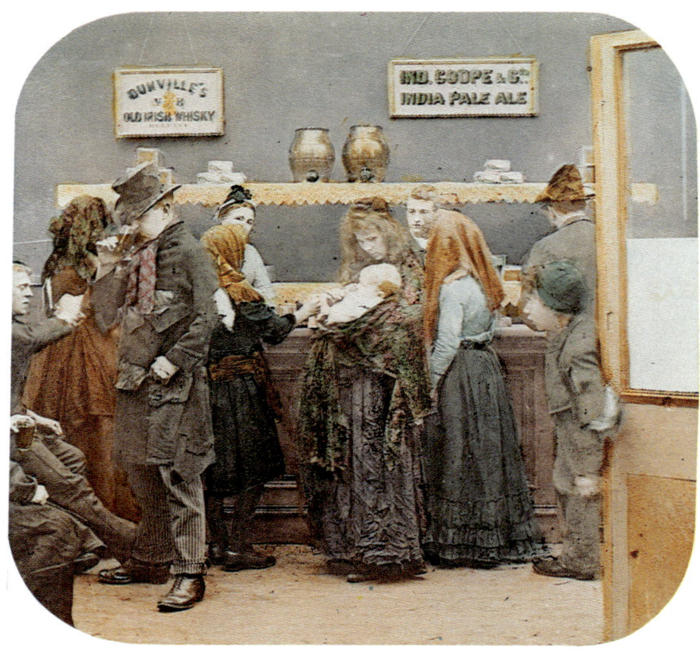

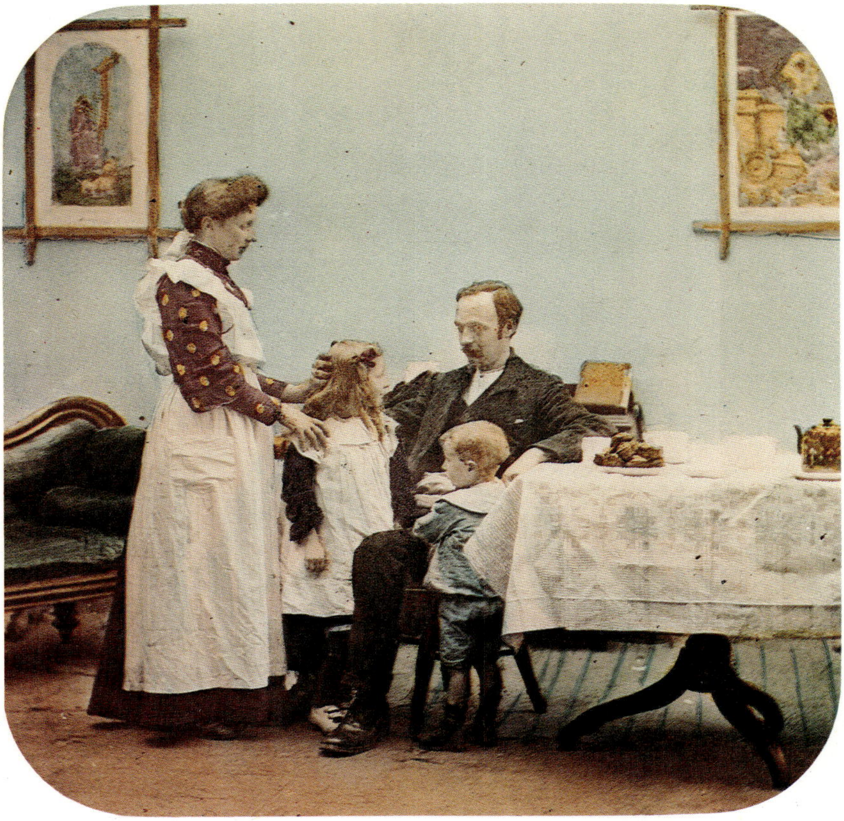

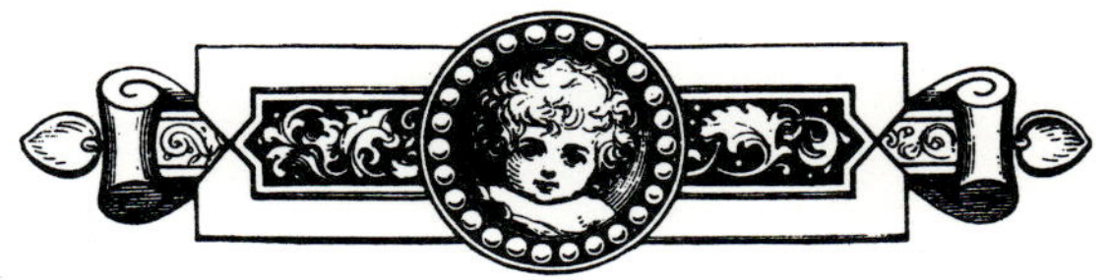

John Varley now has money saved, that buys good food and clothes,
And long has felt the gain that from a tender conscience flows;
His promise he has bravely kept, that the beerhouse he would shun,
And ne'er forgets the lesson taught by little Bessie's bun.

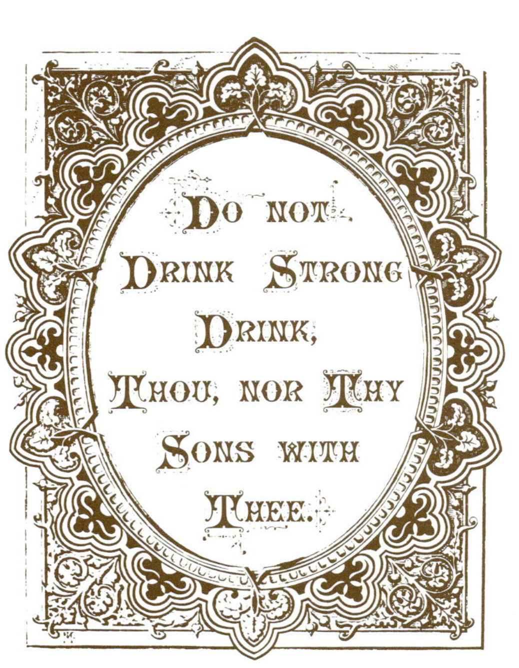

Do not
Drink Strong
Drink,
Thou, nor Thy
Sons with
Thee.

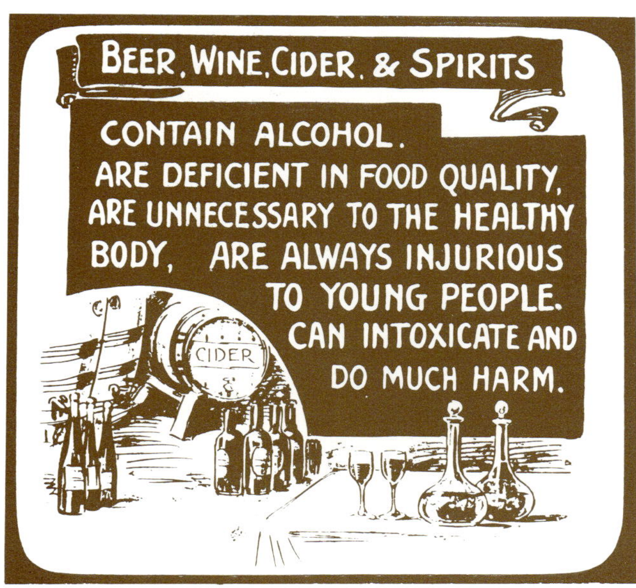

BEER, WINE, CIDER, & SPIRITS
CONTAIN ALCOHOL.
ARE DEFICIENT IN FOOD QUALITY,
ARE UNNECESSARY TO THE HEALTHY
BODY, ARE ALWAYS INJURIOUS
TO YOUNG PEOPLE.
CAN INTOXICATE AND
DO MUCH HARM.
CIDER

The story I'm going to tell you, is truth from beginning to end.
It didn't come under my notice. It was told me by a friend,
A relation, the wife of my brother. And the saddest part that's true
Appeared in the Daily Papers, as dozens such stories do.

*　　*　　*

Thomas, my eldest brother – I don't mind who sits and hears –
Was coachman to Squire Lawrence for years and years and years.
A first-rate man was Thomas. And he married the Dairy-maid.
Yes: that he did: and he loved her, most true. And I'm not afraid
To say that a sweeter creature than Tom's wife, Rachel Dale,
Never set foot on the meadows, or looked at a milking pail!

Tom had saved a bit of money, and he took it out of a bag,
And put it into a Public, that was called 'The Lamb and Flag.'
I'd have called it 'The Net and Fishes,' or 'The Spider and the Fly' –
Those are rare good names for Publics – but the Sign was swinging high
Before Tom and Rachel went there. A Lamb with a Flag of gold,
Glittering above the customers, most dazzling to behold!

It's a common thing for coachmen to enter the Liquor Trade.
I don't know why, but it is so. And Tom and Rachel made
The very best of Landlords. Tom drove his trade along
As well as he'd driven horses. He was sober, and "straight," and *strong*!
And if a man got noisy, and started to swear and shout,
Tom went round very quiet, and simply – put him out!

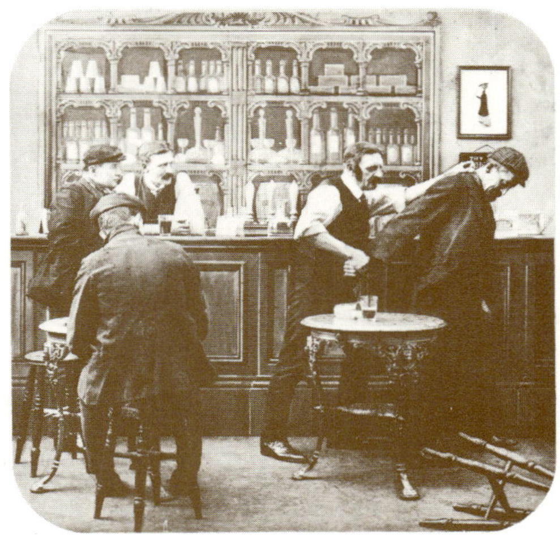

He kept the Law as careful as any Policeman would.
And whether 'twas beer or spirits, all that he sold was good.
When I say "good" I mean . . . well . . . as good as it ever is!
His landlord was the Brewer, and Thomas could say this –
To a finer-hearted gentleman you couldn't pay your rent!
He was all on the side of Temperance, and sat in Parliament:
And passed the Act, and kept it, and no tenant of his would dare
To serve a man on the Black List, any more than he'd fly in air!
Yet Rachel often told me, that all about their way
The drinking was distressing. It grieved her, day by day,
To look into the faces of the poor, drink-sodden souls
Who came from courts and alleys, and drifted in, in shoals,
To all the Public-houses. Their Bar was clean and bright,
But the wrecks and dregs that filled it – say on a Saturday night –
To a tender-hearted woman, were pitiful to see.

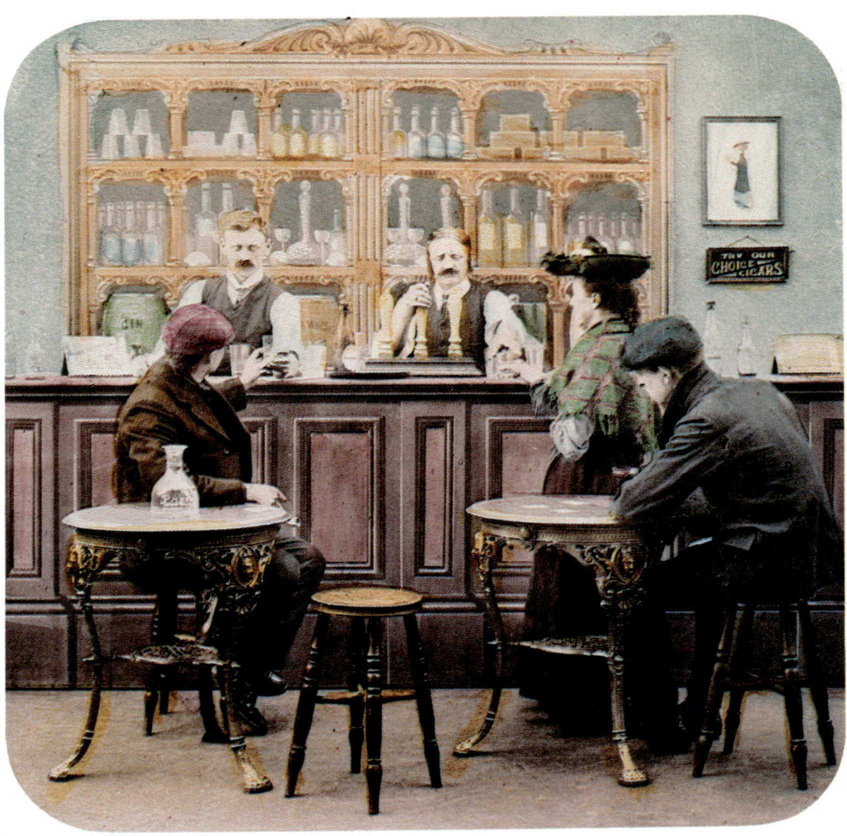

She got to know the people who came there frequently.
And amongst them was a couple she noticed above the rest.
She found they were wife and husband: though that she wouldn't have guessed,
As they never came in together. The man was a surly lout,
And quarrelsome. And Thomas had had to put him out
Not once, or twice! she told me. The woman would slink in, sly,
And suck down gin and whiskey, when nobody was by.

She was mother of seven children, and middle-aged, and poor.
The man earned decent wages: but Rachel was certain sure
They wasted half on drinking.
                    One foggy winter day,
It chanced that Fred, the barman, and Tom, were both away,
And Rachel took the serving. This woman comes creeping in,
And asks in a husky whisper for two-pennyworth of gin.
And Rachel Dale leans over, and says she, in her pleasant way,
"Let me make you a cup of cocoa, or tea. It's got more stay
Than spirits. The kettle's boiling. Just come in as you are!"
And into the cosy parlour she'd got behind the Bar,
She had her in half a twinkle!
                    "Now, Mrs Hames," says she,
A setting out the tea-cups, as cheerful as could be,
"You spend too much on spirits, and not enough on food.
I've watched you and your children. You're doing yourself no good.
Give it up! And turn teetotal!" "My very heart and life!"
Gasps the woman. "Turn teetotal! And you a Publican's wife!"
"A Publican's wife I may be, but NOT," says Rachel Dale,
"A Vampire sucking life-blood! My husband sells his ale
And has to make his profit. And I wish with all my soul,
That he was paid a salary, and got his money whole
And free from the sale of liquor: – but we sell drink, nevertheless,
For honest thirst, remember, and not for drunkenness.
We've got a heart and conscience! Do you think I can see you drift
Here at our Bar, to ruin, and never so much as lift
A hand to try and stop you! –"
                    And the woman was *so* upset
And touched, and fair astounded, she cried her apron wet.

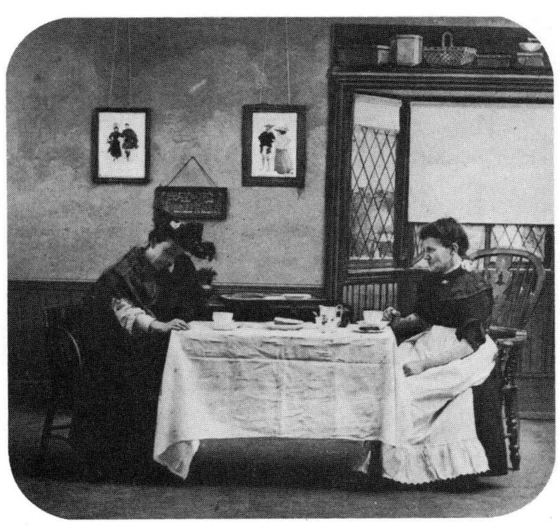

"It's true," she says a sobbing. "I'm doing myself no good.
I'd give it up tomorrow, if I could: if I *only* could!
But Oh! The craving's awful! You don't know what it is to feel
The Public Houses drawing you, inside, with cords of steel.

If I didn't pass them constant, and catch the smell of beer,
Maybe I'd lose the craving. But, Mrs. Dale, round here,
They seem to meet you all ways! We live next door to you –
'The Lamb and Flag.' And behind us, we've got 'The Wooden Shoe,'
And 'The King's Head' at the corner. I can stand outside our door
And count – 'The Cape,' 'The Magpie,' 'The Crown,' 'The Plough,' that's four!
And you know there are others handy," *And Rachel knew it well.*

She tried to help that woman. It's a funny thing to tell
Of a Publican's wife – but she did this:- She went to a lady near,
Who worked amongst the people. And for over half a year
They visited the Hameses, till they got them to sign the Pledge,
Then to help them to keep steady, to drag them from the edge
Of the Pit that's swallowed millions – they advised them, for their good,
To take another lodging in a different neighbourhood.
And man and wife were willing. And they tried to find a place
Where the open doors of Publics wouldn't stare them in the face
At every turn and corner: a lodging near Hames' work,
And not above his rental . . . Friends! I'm not going to shirk
The facts . . . *They couldn't find one.* They couldn't find a street
In the whole of that wide district – nor would they, I repeat,
In the length and breadth of London – a street where the *poor* could bide,
Without a beershop, beckoning, on this or the other side!

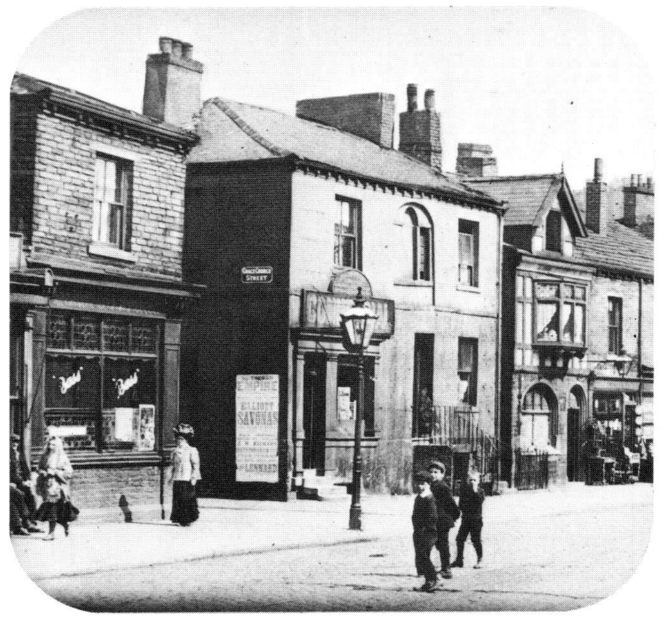

And we call this Christian England! For the sake of gold, of gain,
We take our poor weak children, drink-cursed in body and brain,
And we *swamp* them with Temptation! We roll the barrel down,
Till they sink in drink, like drenched flies, and we watch them – while they drown!

But I mustn't talk in this way. I've got to tell the tale.
The Hameses stayed, and struggled, till the sight and smell of ale,
And stout, and rum, and whiskey, and everlasting gin,
Broke down their resolutions: lured the poor wretches in:
Back to more desperate drinking: back to more reckless sin.

One evening in the Spring-time: The holiest time o'year.
When love and Peace seem calling to those who have ear to hear.

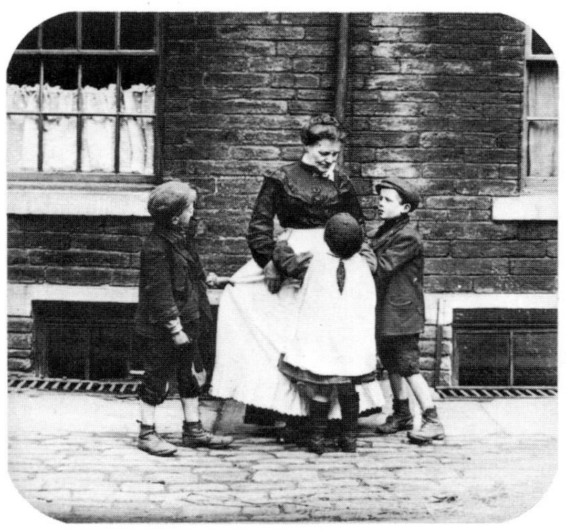

Rachel heard children screaming, so wild, she ran outside –
And the ragged little Hameses, three of them, terrified,
Clung to her, sobbing – "Mother! Oh come to Mother! Quick!"
And Rachel went with the children, and saw . . . what turned her sick,
And dumb with helpless horror . . .

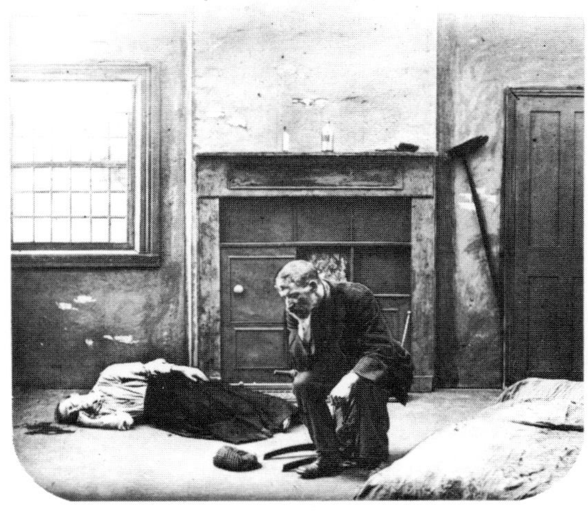

                In a room with scarce a stick
Of furniture inside it, save a bed and a broken chair,
Sat the man – the husband – tipsy! And near him, fallen there,
On the floor, before the window, where the Spring light touched her head
With its pure and radiant glory . . . lay the wife – the woman – DEAD!
In a pool of blood, that trickled, and dyed the bare boards red.

There was Coroner and Inquest. And Hames gave evidence.
They had to wait a little before they could get at sense
Out of his fuddled fancies, and sottish sulks and qualms.
His wife had been out drinking, he said, at 'The Stanley Arms.'
And he had been out drinking, he owned, at 'The Holly Bush.'
When they came back she struck him, and he gave her "a little push" –

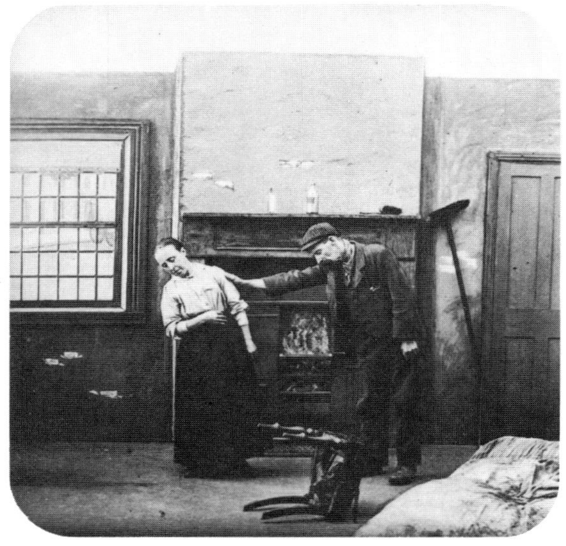

"No more than he'd often given" – and she caught her foot in her gown,
And cracked her head on the fender, he thought, as she tumbled down.
That was all he knew about it, he'd swear, with his dying breath –
And the Jury gave a verdict of "Accidental Death."

* * *

A fortnight after that happened, Rachel came round to tea.
Though we both of us lived in London, 'twas seldom she and me
Could have a chat together. She looked so pale and weak,
I made her eat a crumpet before I let her speak.
She told me all this story, and trembled like a rag.
And when she'd done, she says – "Annie! We're leaving 'The Lamb and Flag.'
We are going out of the business. We've done our very best
As Publicans; I say it; let you search from east to west.
Our House was well conducted. We've closed at the proper time.
We've kept the Law. We've battled, against drunkenness and crime.

But I feel it, and so does Thomas, if we held to the House, and stayed,
It would break the hearts within us – *for it's too sad a Trade*.
Oh! I can't tell what I've suffered!" says Tom's wife, Rachel Dale.
"Look at the name on the Sign-board! – Annie, it's made me quail!
That ever a sign so sacred as the Lamb, and the Flag, we see
A shining in our Churches, should look on the misery
And shame of the Public Houses! –" She says – "It's blasphemy!
That's what it is to my thinkin'. Oh no! We are going away.
We've done with the Liquor Traffic for ever and for aye.
We are going into Coffee! And you'll find we shall make it pay!

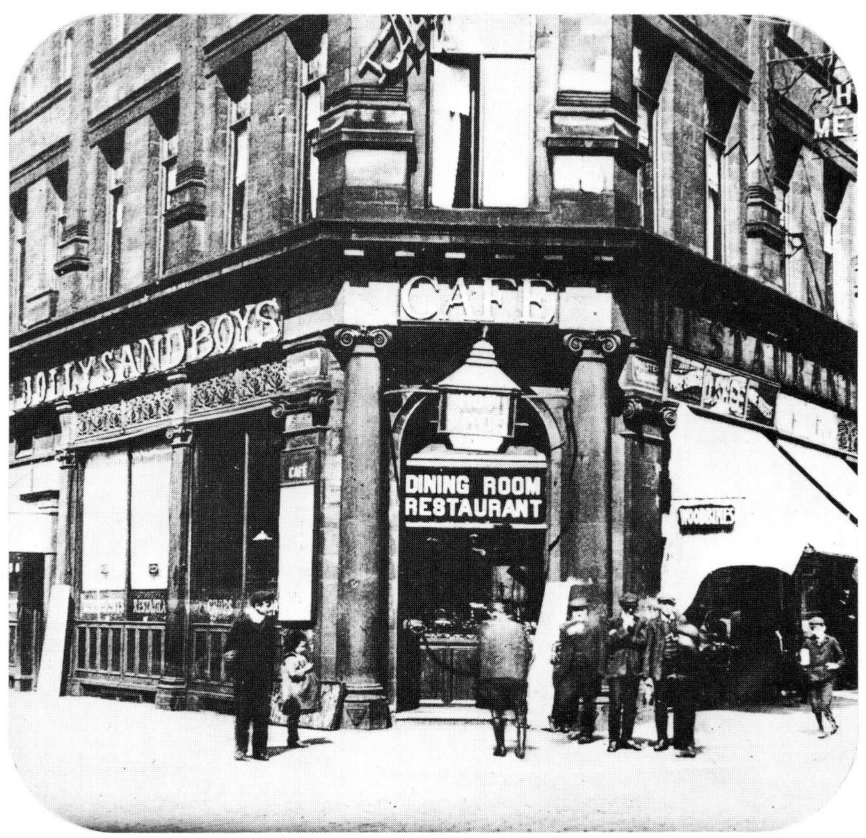

And so they did! Why, bless you! They opened a splendid place,
And called it the "Jolly Sandboys." When Thomas ran the race
He knew the way to win it! – I've seen a Coffee House
Looking that dull and cheerless it wouldn't tempt a mouse,
Much less a thirsty workman! There's one I could show you straight –
With a stale loaf in the window! and one herring on a plate,
That's been there a week to my knowledge! – some sugar full of flies!
A jug with nothing in it! And two mouldy-looking pies,
On dirty bits of paper! You can wait there till you're old,
And when you get the Coffee, it's always thick . . . and cold!

Now go to the "Jolly Sandboys," and you get it quick and hot!
The Bar a perfect picture. Food ready on the spot.
Iced drinks in the heat of summer. Hot soup on the winter days.

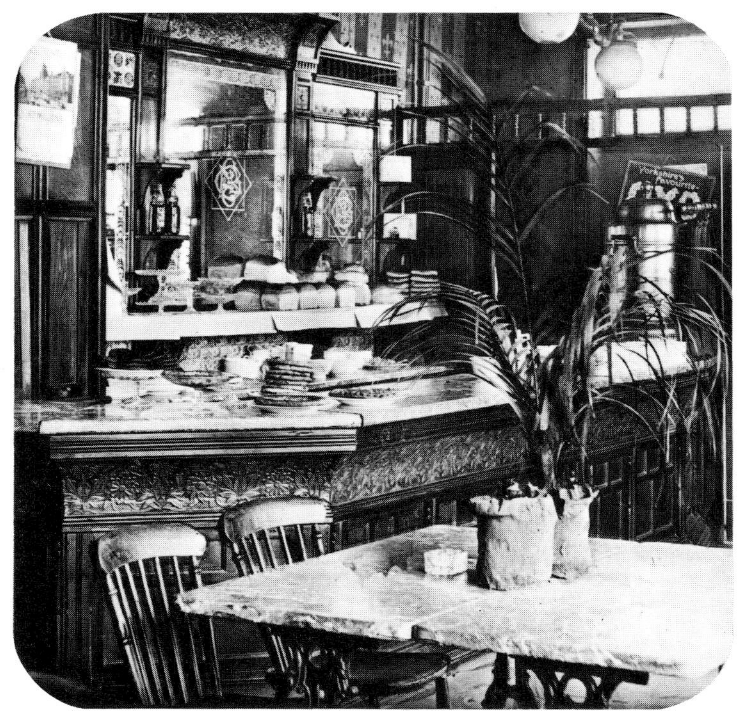

And the money they turn over! in a twelvemonth! would amaze
Those who think Coffee Houses can never pay their way.
Why! Tom has eggs for breakfast, and rashers, *every* day!

But just a word to finish. That "Accidental Death"
Was not Accident, but Murder. A fight – a blow–. The breath
Dashed from a tipsy woman, in a moment. Yet – think clear –
Not Murder born of Malice, but Murder born of Beer.
Don't judge Hames. Judge the Nation. For what doth Scripture say? –
"Woe to those who put stumbling-blocks across a brother's way."
Well may we cower and tremble, lest at the Judgment Day
We answer as a nation for the wealth which we have made
Out of our brother's stumbling! Out of this piteous Trade!

Yet the time is surely coming, when the country shall be free
From drink-born crime and madness, and bare-foot poverty,
And the dead weight of Temptation. Oh! pray for it! Pray and pray!
Till our noble England, rising, rolls her reproach away
And leads her sober People, nourished, and clothed, and shod,
Out of the dark of Evil into the Light of God!

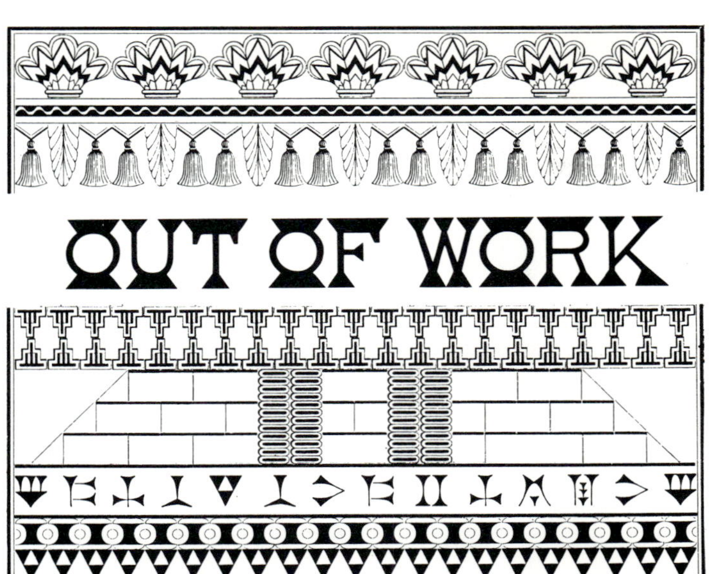

OUT OF WORK

I suppose it ain't becoming, for a wife to stand all day
A-praising up her husband, but I feel I just must say—
Although I say it that shouldn't—that placed longside my Jim,
I never see another that can be compared to him!

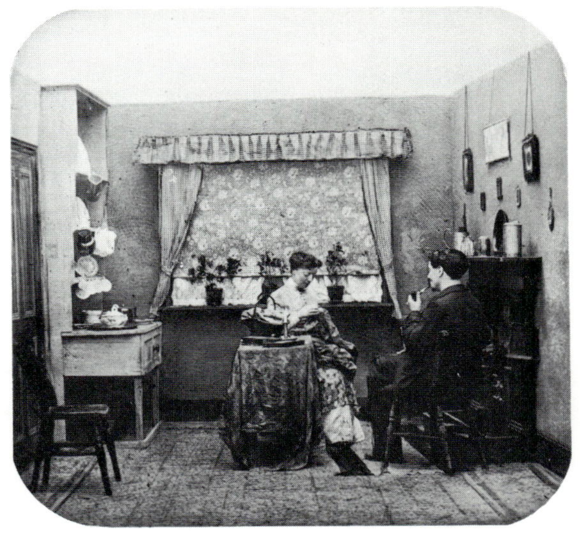

There's many a Summer husband! Do you know what I mean by that?
A man who can make home cheerful, with his evening pipe and chat,
As long as times are easy. But let the times get bad,
And you find your Summer husband quite another sort of lad!

And I will say this of Jimmy, he don't deserve the name:
For take him Summer or Winter he's pretty much the same!

I should like to tell you the story of the trouble we went through,
When both of us was younger. It's nothing very new:
It's a common sort of story; you may think it dull and slow:
But I'll try to hurry through it as quick as my tongue can go.

We'd been just eight years married, and the baby, little Sal,
Had reached her seventh birthday (such a clever little gal!
I'm mortal proud of Sally, though that's neither here nor there);
And we'd two more children—Harry, and Dick with his father's hair.

There were several other lodgers in the house, as well as we,
And us and the floor above us were neighbourly, d'you see?
I laughed when first they come there; for it just was Timothy Crab!
Him as was sweet upon me once, and drove a hansom cab.

I played him off upon Jimmy, for a joke, in our courting days!
But he'd never have done for me, you know, in no sort of a manner of ways.
I'd my own ideas of Timothy. He was fond of taking a drop.
And another drop; and another. Till he didn't know where to stop.
And thinks I, "He may be good-looking, and soft with his tongue, and free,
But he'll never make a good husband, and never the one for me!"

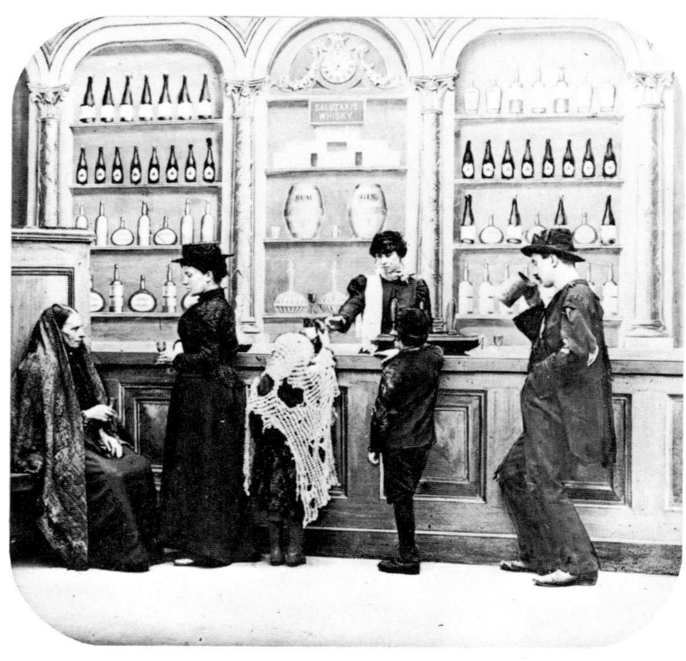

And I thought right; for I tell you, his home was a wretched place;
It made my heart ache, often, to look in his poor wife's face;
She'd been a pretty creature, that little Mrs Crab,
But he drank away her beauty, and he drank away his cab,

And he drank away his furniture, and his children's bread and cheese—
There were four of them, poor darlings, as pretty as you please—
And what with work and worry his little wife fell ill,
At the ending of the summer, when the days grow damp and chill.

I made some soup one evening, and took it for her to try,
And I found her in such a trouble, it was fit to make you cry.
The eldest child, Eliza, turned nine, or thereabout,
Was down with burning fever. The doctor had just gone out,

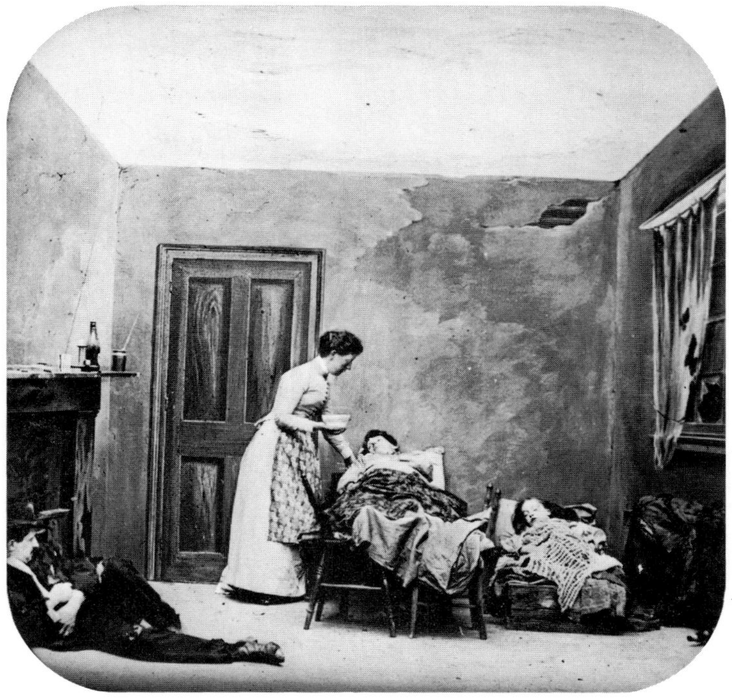

And left an order for the hospital, that one by the Grey Nag's Head,
The mother couldn't take her, for she couldn't leave her bed,
And the father, who should have done it, (Ah! to what that man had sunk,)
The father, who should have done it, was down in a corner—DRUNK!

Drunk, and stupid, and grinning. There! I couldn't look at him;
But I left the soup with the mother, and I flew downstairs to Jim,
And my face was just that scarlet that Jim, he cries, "Hallo!
Whatever is the matter, to make you colour so?"

"Matter," I says, "My goodness! Matter to make me red
And white and black together. There's that poor soul in bed,
And Lizzie down with the fever! She must go to the hospital, quick;
And there's that hulking Timothy—to name him makes me sick—

What calls hisself a father! a-lying like a log,
And helpless as a baby, and more stupid than a dog,
And perhaps his child a-dying. The lazy loppetting lout!
The muddled, fuddled villain! I'd go and shake him out
And PUMP on him, I would, if it chilled him to his death—"
And Jim says, "Gently, Annie. You'd better fetch your breath."

"I can't talk gently, Jimmy. I'm mad enough for two—"
And Jim says, "Stop a minute. Let's see what we can do.
If the child must go to the hospital, I'll carry her myself."
And he went to fetch a blanket, and his cap from off the shelf.

He'd scarcely eat a mouthful since he'd come in to his tea,
And he'd been a trifle poorly, the last two days or three,
And I didn't like his going. But he kind of looked me through—
"Do unto others, Annie, as you'd like them to do to you.
That's in the Bible, ain't it?" "Oh dear," says I to him,
"There! Throw me down my bonnet. We'll go together, Jim."

After all, there was nothing in it. 'Twas just a neighbourly act.
There's hundreds would do similar. You know it for a fact.
But it seemed a little hard, when I tell you what is true,
THAT IN LESS THAN A WEEK FROM THAT EVENING, MY JIM HAD THE FEVER TOO.

Ah! that was a trouble for us. I'd never known before
What it meant to have your husband a-lying at death's door.
I learnt the power that Autumn, of simple, earnest prayer,
And his life was spared, thank Heaven! though our troubles didn't end there.

He was two whole months in hospital, and of course not a shilling of pay,
It was lucky we had a little saved up for a rainy day.
They filled Jim's place at the factory: they acted fair and kind,
For they kept it three weeks open—they wouldn't have done that, mind,
If they hadn't known he was steady, and worth the wage he got:
But they couldn't keep it longer for one of the usual lot.

There's some here may know what that means. I stand as a wife, and say
God help the *honest* husbands, who tramp for it day by day;
Tramp when the sun is rising, tramp till he shines aslant,
God help the poor brave fellows who TRY to get work, and CAN'T.

I earned a trifle by sewing through many a night till dawn,
But we had to keep on putting our bits of things in pawn;
And one day Jim says, "Annie, I'll go to the factory door,
Maybe they want a hand now, and will take me as before."

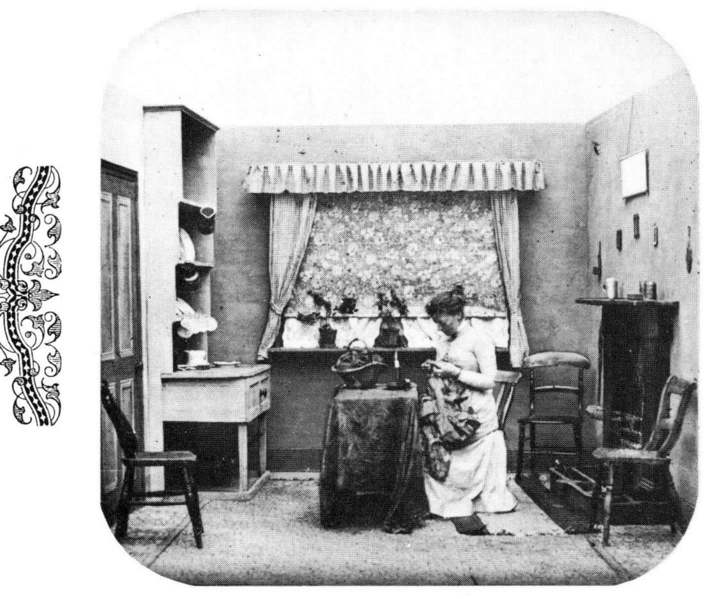
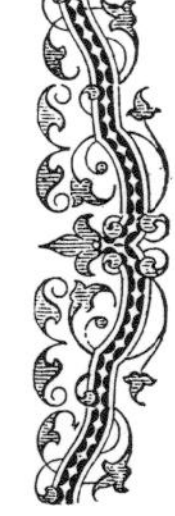

He went, and we sat waiting, Harry, and Dick, and me.
(Sally had taken some work home.) It was cold as cold could be,
And we hadn't a morsel of fire, for our coals had all run out.
And the children whispered, "Mother, ain't it tea-time now, about?"

It made me cry to hear them, for I knew the shelf was bare.
A tear run down my lashes and fell on Dicky's hair,
And the boy looked up so cheery—he was a plucky little lad—
"I ain't VERY hungry, mother; you needn't feel so bad."

I listened and longed for Jim's footstep, and I heard it coming slow.
I didn't ask if he'd got work, for a look in his face said No.
"They couldn't take me, Annie: the master is away.
They've a dozen applications for work in a single day.
And trade is low and flagging."
                              Then he crossed the room to me,
And placed his hand on my shoulder. "Annie, my girl," says he,
"I told you I'd work for you faithful, when I asked you to be my wife:
And I've tried my best to do it, God knows, through our married life:
But the times are dead against us: we've got to face the worst:
Can you bear up through it, Annie?"
                              I thought my heart would burst:
For when a man speaks tender you seem to feel it more.
I just turned round and kissed him, as we'd never kissed before.

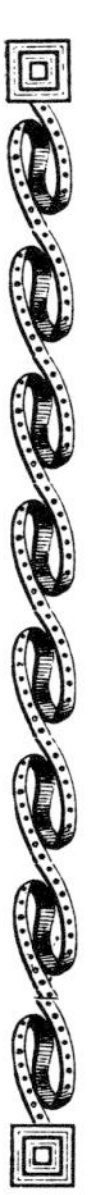
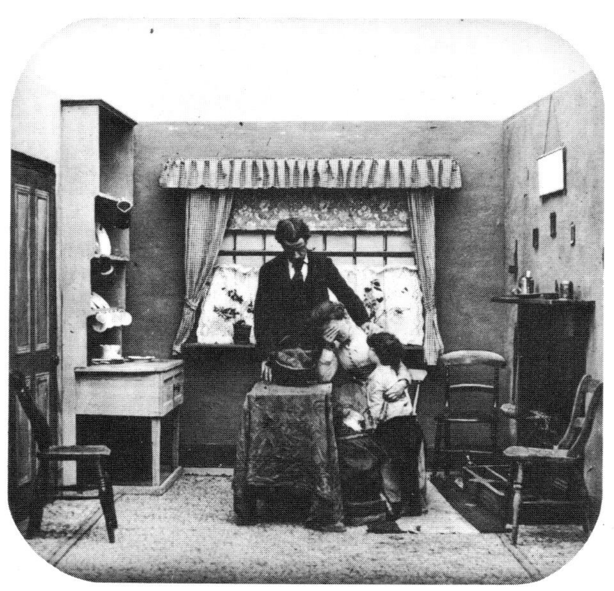

As we stood together, a sound came down the street—
A child's steps, running, running, so eagerly and fleet—
And a minute after, Sally, came rushing, flying, in,
So breathless and excited she scarce knew how to begin.

"Oh mother, look! Look, father! Look what I've got to show!
I saw a lady drop it . . . I couldn't tell her so . . .
For she stepped into her carriage, and drove right out of sight.

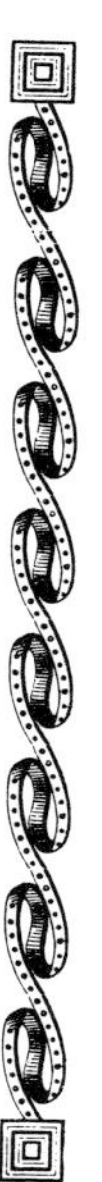
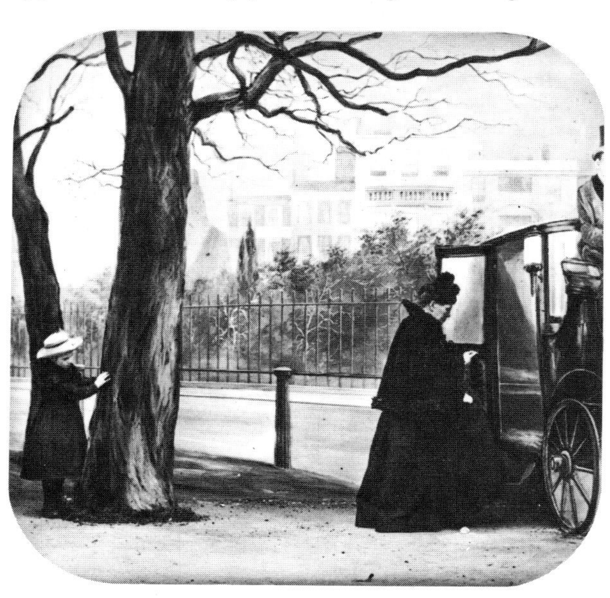

I snatched it from the gutter . . . and I've run with all my might . . .
Oh mother, ain't it LOVELY?"
                       'Twas a purse the child had brought.
A purse of solid silver, fit for the Queen at Court.
And when I took it from her, and opened it, there lay
FIVE SHINING GOLDEN SOVEREIGNS. I remember to this day
The joy that shot all through me. "O Jim!" says I, "O Jim!"
I was fit to start a-crying, and my eyes went dazed and dim.

"Here's food for you and the children, and the rent, and fire, and light,
And enough to get our things out, and make our Christmas bright.
Five golden sovereigns, Jimmy. Here, count them after me.
They're sent straight down from Heaven to help our misery!
Speak man!"
             And Jim spoke sudden. His voice rang firm and clear.
"Not Heaven," he says, "Not Heaven, but the Devil, sent it here.
That money isn't ours: it isn't ours, I say,
And not a single penny shall be spent if I die to-day!"

I thought he'd lost his reason. "Not ours! When 'twas fairly found
Dropped out of a lady's carriage, and lying on the ground.
A lady who'd never miss it. Perhaps a countess, or one as high
And rich. If you *don't* spend it, you're a blessed fool," says I.

I said that: yes, I said it. His eyes were like the sun—
"If I'm a fool then, Annie, I'll be an honest one.
I don't care who was the lady: it may seem desperate hard,
But the right place for that money and purse is Scotland Yard.
And it shall go there, Annie. It ain't at all like you
To hold me back from doing what's the honest thing to do.
I've read that much in the Bible."
                        He turned to the children then—
"Boys," he says: "Dick, and Harry: you'll both of you grow to be men,
And you're old enough to remember. Do you see this here silver purse?
It's going to be given up, for fear we should do what's worse
Than bearing cold and hunger. I've nothing to leave you boys
But what's worth more than money, and whips, and tops, and toys,
And that's an honest name. God help you to keep it so."
And he walked straight out that minute.
                        I was dumb when I saw him go.
I knew he was right. I knew it. I could hear the Bible speak.
"Thou shalt not steal," it was saying, and the tears ran down my cheek.
"Children!" I says to them. "Sally. And Dicky, you're not too small—
You mind that you mind your father, for your mother's no good at all!"

Well! we thought it was over and done with, but the very next afternoon
As I sat sewing lonely, feeling sad and out of tune,
There came a knock at the door: and when I went to see,
I saw a lady standing. "Are you Mrs. Hyde?" says she.

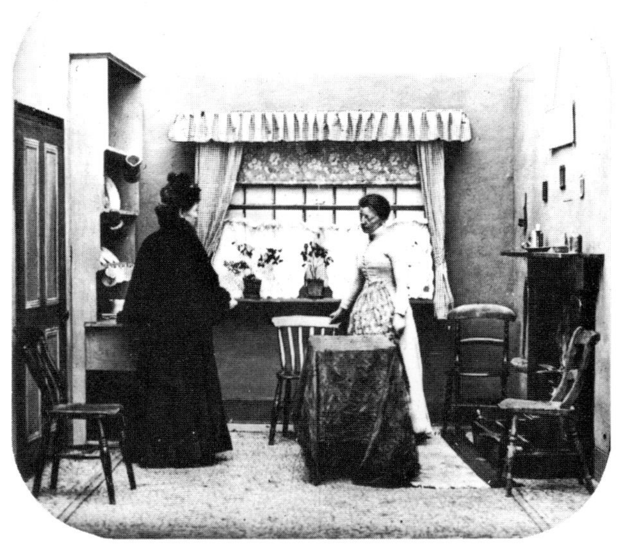

"Jim Hyde's my husband, ma'am," says I, with a sort of stare.
And in she stepped quite friendly. She was slim, and pretty, and fair.
"I want to see your husband. I've just come from Scotland Yard.
They gave me his name and address—I wrote them on this card—
I hear he brought my purse back." And then she smiled, and stopped.
And I felt that astonished! I thought I should have dropped!

She would hear all about it, and so as Jim was out,
I told her straight and simple just how it came about.
And this is what's so wonderful, as you will all agree,
Of all the ladies in London, who should she chance to be
But the wife of the Head of our Factory! And when she went, says she—

"You'll prosper, Mrs. Hyde, for your husband's an *honest* man.
I'll speak for him, for certain, and do the best I can."
And she spoke for him to her husband—that's Mr. Arthur Prince—
And they took Jim back at the Factory, and he's been there ever since!

Yes! And there's more to follow, for just before Christmas Day—
The sky was fixed for snowing, a chilly sort of grey—
A man came up with a hamper, and brought it to our door.
We'd never had such a hamper in all our lives before!

'Twas Mrs. Prince had sent it: 'twas crammed to the very lid,
It took us all an hour to unpack it, that it did.
There was a lovely goose for dinner. And a pudding. And a ham.
And some mince-pies. And some bacon. And *such* a pot of jam!

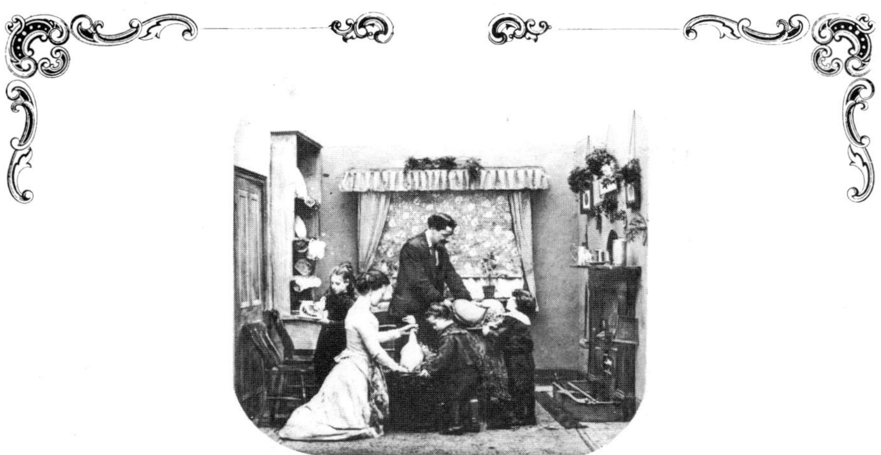

And clothes and things for the children. And a gown and a shawl for me.
And an overcoat for Jimmy. And a couple of pounds of tea.
And—I don't know what there wasn't! And there! I can only say
I wish you could all be as happy as we were that Christmas Day.

That's the ending of my story. But because it's ended bright
Don't think that giving up that purse that bitter winter night
Was something light and easy. I say 'twas a HERO's deed.
I say it is placed on a record the Angels in Heaven read,
Though 'twill never be read in our papers.
                                     I know Jim's a working man.
I know he ain't a soldier, to fight as soldiers can.
But what he did was a braver, ah! and a *harder* thing to do
Than many a gallant action that's brought into public view.

God rewards such heroes, mind you, in His own time, long or short.
And I ain't ashamed to say it—though I says it as didn't ought—
That I'm just as proud of Jimmy as if he was Prince of Wales!
And here's wishing you Good Evening! before your patience fails!

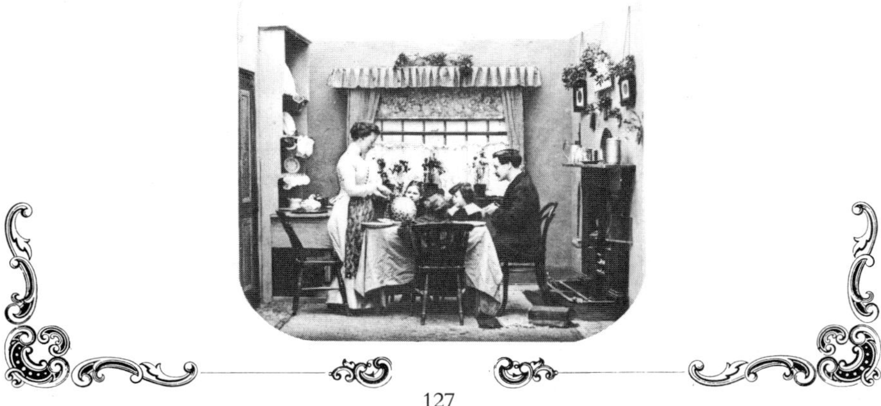

THAT FELLOW JONES

I heard the bells a-ringing as I come down the street,
Ringing a Merry Christmas, so friendly and so sweet,
And it set me off a-thinking of a certain Christmas Day
When I learnt a Christmas lesson in a very sing'lar way.

It must be now, I fancy, some three or four years ago,
That friends of ours were living at the bottom of our Row.
The husband worked at the factory, the same as my husband Jim,
And Jim he looked a giant when placed 'longside of him.

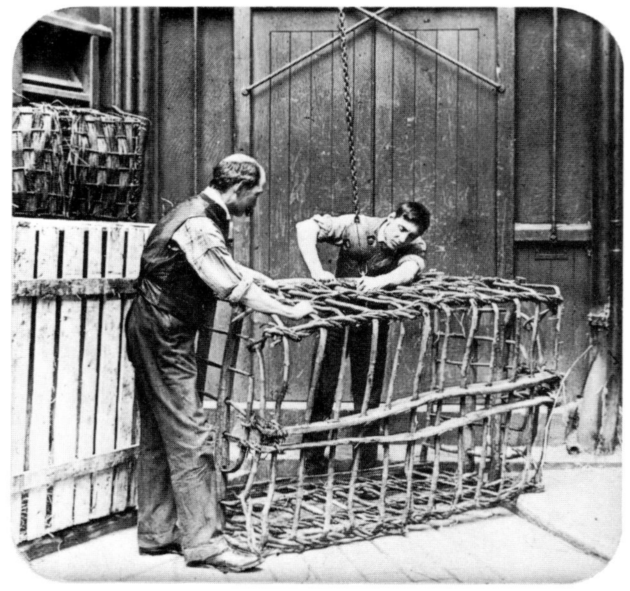

For he wasn't a dwarf exactly, this chap – his name was Jones –
But undersized, and sickly, and nothing but skin and bones.
Still I'm bound to say he was pleasant, and steady through and through,
And though he was Jimmy's junior, a very good workman too.

They were poor, for they'd lots of children, and Mrs Jones, poor thing,
She didn't know how to manage. She was one of the sort who'd fling
An onion into some water and call it Irish stew!
And Jones would have to eat it! And I'll tell you what she'd do –

She'd put a chop on the fire, and go out and buy the bread,
And say "lor!" When the chop was a cinder! There, she hadn't a scrap of head:
But she made a pleasant neighbour: and often Saturday nights
I'd run in for a minute and help her get to rights.

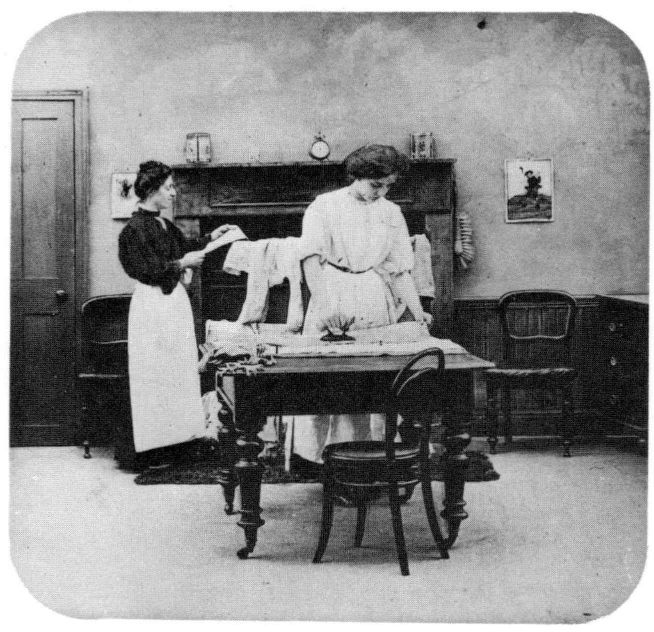

I'd make the Sunday pudding, or I'd iron out the clothes,
She often washed on Saturdays, as you might well suppose! –
And sometimes for our supper when I'd got a dish of sprats,
Done crisp, you know, and peppered! (I say folks must be flats
That like them fat and greasy.) I'd send Jim down to see
If they'd have a bit of supper along with him and me.

And they'd come a-saying as how they couldn't refuse.
And the men would smoke together and chat about the news.
And we'd all be just as friendly as anyone could choose.

   *   *   *

Well, one day at the factory an under-forman died,
And left of course a vacancy, for which Jim straight applied.
There were others trying for it, and 'twas in the master's gift,
But not a man in the factory as well deserved a lift.

As Jim, we knew for certain. The character he had!
Not one could say against him a word of what was bad.
Six years he'd worked, and never had a stroke of blame,
There, 'tain't for me to praise him: but others said the same.

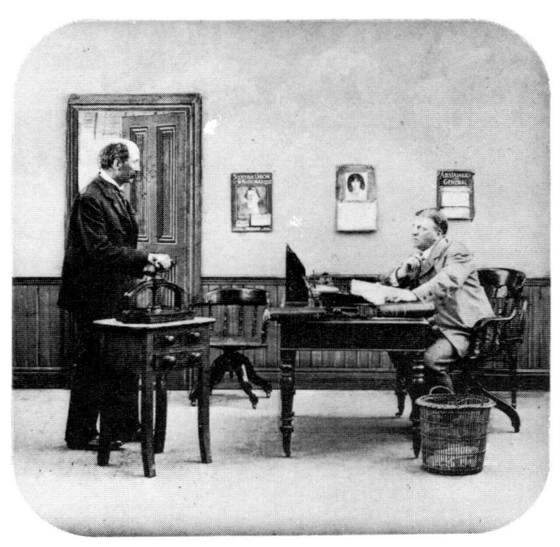

One night, as we were talking, Jim says, "Why, I've heard tell
As Jones, of all chaps, Annie, is in for the place as well!
But I think he would have told me, seeing we live so near."
"Of course he would," I answered, "you can't believe half you hear."

And Jim, he laughs, "Why, Annie, we'll be most too fine to speak,
With five-and-twenty shillings paid reg'lar every week.
I'll have a coat for Sundays as smart as Foreman Gray,
And I'll buy you a new bonnet, whatever you may say."
"Oh, Jim," I says, "don't talk so. You take my breath away!"

Next morning, I remember, I scarce knew how to bide,
With feeling so excited and fluttery-like inside;
For Jim had said, at leaving, "We're pretty safe to hear
Who's got the place to-day, Annie, and there isn't much to fear."

I'd just got dinner ready, when he comes tearing back.
He burst the door right open, and his face looked black as black.
He says, "It's settled, Annie." And I started at his tones.
"And who d'ye think has got it? Why, that there fellow Jones."

"Jones!" I says, "Jones has got it! *Never!*" I says, and oh!
However we may laugh now, it was a dreadful blow.
Jim took on something awful. "The wretched little rat!
To think they should pass me over for a miserable chap like that!
Him to be made my master! Him to be bearing rule,
As doesn't know what I know, and is nothing but a fool.
Him to be made under-foreman, and ME to be laid on the shelf!
It's shameful" – and that minute there walks in Jones himself.

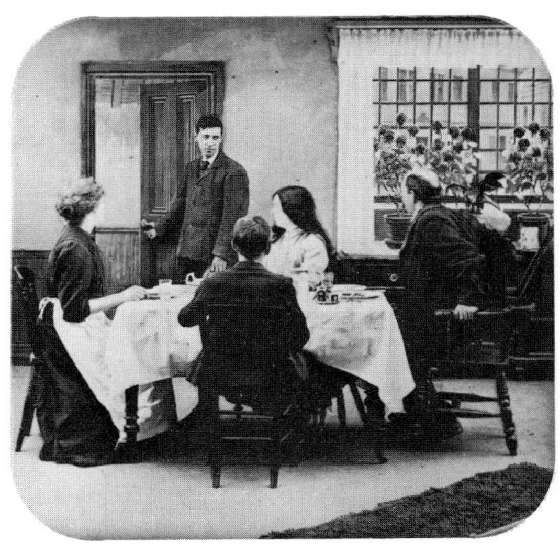

He'd come to make things pleasant, as I've since understood,
But he'd not a chance of saying what he had thought he should:
For Jim was in that passion, he turned on him then and there –
"Don't you come here a-sneaking, and thinking to make things square.

You've sneaked enough," he thunders. "You've kept it close and tight,
You couldn't say out honest you meant to make a fight,
And oust me if 'twas possible. No, you've been on the tack
Of whining round the master, and lying behind my back.

Ain't you ashamed to stand there and look me in the face?"
"I'm sorry I didn't tell you I was trying for the place,"
Says Jones. And Jim roars, "Sorry! Sorry! Don't make me sick!
Do you think that cant will cover your mean and dirty trick?

There! Leave my house this instant, before I kicks you out."
And Jones spurs up – "You kick me! You great insulting lout."
And they glares at one another. And Jim says, "Do you think
I couldn't send you flying before you'd time to wink?
Do you think I couldn't shake you and rattle all your bones
Into a blessed jelly, as sure as your name is Jones?
But I'd scorn to lay a finger on a little cur like you.
Be off, and thank your inches that you ain't black and blue.

Be off! I say, and never cross the step of this door again."
And Jones walks out a-swearing quite terrible and plain.

*   *   *

131

Well, after that you'll reckon we weren't the best of friends,
And when a quarrel's started you can't tell where it ends.
I took Jim's part, 'twas natural, and Mrs. Jones and me,
We turned the greatest strangers that ever you could see.

She'd pass me so superior. And I'd look proud at her.
And one day, I remember, there was such a mighty stir
Because my little Sally had been playing with her Jane.
"Sally," I says, "remember, you must never do that again.

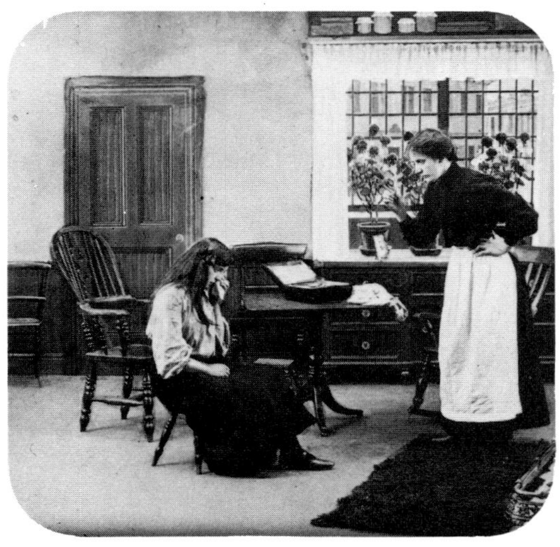

There ain't one of them little Joneses," says I, "fit to play with you.
And Mrs Jones she said the same about our children too.
And Jim was never tired of sneering at what Jones did.

"He hasn't the sense," he'd tell me, "that's in your saucepan lid."
"No more he has," I'd answer. "And as for his wife," I've said,
"It isn't brains, it's sawdust, that she's got in her head!"

Twelve months we lived like that, mind, and lived in the self-same row,
And never looked, and never spoke so much as a Yes or No.

I don't say it was Christian. I think now it was wrong
For neighbours to be quarrelling so bitterly and long.
But there's many a quarrel like it, and for smaller reason too.
And the time came round to Christmas, the same as it always do.
About ten days before it, Jones fell and broke his arm.
"And serve him right," says Jimmy, "I knew he'd come to harm."
And then on Christmas morning, as the sun shone bright and clear,
We walked to Church with the children, as we'd done every year.

And oh! We felt that pious! And Jim says, "Jones won't go
To Church nor yet to Chapel." And I say, "Oh dear no."
And Jim he adds complacent, a–looking at the sky,
"He's no better than a heathen." "He's a great deal WORSE," says I.

And then we took our places in the Church all warm and bright,
And we joined in the prayers quite hearty, and we sang with all our might.
And then there came the sermon. I may live till I'm old and grey,
But I'll never hear such another as I heard that Christmas Day.

A stranger was in the pulpit. His text was "Goodwill to men."
There's parsons, and there's parsons, but there isn't one in ten
Can put it straight as he did.
            He says, "It's the time of year
When you're all of you thinking of pudding, and beef, and tips, and beer.
Now, Christmas," he says, "ain't eating. And Christmas," he says
            "ain't drink.
There's something besides that in it of which you've got to think.

Christmas," he says, "is kindness. And Christmas," he says, "is love.
For 'twas love that brought our Saviour down from His heaven above.
And if He hadn't loved us, and died for us, great and small,
There'd never have *been* a Christmas," says he, "in the world at all!"

And then he leant right over, and he seemed to look hard at we,
"Now is there someone sitting, down here in front of me,
WHO HAS QUARRELLED WITH A NEIGHBOUR?" he says, "or feels a grudge
Against a fellow–creature? If so, don't let him budge.

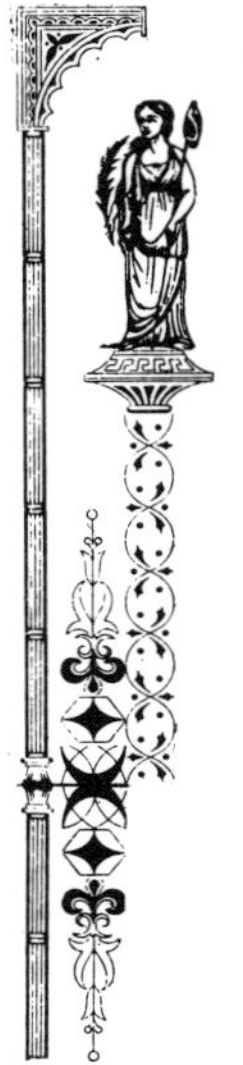
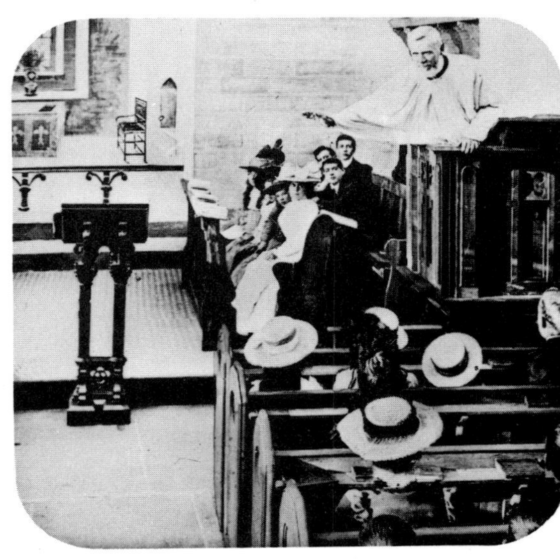
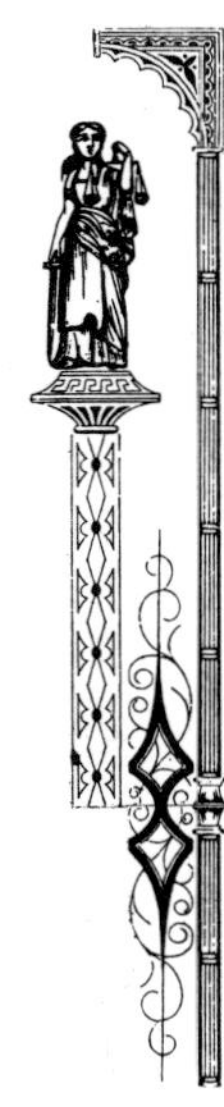

From this here Church this morning, till he feels that he can stand
And wipe out that score for ever by the shake his neighbour's hand.
For unless you're a lot of heathens," he says, "there's no other way
But friendliness, and kindness, for keeping Christmas Day."

I walked home very quite. And Jim, not a word says he.
But when 'twas time for dinner, he got sort of fidgety.
"I'll go down street," he says. And I says, "I'll come too."
For it struck me all of a sudden what he was going to do.

And down we walk'd together, and in at the Jones's door.
They stared to see us enter as they'd never stared before.

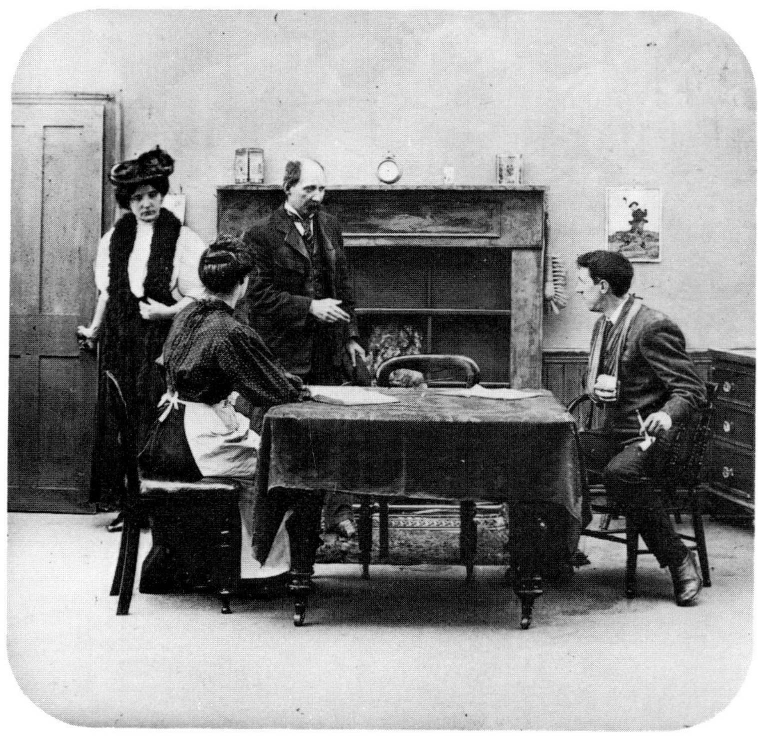

And Jim speaks out that minute – "Jones," he says, "you and me
Have quarrelled for a twelvemonth in a way that shouldn't be.
I own 'twas my fault mostly, and now I've come to say –
Let's shake hands, and forget it, because it's Christmas Day."

And oh! You'd never think it; we felt I don't know how.
And Jones he nearly blubbered, as stupid as a cow,
And he shook Jim's hand so hearty, with the arm that wasn't broke,
That we wives fell a-laughing, and a-crying, fit to choke.

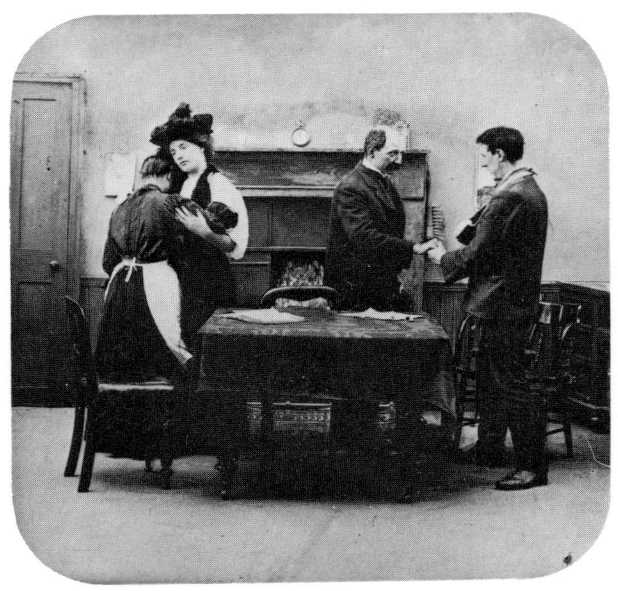

And then I thought of my oven, and what there was inside,
And says I, "Our dinner's simple but without improper pride
I'll answer for the cooking, and though our room is small
If you'll eat your dinner with us, you're welcome, one and all."

And we had a jolly dinner: and songs: and lots of fun:
And of all the Merry Christmases that was the merriest one
That ever I remember.

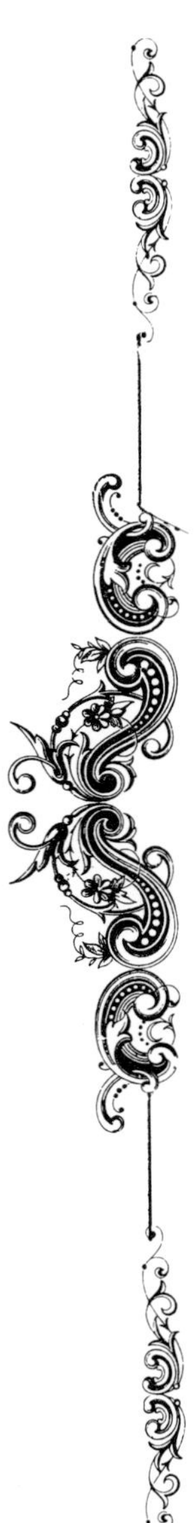

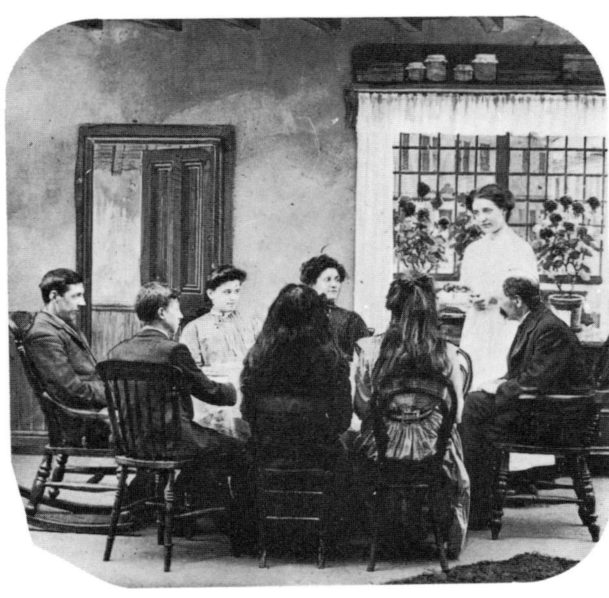

James Peglar

"Oh, mother!" says my Sally, as she sat and sipped her tea,
"May little Daisy Peglar come to Sunday School with me?"
"Surely," says I, without thinking: for the child was lone and lorn,
And had never known her mother—who died when she was born—
And I thought 'twould be a pleasure and would cheer the little thing
To hear Bible stories, and learn the hymns, and sing.

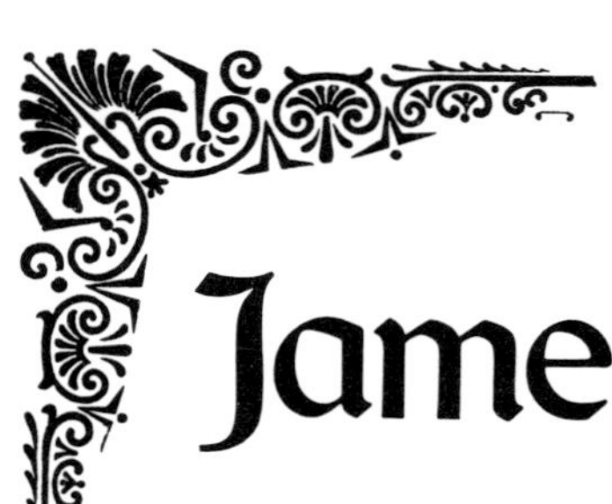

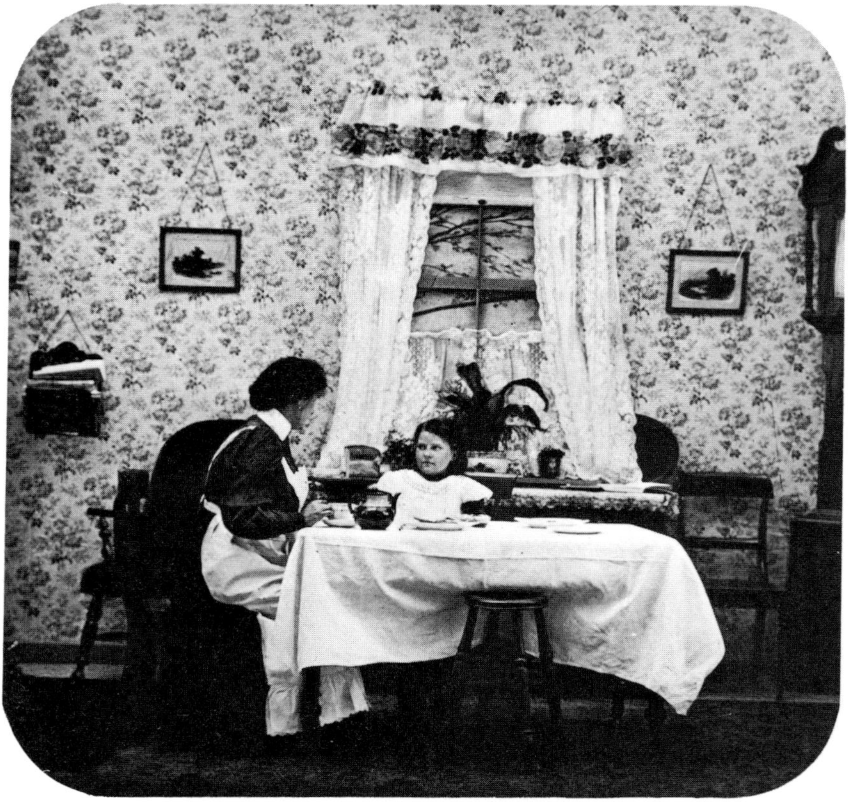

But I reckoned without her father! when I gave her leave to go.
And the very next evening, Monday, he came and told us so!

He was Foreman at our Factory: and was sharp, and knew a lot.
He'd had a deal more schooling than my Jim ever got.
He used to speak at Meetings, and put the others right!
He sat beside our table, and he talked to us that night—

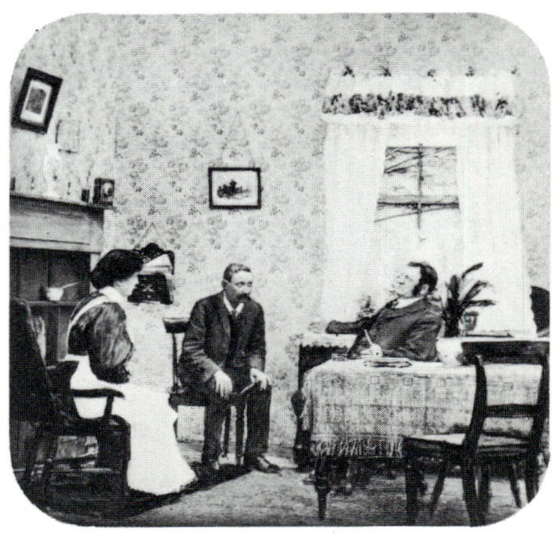

Smoking his pipe with Jimmy—he talked as you've never heard!
A Sunday School was poison!! If we actually preferred
To have our child taught rubbish, we could do as we thought wise:
He wouldn't let his Daisy learn superstitious lies,
Not while his name was Peglar!
                                    Jim stares with both his eyes!
"Well!" he says, "we send Sally where there ain't no rubbish taught:
Naught but the simple Bible—"He cut Jim pretty short.
That was just the mischief of it. He'd not row in the Parson's boat.
He wouldn't have the Bible shoved down his daughter's throat.
He'd never been better for the Bible he could swear,
And he'd train his child without it.
                                    I got up from my chair.

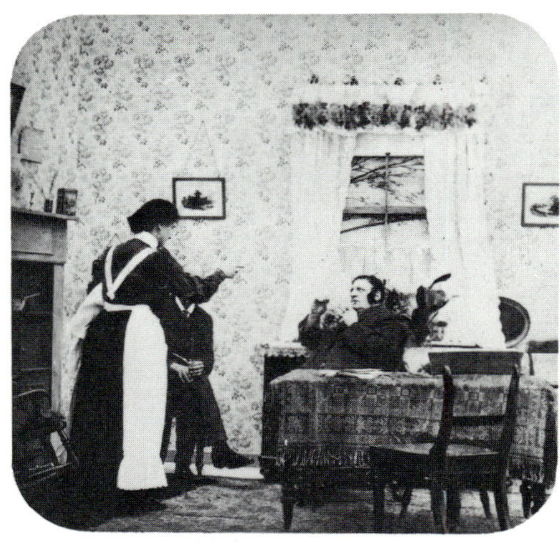

"Sir!" I says, "Mr Peglar. You're our Foreman, I'm aware.
And I've no wish to insult you, for civility's our rule,
And likewise you're a neighbour—but, "I says, "you're a FOOL!
Is your child to learn her duty to her home, herself, and you?
Do you want her good? and happy?"—"Yes!" he says. "Of course I do.
And she'll BE that without the Bilbe."—"No"! I says. "She will NOT!
You're our Foreman, Mr Peglar, but you're talking . . . simple *rot!*
You might as well sow tin-tacks, and expect a row of peas,
As preach such one-eyed doctrines and think that out of these
There's happiness a coming! To keep God's Word away
Is to keep your child in a cellar from the air and the light of day.
What does the Psalm say? Listen! 'Thy Word is a Lamp to my feet.'
And a Lamp it is: and a Lantern: as we jostle in Life's dark street.
All honesty, all honour, all truth, all purity.
Is found in the Holy Bible, God's Message to you and me.
I'm nothing at all to boast of," I says, "but this is true:—
There's not a spark of goodness in anything I do,
Not a kind act to a neighbour, not so much as a pleasant look,
That I don't owe to the teaching I've drawn from that sacred Book,
And I'd die for what I'm saying. And though hearing it makes you wild,
If you *dare* to keep back the Bible from the soul of your motherless child,
You will rue the day you do it in your stubbornness and pride,
As sure as your name *is* Peglar, and as sure as my name is Hyde!"

And then I said "Good evening:" for I did feel that upset
I couldn't stay there any longer. No. And I shan't forget
How the children cried about it when they heard they couldn't go
To Sunday School together. And Sally brought her row
Of Sunday cards for Daisy, and picked her out the best.
'Twas the picture of a Shepherd with a lamb upon His breast:
And the old sweet words—"Come unto Me and I will give you rest."

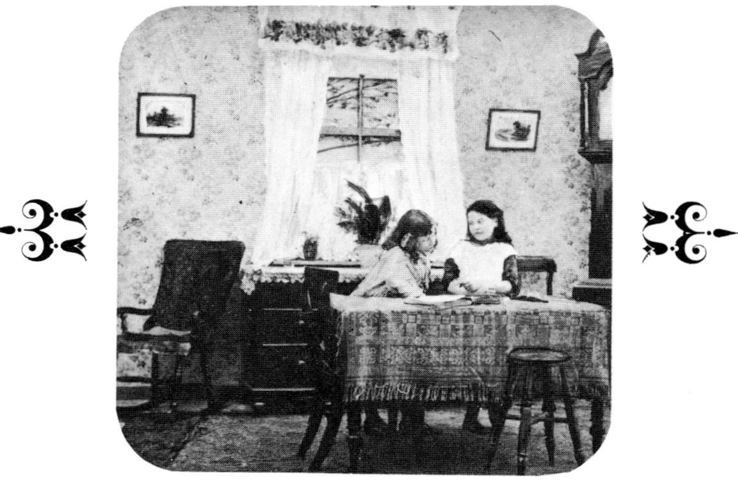

There's a deal to tell in this story. And yet I think I ought
To tell it full and faithful, and not try to cut it short.

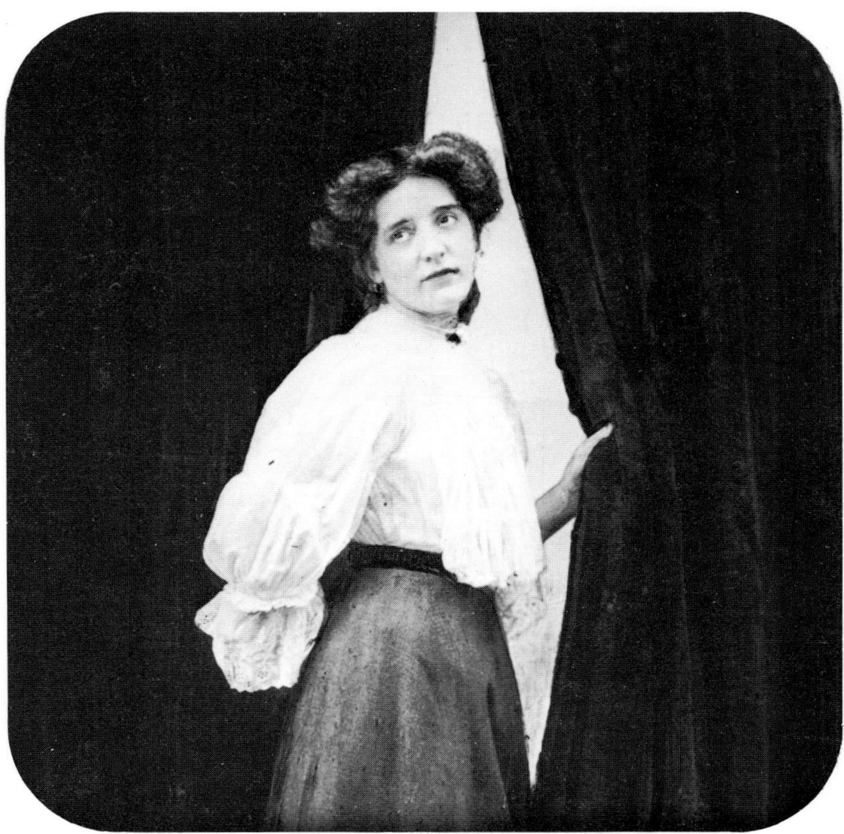

That little Daisy grew up as my children grew.
As pretty a girl as ever I saw, and I've seen a few.
Her father lived to spoil her, and humour her, night and day.
He thought he could make her happy by letting her have her way.
She might spend as she liked, and do as she liked, and live to enjoy.
And that's not good for a young one: be it girl or boy.
She wasn't taught the Bible. He had his way in that.
Nor was there a place o' Worship I ever saw them at.
We used to pass them Sundays. They going for a walk.
We going to Church. And if ever you've seen a pink rose on a stalk!
A blooming in light! that was Daisy—as she hung on her father's arm!
Her hair in golden glory! and her blue eyes like a charm!
And many's the time my heart's ached to think that pretty child,
Who hung on his arm so loving, and looked in his face and smiled,
Would have nothing at all to steer her where the breakers of evil foam,
But the love she had for her father and the love she had for home,
And that isn't enough to steer by : strong though it is, and good :
For human love, by itself, the best of it understood,
In the Breakers of Temptation . . . will smash . . . like rotten wood.

And she met temptation early. She worked at the millinery,
For a year or so, apprenticed, as Sally had to be,
And the two young things were friendly as did me good to see.

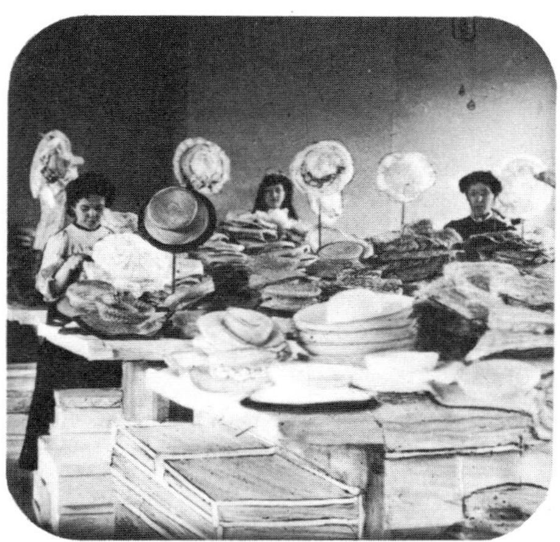

And it came about one summer, a man loafed round our way,
Who made his money touting, and betting, we heard say.
A foreign chap to look at, but handsome—I will allow.
And Daisy she picked up with him (goodness knows when or how).
And she passed him on to Sally.
                              Now me and Jim, you know,
Don't make acquaintance that way; and we told Sally so.

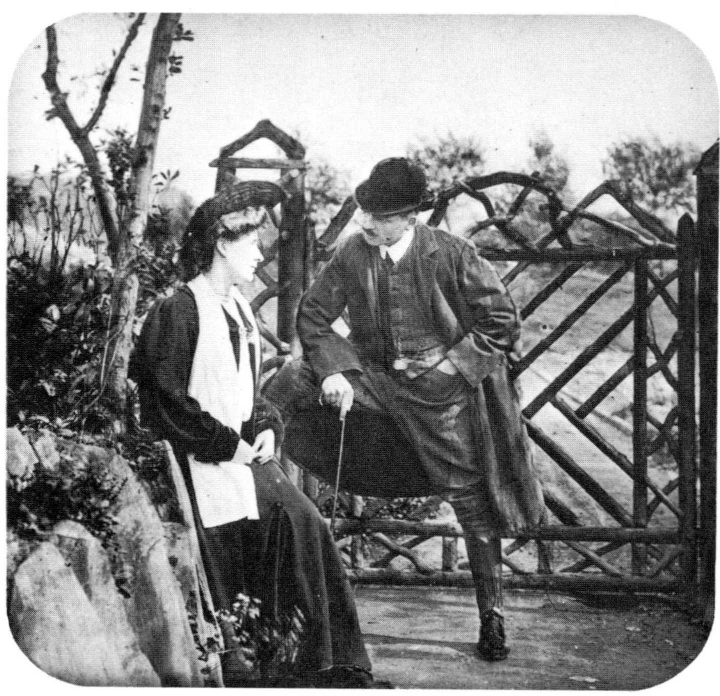

"But he gave me a brooch," says Sally, "and he's given Daisy, six!
And he says he could make her a lady." And Jim says, "Fiddlesticks!
Could he make her an honest woman? It's come out pretty clear
He don't earn his living honest. Now Sally," he says, "my dear,
You're to drop him from this minute. So do as you are bid.
And I'll give a hint to Peglar, to warn him." And he did.
And Peglar spoke to Daisy, and forbade her to walk or speak
With this flashy Jack-a-dandy she'd barely known a week.

Friends! you would scarce believe it,—but the long and short is this:
She ran away from her father without a farewell kiss.

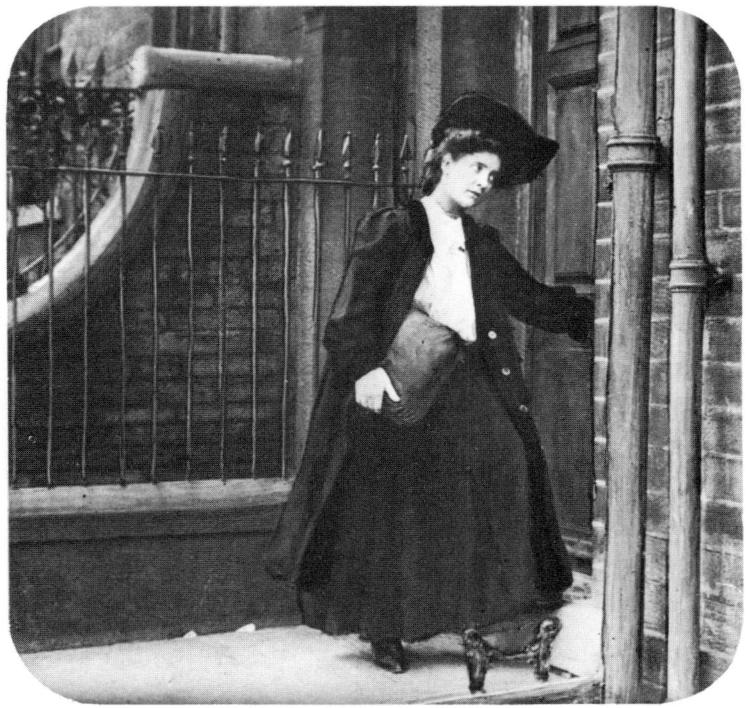

And under that fellow's tempting, she robbed him, left and right,
Of all she could lay her hands on!
                              He came to us that night
And he sat like a man with the palsy.
                                   And I durstn't speak a word
I felt that sorry for him. But I think he must have heard
A Voice which rolled in thunder out of the Word of God—
"*Fathers . . . bring up your children in the nurturing of the Lord.*"
And the fruit of Bible training was our Sally, sitting there,
Sweet and safe, with her sewing, in her Grannie's rocking-chair.

*   *   *

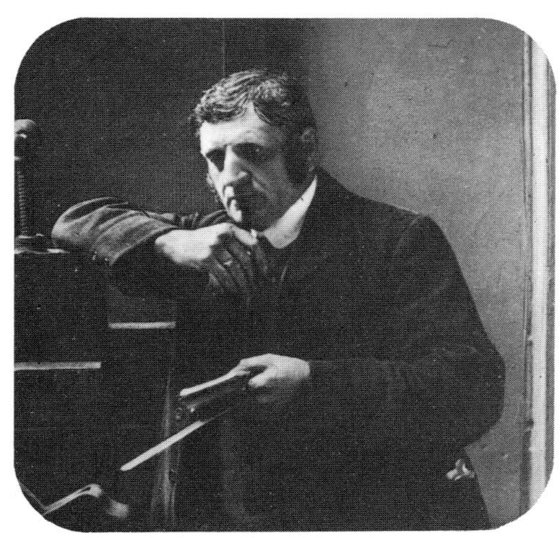

They said about our Factory, James Peglar's hair went white
In the four and twenty hours that followed his daughter's flight.
But he kept his trouble secret, and hidden out of sight,
And we didn't ask him questions.
                              But friends, an evening came
That's stamped upon my memory in prints of living flame.
An evening when James Peglar, and me, stood side by side,
By a beggar's bed in the Workhouse. A woman who wept and cried
And asked him to forgive her. A wretched fallen wreck,
And I shouldn't have known it was Daisy. But her father knew, and fell
Down on his knees by her bedside, and sobbed, as I couldn't tell,
And kissed her. And she gasped out—"Father . . . I've been in Hell . . .
And I've found the way to Heaven . . . by this—" and she'd got to show
The little card that Sally had given her years ago.

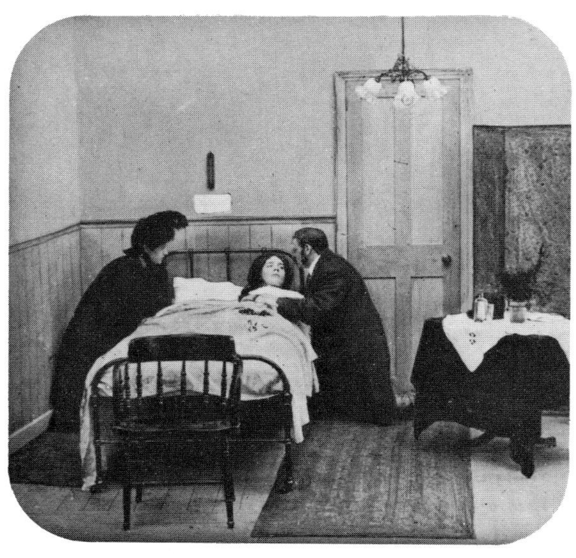

The picture of a Shepherd with a lamb upon His breast,
And the might words—"Come unto Me and I will give you rest."
"I found those words in the Bible . . . and wonderful words beside . . .
And I clung to them," she whispered, "and they saved me from suicide . . ."
And then she lay like a dead thing. But just before she died,
She lifted up her baby with her dying strength, and cried—
"Oh! somebody give my baby what his mother never had.
Oh! teach my boy the Bible and save him from being bad."
"I promise I will," said Peglar.
                              And the woman died at rest.
And we laid her in her coffin, with that picture on her breast.

        *   *   *

    This tale's not easy telling, but it ends more happily.
There's a sight I often witness in a house near our Factory,
When I look in of an evening. An old man sits in his chair,
And his Grandson stands beside him. A little chap, with hair
The colour of his mother's, and his mother's lovely eyes.
And he spells out a Pslam from his Bible in a way that's a surprise!
And when the reading's over James Peglar looks at me—
As he gives the child a penny and sets him on his knee—
"It's better late than never: it's better by far," says he!

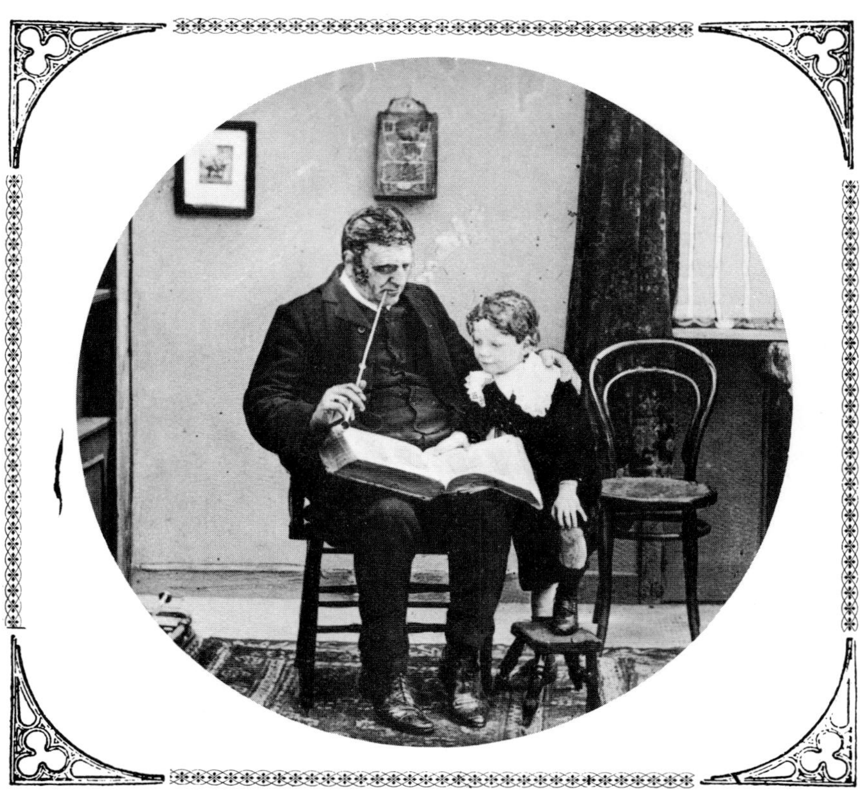

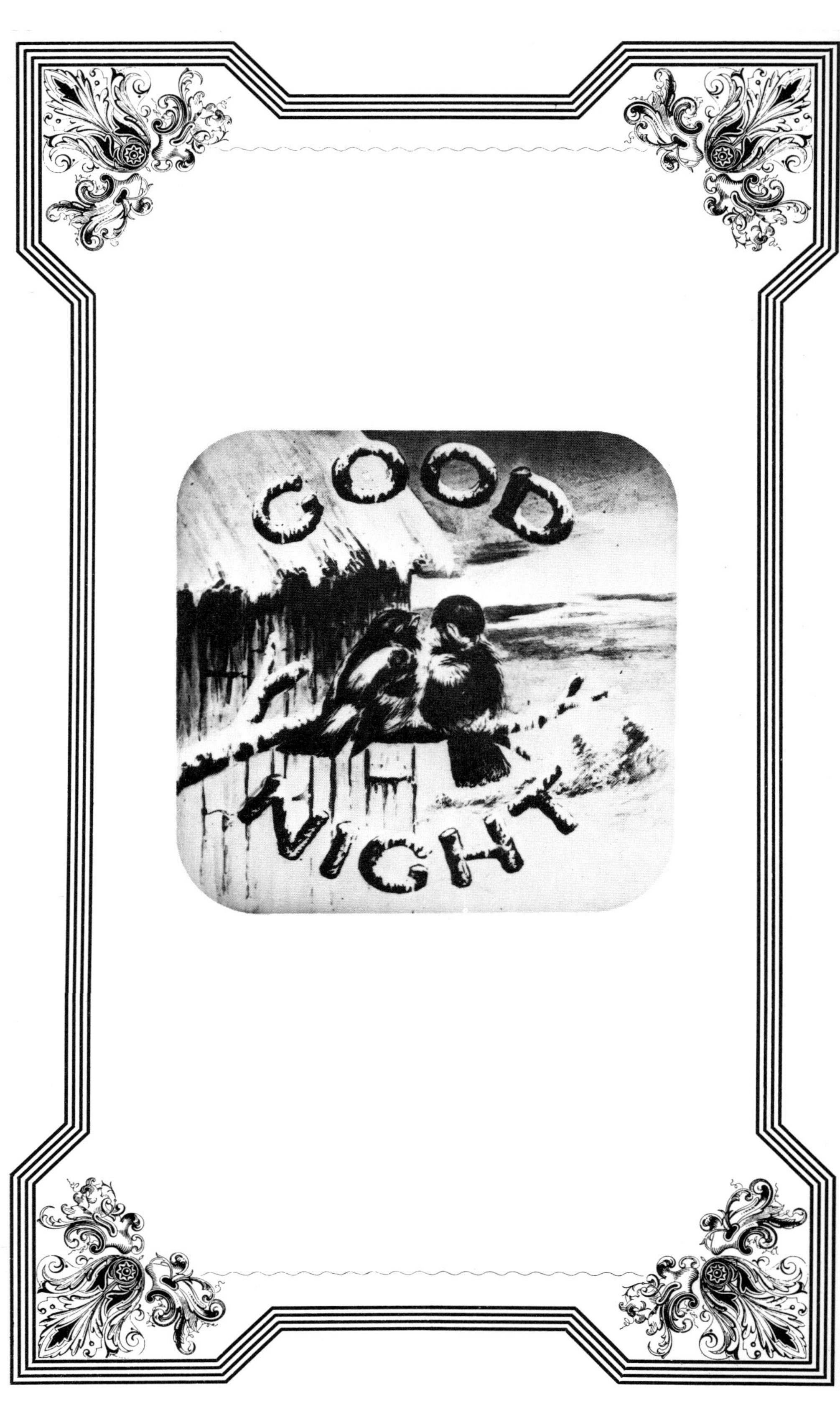
GOOD
NIGHT